BUSINESS
STUDIES

Peter Fearns has wide experience in industry and teaching. A former chief examiner for A level Business Studies at the AEB, and an HMI in Business Studies, he helped to formulate the BTEC National module 'The Organisation in its Environment', and was consultant to the BBC/BTEC series *Business World*. He is currently Principal of Burton on Trent Technical College.

D1586455

TEACH YOURSELF BOOKS

BUSINESS STUDIES

Peter Fearns

TEACH YOURSELF BOOKS
Hodder and Stoughton

First published 1980 as
Business Studies: An Integrated Approach
Second edition 1984
Second impression 1985

British Library Cataloguing in Publication Data

Fearns, Peter
Business studies.—2nd ed—(Teach yourself
books)
1. Management
I. Title
658.4   HD31

ISBN 0 340 34307 9

Printed and bound in Great Britain for
Hodder and Stoughton Educational,
a division of Hodder and Stoughton Ltd,
Mill Road, Dunton Green, Sevenoaks, Kent,
by Richard Clay (The Chaucer Press) Ltd,
Bungay, Suffolk.
Photoset by Rowland Phototypesetting Ltd
Bury St Edmunds, Suffolk

Contents

PART TWO *The Formation and Management of*   41
Organisations

PART THREE *The Organisation and its Resources* 87

organisations manage people . The welfare of employees .
The informal organisation . The Human Relations School .
Employee/employer relationships . Termination of
employment .

Introduction

One of the problems in learning about Business is that there is no generally accepted definition of what constitutes 'Business Studies', since it encompasses many different disciplines and at the same time embraces many different forms of organisation. A study of the diverse and yet integrated nature of business activity is the key to understanding Business Studies, and the aim of this book is to provide the foundations for such understanding.

The text integrates five disciplines: Economics, Accountancy, Law, Government and Administration. *Economics* is similar to Business Studies in that it is composed of knowledge from a wide variety of concepts and topics such as public finance, inflation, unemployment and international trade, and all these are included in the text. In addition, the book examines the resources which are required by business, and analyses the relationship between market forces. *Accountancy* is dealt with as a traditional business subject which provides the techniques for analysing and controlling business performance. Information on *Government* and *Law* is included because it covers the legal, political and constitutional framework of business activity. This framework not only includes government intervention into private organisations, but also the business of Government itself: the provision of social services, the administration of government regulations and the commercial activity of public corporations are treated as subdivisions of Business Studies. The principles and information from the less well known disciplines of *Administration* and *Supervisory Studies* run through the text. Business functions such as personnel management, financial control, production and marketing are, in some way, common to all public and private organisations.

In practice the disciplines of Business Studies are not conducted independently of one another: they are interdependent activities, and the book highlights their integrative nature. Similarly the operations of commercial and non-commercial organisations are interdependent, so the text considers all forms of public and private organisation and emphasises their interdependence.

The book is a practical introduction to Business Studies; and is particularly appropriate for those who are studying a Business and Technician Education Council course or GCE 'A' level in Business Studies. The text covers all of the course specifications of the BTEC National level core modules 3 and 4: 'The Organisation in its Environment'; and includes some specifications of the core modules 1 and 2. It also covers the syllabus of the AEB Business Studies 'A' level. Integration of the subject matter is achieved by several features: firstly, by giving many examples which illustrate the relationship of the disciplines to all types of organisation; secondly, by providing cross-references in the text which show the interrelationship of the chapters; thirdly, by including a comprehensive index; and lastly, by providing questions at the end of each Part which test the student's ability to appraise and explain business activities. The basic information for each question can be found in the respective Part and in other sections of the book. However, it is not assumed that the text gives all the answers: it provides the basis for the evaluation of business problems and the analysis of the business environment. Business Studies students should use the book as a basic text but, in addition, should refer to textbooks of the various disciplines, as well as read newspapers and journals and obtain current ideas and information from television and radio.

Business Studies is a dynamic subject which requires constant observation of current business activities. The book emphasises the nature of change, and at the same time gives students an insight into the spirit of modern society; it complements other social studies by attempting to provide a better understanding of the social and economic environment.

Acknowledgements

Tables and diagrams from *Social Trends*, *1979* and *1983* are reproduced in this book with the permission of the Controller of Her Majesty's Stationery Office.

PART ONE
Customers and Clients

1

The Population

Sources of UK population data

1 The census of population

Population statistics are collected by the Office of Population and Census Surveys. To carry out a complete count (census) of every person in the country is complicated and expensive. Consequently the census is only fully conducted once every ten years, when, on a given night, account is taken of every person in the United Kingdom. There is a statutory obligation on every household to provide the following information:

(*a*) The type of housing, the number of rooms, toilets, etc.
(*b*) The number of people in the house.
(*c*) Each person's age, sex, marital status, occupation, educational attainment and country of birth.

2 Vital statistics

In addition to the main census, other information – on births, deaths and marriages – is constantly being obtained by the Registrar General's Office. These statistics are known as 'vital statistics', and provide up-to-date details of the population structure. The population picture is made complete by the information on immigration and emigration which is collected by the Home Office.

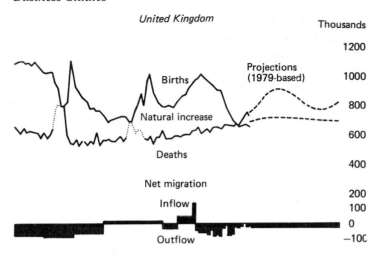

Fig. 1.1 UK population changes and projections (source: *Social Trends*, 1983)

Change in the UK population

The organisations which are responsible for planning in the economy are concerned about *relative* changes in the population rather than the absolute statistics. Consequently the information which is provided by the Registrar General on births, deaths, and marriages, is quoted in *rates of change*:

1 Birth rate: Fertility
During the past 70 years birth rates have declined greatly. In the early part of the century the average number of children for each married woman was six, compared with the modern level of two. However, this trend has not been constant, and Fig. 1.1 illustrates how birth rates have fluctuated during the twentieth century.

2 Death rate: Mortality
Discoveries in medicine and improved hygiene caused life expectancy to increase during the first half of the twentieth century. In

recent years, however, there has been a tendency for mortality, at some adult ages, to become worse rather than better – for example, the death of men in their fifties due to heart disease. Even so, the expectation of life has improved as the century has progressed. For example, if we compare the chances of survival in the 1930s with the 1980s, during these fifty years the chances improved for babies by 13%; for men and women up to the age of 60 by 25%; for men up to 77 by 7%; and for women up to 77 by 20%. Improvements have not taken place for those over 90 years of age.

The most significant feature of the United Kingdom death rate is that, for many age groups, people have a 25% better chance of reaching a given age than they did fifty years ago.

3 Migration rate: Mobility

Traditionally emigration has exceeded immigration in the United Kingdom. However, during the early 1960s there was a substantial inflow of immigrants from the Commonwealth. This inflow of people was reduced by legislation, which restricted entry into the United Kingdom; and the traditional trend was soon re-established. For example, during the decade 1964 to 1974, 2.8 million people left and 2.3 million came to the United Kingdom to live.

Total population changes

These rates of change in births, deaths, and migration determine the total population. Fig. 1.1 illustrates the population changes from 1901 to 1979, and projects the forecasted trends to the year 2011. The gap between births and deaths provides the net natural increase in the total population. From this total the net migration numbers should be added or subtracted to give the total population.

Optimum population

Much discussion has taken place on what would constitute an optimum or ideal population for the United Kingdom. However, there is no consensus either on what would form an optimum population, or on how it could be achieved. Obviously changes in the structure of the population affect the provision of public services such as education, housing and health; and all governments hope for stability in the birth rate. But there is little that democratic governments can do to control birth rates directly.

Recent changes in the population structure

	1941	1961	1981
Total Population:	48m	53m	56m

The total population in the United Kingdom has been increasing since the Second World War. A sharp decline in the birth rate during the 1970s interrupted the trend; but the projections for the rest of the century show a continuing, if slower, growth.

An implication of net growth of the population is that there is an increase in demand for all types of product and services; this is particularly true of the need for housing. During the thirty years 1951 to 1981 the total number of dwellings in the United Kingdom will have increased from 12m to almost 19m; and the size and standard of accommodation has also improved. Thus the problems which a growth in population can cause, such as overcrowding and homelessness, have been greatly relieved since the Second World War.

The increased demand for food is another important implication of population growth. The United Kingdom produces only half of its requirements for food, and so increases in the population not only require home producers to become more efficient, but also put pressure on the Balance of Payments to pay for imported food.

Under-sixteens

Children between the ages of 5 and 16 years must, by law, attend school. Therefore any variation in the number of those under 16 years has significant implications for the education service. The figures given below show how the number of children who require education has fluctuated since 1941.

	1941	1961	1981
% of the pop. under 16 years	21%	25%	22%
Actual number	10.1m	13.1m	12.3m

It is these fluctuations which cause problems: when the school population is increasing, then there is pressure to build more schools, to purchase more educational equipment, and to train more teachers. However, when the school population declines – as it did in the United Kingdom during the 1970s because of the falling birth rate – then some of these expensive resources become redundant.

A second major difficulty occurs when a large proportion of people aged 16 years leave school and are unable to find employment. For example, the children born in the 'bulge' in the birth rate which occurred in the early 1960s (see Fig. 1.1) became part of the working population during the late 1970s. Many of them could not find jobs, and the government, in an attempt to solve the problem, set up Youth Opportunity Programmes, paid youth employment subsidies to employers, and in 1983 introduced the Youth Training Scheme.

Retired people – men over 65 years, women over 60 years

	1941	*1961*	*1981*
% of the pop. who are retired	12%	15%	18%
Actual number retired	5.7m	7.7m	9.8m

Children and retired people are part of the *dependent population* – that is, they have to be supported by the working population. The statistics show how the proportion of elderly people has steadily increased since the Second World War. The main implications of this growth are for the social services and the National Health Service.

The expenditure on the social services has increased dramatically since the 1940s; and the increase in the numbers of elderly people has been a major factor in this increased spending. For example, half of the Government's expenditure on social security is spent on the elderly. In addition to this support, retired people often need hospital treatment or visits from GPs; as the proportion of elderly people grows, so does the need for more geriatric treatment and other forms of health service.

The working population

The working population includes all those who are in employment, those registered as unemployed, and the self-employed. Fig. 1.2 shows the composition of the labour force from 1951, projected to 1991.

Since the Second World War there has been a gradual increase in the working population from approximately 20m to around 26m in the 1980s. The most significant change in the composition of the United Kingdom's labour force has been the increase in working married women. More than 4m more married women were working in 1980 than in 1950.

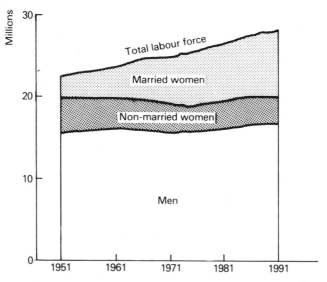

Fig. 1.2 Composition of the labour force, Great Britain 1951–1991
(source: *Social Trends*, 1979)

The change in the composition of the working population has implications for all types of consumer markets. For example, working women have more money to spend on clothes and cosmetics; and, because their time at home is limited, they will tend to buy convenience foods rather than fresh food. There are also social implications. For example, the Equal Pay Act, 1970, and the Sex Discrimination Act, 1975, illustrate how the government has had to formulate social and economic policy to meet the increased political power of female employees.

Demographic change, attitudes and beliefs

Changes in the structure of the population cannot be separated from changes in people's attitudes and beliefs. People's opinions about such things as marriage, material needs or politics can influence the nature of the population structure. Two examples of recent changes in attitudes which have social, political, and economic implications are attitudes to marriage and family life, and attitudes to rural and urban living.

Example 1   Attitudes to marriage and family life: Birth rates

The pressure to liberate women from certain roles in society has led to changes in the economic power of working women. Legislation has helped to enforce these changes: the Equal Pay Act, 1970, prevents discrimination against women in the terms and conditions of employment; the Sex Discrimination Act, 1975, set up the Equal Opportunities Commission to ensure that discrimination in employment does not occur. These changes in the law have themselves altered the economic status of women and, in turn, have affected attitudes to family life and to child rearing. In addition to legal changes, improved techniques in contraception, as well as a greater understanding of family planning, have led to changes in attitudes concerning the size of families. These legal, social and economic changes certainly influenced a dramatic fall in the birth rate during the 1970s, a fall which will have long-term consequences for employment and social policy, and immediate consequences for education policy.

Example 2   Attitudes to rural and urban living: Migration

Far fewer people now choose to live in the centres of cities and inner urban areas. Richer members of society have been able to find homes outside these areas. As a result, city centres have the problems of decaying and derelict homes, poor schools and high crime rates. Many of these problems are related to 'problem immigration', because a large proportion of poor immigrants settle in the urban areas where accommodation is cheapest.

Associated with urban decline are the problems of overcrowding and poverty; the slums of the inner cities create homelessness, poverty and destitution. In addition to urban decay are the problems of traffic congestion and pollution, which make planning and re-development imperative.

Successive governments have tried to solve these problems. For example, the provision of employment assistance and the social services helps the disadvantaged in the inner cities. In addition, in the 1970s the government established programmes to improve the urban environment. The Inner Urban Areas Act, 1978, designated the city areas which required the most help, and provided finance to improve premises and transport facilities. The long-term aim of the government is to attract business back into the inner city areas.

These two examples illustrate the important point that population changes and changes in attitudes are linked; and that both have a direct and indirect effect on public and private organisations.

2

Social and Material Needs

In Business Studies, wants and needs are referred to as 'markets'. In general the term 'market' is used in connection with commercial activity; however, in a broader sense, there is a market for hospital beds, or for places in university, or for any other public service. Thus all organisations, both public and private, have some form of market in which they 'distribute' their product or service (see Fig. 2.1). Organisations exist because customers and clients have wants and needs.

Home demand for goods and services

As a general rule, when people purchase goods they are *customers*; when they receive a service they are *clients*. This distinction between customers and clients is not rigid. Many industries such as Hotels and Catering, Transport, Entertainment and Retailing provide a service, but serve customers.

An important theoretical difference between a customer and a client is that a client receives specialist advice or help which is administered on a personal level. For example, people's *social needs* are mainly provided for, on a personal basis, by government services such as education, health and welfare. In addition to public social services there are private organisations, such as those engaged in banking, accountancy, insurance, and legal advice, which provide professional and commercial services for clients.

People's *material wants* are satisfied by the production of goods. The best illustration of the type of goods which people primarily need or want is given by the items which are included in the Index of Retail Prices. Table 2.1 shows the approximate proportion of total consumer expenditure which is spent on the six main items:

Table 2.1 Proportions of total consumer expenditure

	%
Food	20
Housing	15
Clothing and footwear	8
Alcohol	8
Durable household goods	4
Tobacco	4

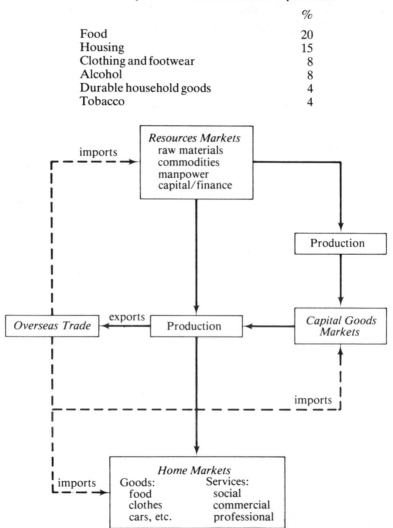

Fig. 2.1 Markets: the main areas of demand

Capital goods markets

It is important to realise that organisations themselves act as customers and clients. There are many firms which do not serve the public directly, but are involved in producing goods and services for other organisations. For example, the government is a customer for computers, private corporations are clients of external auditors. Almost all producers have to buy finished, or partially finished, goods in order to complete a stage of production: a car manufacturer requires steel plate in order to make car bodies; a farmer requires a tractor to produce grain. Goods which are produced for other producers are referred to as *producer goods*.

Overseas markets

Britain is one of the world's leading trading nations, and has traditionally bought and sold goods all over the world. However membership of the Common Market is changing the pattern of Britain's trade, and more and more trade is taking place within the EEC. Almost two-thirds of the United Kingdom's overseas markets are now situated either in Europe or in North America. The nature of the United Kingdom's export markets, and the destination of the exports, is illustrated by Tables 2.2 and 2.3.

Table 2.2 The nature of the UK's exports

Type of export	% of total exports
Manufactured goods	27
Machinery and transport equipment	19
Fuels and lubricants	18
Food	16
Crude raw materials	9
Chemicals	6
Drink and tobacco	2
Others	3
Total	100%

Table 2.3   The destination of the UK's exports

Destination of exports	% of total exports
European Economic Community	32
The rest of Western Europe	17
Developing countries	15
North America	12
OPEC countries	11
Other developed countries	9
Centrally planned economies	4
Total	100%

The demand for resources

In addition to producer goods, every organisation requires resources in order to produce. Resources, or *factors of production*,
fall into three categories:

1   The labour markets

Everyone who can work belongs to at least one labour market.
Labour markets range from the demand for labourers to the
demand for highly skilled people such as doctors and architects.
There is an immense variety of occupations, and Table 2.4 gives a

Table 2.4   The UK's labour markets (males)

Types of labour market (males)	% of total
Engineering and allied trade workers	16
Professional and technical workers	11
Transport and communications workers	8
Sales workers	8
Clerical workers	7
Labourers	6
Service, sport and recreation workers	6
Administrators and managers	5
Farmers, foresters and fishermen	4
Construction workers	3

general idea of the nature of labour markets which employ almost three-quarters of the male working population.

The main factors which determine to which market or markets a person belongs are education and training, previous experience and personality (see Chapter 11).

2   Raw materials markets: The commodity markets

Some of the most important goods in the raw materials markets are natural products, although developments in synthetic products are causing structural changes in the natural product markets. All material products contain natural ingredients, and the demand for these ingredients tends to remain steady throughout the year. The production of natural products is, however, often on a seasonal basis; consequently many commodities are sold through formal markets or *Exchanges*. For example, the London Commodity Exchange deals in more than twenty commodities including coffee, sugar, spices and gums. Other Exchanges concentrate entirely on one type of product, such as the Rubber Exchange and the Metal Exchange.

3   The finance markets

Many organisations require funds to finance production (see Chapter 10), and there are two main finance markets. The *Money Market* deals in short-term loans, and this market involves the Bank of England and the commercial and merchant banks, as well as the Discount Houses. Most loans which exceed 91 days are obtained from the *Capital Market*: organisations acquire medium- and long-term loans through such institutions as the Stock Exchange and Finance Corporations.

3

The Mechanism of the Market

Demand

The various forms of market which were described in Chapter 2 exist because people want that range of goods and services: the demand for goods and services is the basis of all business operations. However, people's wants and needs are never constant. The first part of this chapter examines the factors which determine demand; and analyses how and why people's wants and needs change.

Factors which influence demand

1 The producer's influence

Demand, in this context, means that customers and clients have the intention of acquiring the goods or services, as well as the money to pay for what they want. An analysis of the market as a mechanism does not include the wants and desires which people cannot afford. Having stated this assumption, it follows that the lower the *price* of a product then, generally, more people will be able to afford it, and consequently the demand will increase. Conversely, when the price increases, fewer people will buy the product, and the market will contract.*

Elasticity of demand   The relationship between price and demand is not straightforward: the extent to which demand responds to changes in price varies. For example, goods which are 'essential',

* See Appendix 2

such as tobacco, will be bought almost regardless of their price. When the price changes and change in demand is small, demand is said to be *inelastic*. On the other hand, if a product, such as fresh fruit, is produced by many competitors, then an increase in the price by one producer will probably lead to a reduction in the demand for that producer's goods, because people will simply buy the alternative producers' products. When demand does respond easily to changes in price then it is said to be *elastic*.*

Price, then, is one of the main factors which encourages or discourages people from buying a good or a service; and producers can influence the demand for their products by altering the price. When competition is keen then the market mechanism influences the producer's price decisions. Because where there are many producers competing in the same market, any one can price himself out of the market: a high price will make people turn to alternative producers, or even to different products. When a producer dominates a market (monopoly), then market forces play a smaller part in price decisions (see Chapter 4).

2 The customer's/client's influence

Price is not the only factor which influences demand. Members of the public are always changing their minds, and altering their ideas. Even when the price remains constant the demand for a product can change. Such changes are called *shifts* in demand, because the whole relationship between demand and price changes.

The producers of goods and services are aware that popularity is one of the most important external influences on demand; consequently they attempt, through sales promotion, to influence the opinions of customers. Naturally, changes in *tastes and fashions* are not entirely in the hands of sales promoters. There are other influences:

(*a*) *Changes in the age distribution* of the population often create changes in demand. This is illustrated by the increasing need for Homes for the Elderly and for geriatric services as a larger proportion of the population becomes older.

(*b*) *The introduction of new products*. People's tastes often

* See Appendix 2

change when products or services are replaced by new alternatives. For example, the development of television caused a sharp decline in cinema attendances; and the invention of the digital watch has almost eliminated the mechanical watch industry. Similarly, passenger ocean-going liners became less popular as jet air travel expanded.

(*c*)   *Public pressure.*   Direct pressure by groups can influence people's tastes. There are groups which attempt to persuade the public to buy, or to avoid buying, certain products. An example of such a body is the anti-apartheid movement which attempts to persuade people not to buy produce from South Africa. Another example is the Campaign for Real Ale (CAMRA), which persuaded many customers to buy beer which is made by small traditional breweries rather than the beer manufactured by the large national companies. An independent pressure group which has a semi-scientific basis for its recommendations is the Consumers' Association. The Association publishes *Which?*, a magazine which analyses products under 'laboratory' conditions, and influences the market by giving guidance on which products perform best.

3   Changes in people's income
An important factor which causes shifts in demand are changes in the real disposable income of customers and clients. Although income can come from many sources – profits, interest, dividends, rent, social security benefits – most income is in the form of salaries or wages.

The factors which influence what people have to spend are:

(*a*)   *Changes in real income.*   Increases in real purchasing power arise from wage and salary increases, and from a change to an occupation where the pay is higher. Increases in real income enable people to become customers and clients for products and services which they previously could not afford. Even when the price of a product increases, people will often buy more of it when their real income increases. For example, the demand for foreign travel increased as earnings increased, even when 'package tours' increased in price. This does not of course apply generally to durable goods – a family would not normally buy a second washing machine, say, except to replace the present one.

(*b*)   *Changes in the price of other goods and services.*   The demand for a good or service is sometimes affected by the price of other goods and services. Some items of personal expenditure are essential (inelastic demand) – for example, most people have to spend money on rent, rates and food. If the cost of these essential items increases, then there is less money remaining to buy other products and the demand for non-essential items, such as entertainment and luxury goods, falls (elastic demand).

(*c*)   *Changes in taxation.*   The State's income is obtained through direct and indirect taxation. All taxation leads to a reduction in people's income, and therefore, when taxation levels are increased, there is an automatic reduction in the demand for the goods and services purchased by private citizens. However, the government does spend the revenue which it has obtained on public services such as education, health and police, which keeps the money in the system.

Changes in tastes and income cause constant shifts in demand, and therefore are a perennial problem for producers. In order to survive, organisations can never remain static: they must always be responding to changes in society.

Supply

Since every organisation exists to serve customers or clients, it is essential that whatever the organisation creates – either products or services – should be consumed or used by people. Organisations function for the benefit of people: if they are unable to meet society's wants and needs, then they go out of business. This fact means that almost all organisations, both public and private, have to be very conscious of the needs and wants of people; and their production must be shaped to meet these needs.

Business activity (production) is usually divided into three sectors: primary, secondary and tertiary. The relative importance of these divisions, in terms of employment, is illustrated by Table 3.1. This shows the trend over the last twenty years for the tertiary (service) sector to expand, and to become the most important sector for the employment of labour.

Table 3.1   Employees in employment: by industry

United Kingdom   Thousands

	1961	1966	1971	1977	1979	1980
Agriculture, forestry, and fishing	710	580	432	388	367	370
Mining and quarrying	727	570	396	350	346	344
Manufacturing						
Food, drink and tobacco	793	797	770	711	698	681
Chemicals, coal and petroleum products	499	495	482	472	482	470
Metal manufacture	643	627	557	483	444	401
Engineering and allied industries	3 654	3 778	3 615	3 295	3 269	3 121
Textiles, leather and clothing	1 444	1 319	1 124	941	897	813
Rest of manufacturing	1 508	1 571	1 511	1 390	1 386	1 322
Total manufacturing	8 540	8 587	8 058	7 292	7 176	6 808
Construction	1 485	1 648	1 262	1 270	1 292	1 265
Gas, electricity, and water	389	432	377	347	346	347
Services						
Transport and communication	1 678	1 622	1 568	1 468	1 494	1 500
Distributive trades	2 767	2 920	2 610	2 753	2 826	2 790
Insurance banking and finance	684	818	976	1 145	1 233	1 258
Professional and scientific services	2 124	2 591	2 989	3 647	3 729	3 717
Miscellaneous services	1 819	2 066	1 946	2 343	2 493	2 519
Public administration	1 311	1 424	1 509	1 615	1 619	1 596
Total services	10 382	11 441	11 597	12 970	13 394	13 379
All industries and services	22 233	23 257	22 122	22 619	22 920	22 511

As at June each year   *Social Trends*, 1983.

Primary production

Primary production is concerned with making use of the natural resources of the country. It is a vital part of the economy in that it produces essential goods such as food and raw materials. This sector is very small in relation to the other sectors: it employs only 3% of the working population. The industries which are part of primary production are:

(*a*) *Extractive industries.* The main extractive industries are engaged in mining, drilling and quarrying: and they extract products such as coal, oil and gas directly from nature. An important feature of these industries is that they are short term: the resources which they extract are limited in supply, and once they have been extracted they cannot be replaced.

(*b*) *Agriculture and fishing.* Agriculture is similar to the extractive industries in that it uses a natural resource – land – to produce; but unlike them it also uses climatic conditions. This means that, with careful planning, the production cycle can go on indefinitely, though care must be taken by farmers to avoid soil erosion and pollution, otherwise production could be impaired. Generally the crop production cycle is annual; but some products, such as trees, require a cycle of thirty to forty years. The fishing industry is similar to agriculture: provided fishing grounds are not overfished, stocks will last indefinitely.

Secondary production

The industries which are engaged in secondary production utilise the raw materials which are obtained through primary sources, either in the UK or overseas; and by employing men, machines and materials they produce manufactured goods. It is the sector which

Table 3.2 Employees in employment in the secondary sector (percentages of total employees in employment)

Industry	% 1981
Engineering	14.4
Construction	5.3
Textiles	3.3
Food, drink and tobacco	3.0
Chemicals	2.0
Gas, electricity and water	1.6
Other	5.7
Total in secondary sector	35.3

creates the material wealth of the country, and the range of products is enormous.

The range of activity in the secondary sector is illustrated by the list of industries which are engaged in producing goods (Table 3.2).

Tertiary production (service industries)

It is in the service industries where customers and clients come into direct contact with organisations. Despite the secondary sector's importance in the creation of wealth, the trend is for a smaller proportion of the working population to be engaged in the manufacture of goods, and for more and more people to be employed in the service industries. The growth of the tertiary sector is one of the most important features of the British economy. More than 60% of the working population are now employed in the service industries, and the number is growing. The growth, and range, of this sector is illustrated by Table 3.3, which compares the proportion of employees in the service industries in 1961 and in 1981.

Table 3.3 Employees in employment in the tertiary sector (percentages of total employees in employment)

Industry	% 1961	% 1981
Professional services	9.6	17.4
Distributive trades	12.4	12.4
Miscellaneous services	8.2	11.4
Public administration	5.9	7.5
Transport and communication	7.5	6.8
Insurance and banking	3.1	5.8
Total in tertiary sector	46.7	61.3

The market as a mechanism

Business is the interaction between those who require goods and services, and those who produce goods and services. This interaction, which allows people's wants and needs to be satisfied, is made possible by the market acting as a mechanism. The degree of influence which market forces exert depends on the nature and extent of competition between producers.

Perfect competition

For a perfect market to exist two assumptions, both fairly unrealistic, have to be satisfied: (*a*) there are many producers, and they are all manufacturing identical products; and (*b*) every customer knows the price of each manufacturer's products. It is rare for manufacturers to produce identical products, and therefore perfect competition rarely exists in business. The best examples are the commodity markets such as the London Metal Exchange and the London Tea Auctions, and the finance markets such as the Stock Exchange and the Foreign Exchange market.

When these assumptions are met, as they are in the examples given, then the consumer is 'sovereign': everyone knows the price of the different products; and with this knowledge customers/clients will always purchase the cheapest item. Those firms which charge a higher price than their competitors, either because they are greedy or inefficient, will automatically go out of business. Competition thus leads to business efficiency. The price which is charged in a perfect market is determined by the interaction between consumers and the most efficient suppliers. The market mechanism sets the price, and determines how much is supplied.

Monopoly

The other extreme form of market control is when an organisation dominates, or monopolises, the market. A monopolist is able either to set the price of his product, or to decide how much to produce. The best examples of monopolistic producers in the UK are the nationalised industries – British Rail, the Electricity and Gas Boards. Although private organisations are legally restrained from monopolising a market, there are some private businesses which are almost monopolistic (oligopoly) – for example, detergent manufacturers (Unilever and Proctor & Gamble), cereal producers (Kellogs and Weetabix), and pharmaceuticals (Hoffmann and La Roche).

In practice, all commercial organisations face a degree of competition. Even the nationalised industries compete – for example, British Rail competes with road and air services, and the National Coal Board competes with other fuel producers. The most important point to remember is that the degree of competition within an industry varies, and therefore the nature of the market mechanism varies. When there are many producers in the same market the consumer's influence is great; when the market is dominated by a few firms then the consumer's influence diminishes.

4

Market Forces at Work

The markets which organisations serve are constantly changing. The demand for products and services is, as we saw in Chapter 3, influenced by many factors which are outside the control of business. In order to survive, organisations have to react to market changes. The elements of risk and uncertainty which exist in business are primarily caused by the shifting nature of demand. This chapter examines how organisations react to shifting demand, and how they contend with market forces.

Organisations respond to shifts in demand by being predominantly marketing conscious. When this occurs the firm is described as being 'marketing oriented'. In order to ensure their survival, organisations develop marketing strategies which often dominate the structure of the organisation to such an extent that the production function is incorporated within the marketing function.

All organisations, whether they are private or public, have to be conscious of the needs of their customers and clients. Many of them will develop marketing functions which include:

(*a*) Research into the nature of the present and future wants and needs of customers and clients.
(*b*) Planning how to meet the changes in the market.
(*c*) Executing the plans by the production of goods and services.
(*d*) Promotion through advertising and other techniques.
(*e*) Distribution of goods and services to the customers or clients.

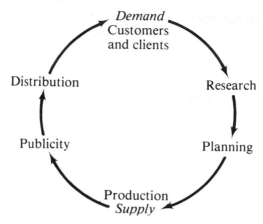

Fig. 4.1   The marketing-oriented organisation

Research into the nature of wants and needs

1   The census of population, and government surveys

The statistics which are obtained in the government's population census, which is carried out in detail every ten years, provide accurate information on the economic and social conditions of the population. Combined with the returns of the Registrar General on births, deaths and marriages, the census forms a factual basis for formulating the government's social and economic policies. Government departments also carry out surveys on a regular basis to ascertain trends – for example, the National Food Survey, the EEC's Consumer Attitudes Survey, the National Readership Survey and the National Training Survey.

2   Field research

Commercial organisations use survey techniques to analyse the market. The process of acquiring information about people's wants and needs is highly technical. First, the market researcher examines a *sample* of the *relevant* population, and then, from the findings on the sample, assesses the tastes, attitudes, and habits of the total market population. *Questionnaires* are the main method used to obtain information, and those who are included in the sample can be asked to give a range of details about themselves and their buying habits.

Well-known examples of this technique are public opinion polls, which forecast the result of general elections. The prediction of the result is actually based on a very small proportion of the electorate. Similarly, many private organisations use field research to try to determine people's *reaction* to their product or service. This type of research is also used by public organisations – for example, the assessment of how many people watched a particular television programme is based on audience research methods using samples.

3 Desk research

Private organisations are interested not only in how customers' tastes are changing, but also in wider developments in the markets. An important method of acquiring information about market trends is to collect data from published sources – journals, magazines and newspapers, as well as specialised publications such as trade journals, company reports and other business publications. The government's Statistical Service publishes details of all aspects of business activity – prices, output, employment – and is one of the main sources of 'desk' or secondary information.

4 Elections

These too are a form of market research. The main method of deciding how the population feels about central and local government services is by having an election, and the future provision of public services (public policy) is influenced by the electorate's reaction to previous policy decisions. Elections are, in effect, extensive and accurate opinion polls.

Forecasting – the application of market research

Forecasting is a semi-scientific prediction of the future. Forecasting shifts in demand is especially hazardous: there is no way of ensuring that the predictions will be accurate, and this provides the risk element in business. The reliability of a forecast depends on three factors:

(*a*)   The *accuracy* of the research information which is used in the calculation of the forecast. For example, when a sample is very small then the information which is obtained from it is less reliable.

(*b*)   The *relevance* of the information which is included. For example, the buying habits of customers in Hong Kong are not necessarily a good indication of what might happen in Australia.

(*c*)   The *number of unknown variables* which form part of the prediction. For example, there are many unknown variables when an entirely new product is being launched, and it is easier to predict people's reaction to existing types of products than to completely new developments.

As a general rule, forecasts in the short term, when more variables are known, are more accurate than long-term predictions. For example, the meteorological office can predict, with 90% accuracy, tomorrow's weather; but the accuracy of the forecasts of next month's weather is considerably less.

There are many types of forecast, of which three are important for businesses:

1   Sales forecasts

These predict shifts in demand. *Long-term forecasts* normally take place when the organisation intends to develop a new product, or to invest in plant or capital equipment. *Short-term forecasts* generally cover a financial year, and contribute to the setting of budget standards. Short-term sales forecasts also enable a commercial organisation to set its prices, and to help avoid cash-flow problems (see Chapter 13).

There are three methods of forecasting sales:

(*a*)   Analysis of market research information; and assessment of the many variables which affect sales, such as the general economic outlook, trends in the existing market, the activities of competitors and recent sales performance.

(*b*)   Statistical analysis of previous sales records.

(*c*)   Speculation by sales executives based on past sales experience, and information from salesmen in the field.

2   Economic forecasts

The government attempts to predict future economic activity by analysing trends in such economic variables as investment and expenditure. Economic predictions are often unreliable because the variables consist of millions of independent decisions which customers and clients make daily.

3 Technological forecasts

Forecasts which attempt to predict long-term technological change are used by the government. For example, the Delphi method of forecasting requires experts to predict possible future problems in technology and related fields. Such forecasts are primarily based on opinions rather than quantitative information, and so tend to be unreliable; their application to commercial activity is limited.

Planning – the application of forecasts

The plans of organisations are based on their predictions of how customers and clients are going to act: plans are prepared courses of action for future events.

Planning at national level

The extent of state planning is determined by the degree of socialist philosophy which is present in the policy decisions. Britain has a *mixed economy*, which means that some state planning does take place; but most economic activity is left to the decisions of private organisations and private individuals (the market acting as a mechanism to allocate resources). The type of state planning which occurs in the United Kingdom is known as *Indicative Planning* – planning by consent. It should not be confused with the rigid five-year plans (Imperative Planning) adopted by totalitarian states such as the USSR and East Germany.

Indicative plans provide guidelines for business to follow: there are no legal sanctions which require the private sector to cooperate in the government's plans. The procedure is to:

(*a*) *Define objectives*. For example, a high rate of economic growth, an improvement on the Balance of Payments, or a reduction in the rate of inflation.

(*b*) *Consult interested groups*. In economic planning, for example, the government, through the National Economic Development Council, consults employers, the trade unions and the City.

(c)   *Determine policy.*   After examining economic forecasts, and after consultation, the government formulates economic and social policy. For example, it will decide the level of public expenditure on such items as education, housing, health and social welfare.

Planning at organisational level

Organisations develop their plans within the framework of government policies. Two of the most important forms of planning at organisational level are:

1   Corporate planning.   The first step in a corporate plan is a systematic study of the organisation's aims and objectives, especially in relation to the needs of customers and clients. Organisations then develop a corporate or unified strategy, which is designed to attain the goals outlined in the corporate plan. Thus corporate plans highlight both objectives and strategies. In recent years local authorities have used corporate planning techniques, and through them they have attempted to integrate the plans of different departments, such as education, housing, planning and transport, into one structure. The advantage of corporate planning is that quite separate departments in an organisation will be united in the pursuit of common goals and strategies.

2   Manpower planning.   Organisations are not only aware of the market in which they distribute their goods and services, but also of those markets which provide them with resources. One of the most important, and costly, resources is manpower. Because of its importance many organisations, both public and private, estimate their manpower needs in relation to:

(a)   Changes in the business environment.
(b)   The *natural wastage* which occurs when employees retire or leave the organisation.
(c)   The changing nature of occupations, and skills which the organisation will require.

The organisation's policy in recruitment, training, promotion and retirement of employees is planned in relation to these estimates.

Marketing and production

Product life-cycle

The changing nature of demand makes cooperation and coordination between marketing and production essential in manufacturing organisations. Most products have a life-cycle similar to the one shown in Fig. 4.2. It is necessary for both the marketing and the production departments to be aware of the product's position in its 'life cycle', so that corporate decisions on marketing and production can be made.

Types of decisions which might be included in a corporate plan are:

Position of the product	*Type of corporate decisions*
1 Pre-production and introductory stage	(i) Capital investment
	(ii) Recruitment of new employees
	(iii) Re-training of existing employees
	(iv) Nature of product differentiation
2 The growth stage	(v) Changes in price
	(vi) Expansion of production
3 Maturity and saturation stage	(vii) New market strategies
	(viii) Change the product's design (marginally)
	(ix) Alter the product's quality
4 Decline	(x) Extend market to overseas
	(xi) Reduce the product's price
	(xii) Cease production

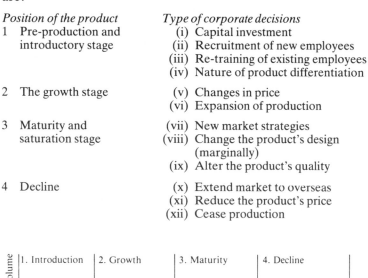

Fig. 4.2   The product life-cycle

The product life-cycle provides a good reason why the marketing and production departments should cooperate. The following topics illustrate the areas where cooperation between the two functions is common.

Production planning

The production of goods requires careful planning: raw materials have to be ordered, machinery has to be bought and maintained, and people with the appropriate skills have to be employed. The capacity of a production unit is determined by the resources which the manager has at his disposal. To ensure full utilisation of resources production managers prefer sales orders to be near to, not above, the capacity of the plant. Therefore liaison takes place between marketing and production departments to ensure that orders do not exceed the plant's capacity. If orders are delayed, then delivery dates are not met and customers become dissatisfied.

Research and development: product design

Decisions on the design and the range of products (*product mix*) also entail cooperation between marketing and production. Production methods are more efficient when products are standardised. On the other hand, new products must have sufficient variety to attract customers. It is, therefore, important for R&D teams to cooperate, not only with the production department on the methods of production of new products, but also with the marketing department on the type of customer the product is likely to attract.

Price and costs

When a product is of a high quality it is generally easier to sell, but is more expensive to produce because *quality control* is expensive. Costs, in addition to influencing quality, determine the price of a product. Often a firm has to decide between high quality/high price products and low quality/low price products. Such decisions require the expertise and judgment of both the marketing and production departments; consequently cooperation between marketing and production on the quality and the pricing of a product is common.

Packaging

An area where cooperation between production and marketing can improve efficiency is in the packaging of the finished product. The distribution of goods is regarded as a marketing function, but the actual despatch to customers is often made by a section of the production department. The nature of a product's packaging affects both despatch and sales. For example, problems in identification could occur in finished stock control if the products are packed in similar packages; on the other hand, identical product packaging can create *brand loyalty* in customers – for example, Heinz foods.

After-sales service

Durable products such as televisions, washing machines, cars and refrigerators have a 'life' of five to ten years, during which time they will require maintenance – after-sales service. Customer satisfaction is improved if the service keeps the product operational. This means that the production department has to manufacture spare parts – sometimes long after production of the model has ceased – and also has to train maintenance engineers. After-sales service is both a production and a marketing function: failure to provide spare parts or service facilities for 'discontinued' lines (for example 'out of production' cars) could deter existing customers from buying newer models from the same manufacturer.

Publicity

One of the most important methods which organisations use to try to change the nature of demand is publicity. The public image of the organisation, and its products or services, is at the root of the marketing function. It is unlikely that many organisations are able to create demand, but every organisation attempts to diagnose what people would like, through market research, and make them aware of its products and services. It may then use subtle methods to *persuade* customers and clients that its own particular product or service will best meet their needs.

There are three main methods of publicising products or services:

1 Advertising

This plays a very important part in business: over 1% of Britain's GNP is spent on it, and the purpose of such expenditure is to:

(*a*) Increase present sales by emphasising the desirable qualities of a product/service.
(*b*) Offset competition.
(*c*) Increase general market awareness of the range of products/services.
(*d*) Create goodwill, and build a corporate company image.
(*e*) Introduce new products, models or services to customers and clients.

Much advertising is handled by specialised *agencies*, which perform the following functions for the producing organisation:

(*a*) Ascertain people's buying motives, and the type of advertising which has the most appeal.
(*b*) Select the most appropriate medium: newspapers, television, films, posters, etc.
(*c*) Create and design the advertisements.
(*d*) Appraise the results of an advertising campaign through market research.

Not all advertising is designed to persuade potential buyers to buy: some commercial advertising, and almost all government advertising, is designed to *inform* people about products or services. Private enterprise uses informative advertising to tell customers about new products and new variations on existing products. The government uses advertising to explain regulations, to clarify citizens' rights and to give health warnings, and so on. However, most commercial organisations are in competition, and most advertising is used to persuade people that a firm's product is unique, and that the product's qualities are essential for the customer.

2 Sales promotion: 'below the line' advertising

Additional promotion methods – 'below the line' advertising – are often used to support an advertising campaign.

Examples are (*a*) displays at the point of sale; (*b*) free gifts, discount schemes and trading stamps; and (*c*) demonstrations and exhibitions.

3 Packaging and product differentiation

Producers often use packaging and labels (*trademarks*) to help customers to differentiate between their products and the products of close competitors. This technique is known as *branding*, and brand names are a common feature of everyday life (for example: Volvo cars, Parker pens, Wimpey houses). This technique can be so successful that customers often refer to a product by a brand name, such as 'Hoover', even when the product (in this case a vacuum cleaner) has been manufactured by a competitor. Producers hope to stress the brand image – 'Don't say brown say Hovis', 'Beanz meanz Heinz' – to such an extent that customers, when buying, ask for the brand rather than the product.

Branding has become such an important feature of sales promotion that some firms, in order to increase total sales, have created 'artificial' competition between brands, all of which are produced by the one firm. For example, there are only two major British manufacturers of soap powders and detergents – Unilever and Proctor & Gamble – but between them they produce eight different main brands. Another indication of the importance of branding is the fact that large retailers such as Tesco, Sainsbury and Boots use their own brand names on popular products like washing-up liquid, cereals and soft drinks.

Distribution – getting products to the people

An integral part of an organisation's marketing strategy is the method it uses to get the products to the customers. Service industries do not generally face this problem, because the production of most services is at the market source. Producers can choose the following *channels of distribution*:

1 Traditional

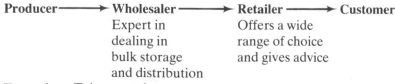

Producer ———▶ Wholesaler ———▶ Retailer ———▶ Customer
                   Expert in   Offers a wide
                   dealing in   range of choice
                   bulk storage   and gives advice
                   and distribution

Example: Tobacco and newspapers.

2   Eliminate the wholesaler

Producer ————————————→ **Retailer** ————→ **Customer**
Example: Marks & Spencer, who perform their own 'middleman'
              functions.

3   Eliminate the retailer

Producer ————→ **Wholesaler** ————————————→ **Customer**
Example: Discount stores, Hypermarkets and Mail Order com-
              panies which combine the functions of the wholesaler
              and retailer.

4   Direct service

Producer ——————————————————————→ **Client**
Example: Most services – banking, insurance, education and
              social services – fall into this category.

A producer will tend to use the full chain of distribution when the following conditions occur:

(*a*)   *High storage costs.*   Some technical products, such as components for cars and electrical goods, are rarely demanded; and they are, therefore, expensive to hold in stock. Similarly, some expensive products such as cars and furniture are not always immediately available, but have to be ordered by the customer. Such products are held by the producer or wholesaler, and delivery to the retailer is made in response to customer requirements.

(*b*)   *Perishability.*   The storage of some goods is often difficult because of their short life span. Perishable produce, such as fish, fruit and vegetables, are normally distributed through wholesale markets to retailers.

(*c*)   *Seasonal production.*   Where production is seasonal, but demand is constant, stock holding costs can be very high. For example, imported food purchased on the commodity markets, such as grain, coffee, tea and sugar, is stored in large amounts. They are then distributed gradually through the full distribution chain.

Monopoly

Producers do not like the uncertainties and risks of competition: many would prefer to monopolise the market. The reaction of most firms to the market mechanism is to try to minimise its harsh effects, and to obtain the *advantages* of being a monopoly. These are:

(*a*) Prices can be fixed by the producer, and the risks and uncertainties of price competition can be reduced or even eliminated.

(*b*) The benefits of price control make it possible for monopolistic producers to make larger profits.

(*c*) The monopolist is in a position to set output at a certain level, which makes production planning and control easier.

(*d*) Monopoly of a large market means that large-scale production can take place within one organisation. This brings economies of scale: finance is easier to obtain, more skilled and specialist personnel can be employed, distribution costs can be rationalised, and specialist equipment can be bought (see Chapter 12).

In order to reduce competition, producers can either combine with their competitors (integration), or they can agree to cooperate (restrictive practice).

Integration

There are two types of amalgamation: (*a*) *Merger:* the firms concerned agree to amalgamate, and (*b*) *Takeover:* one firm, without necessarily having the consent of the other firm, acquires sufficient shares to have a controlling interest.

Restrictive practice

An alternative to formal combinations between organisations is when firms come to some understanding or agreement with one another to restrict competition. Such restrictive practices can be illegal. Under the Restrictive Trade Practices Acts of 1956 and 1968, all restrictive agreements must be registered with the Registrar of Restrictive Trading Agreements. The Restrictive Practices Court can give approval to agreements when they include the following 'gateways':

Table 4.1   Integration and diversification

	Benefits	Examples
Horizontal integration	Expansion in the organisation's existing activities which increases its share of the market.	AEI and GEC, Boots and Timothy White
Vertical integration	Provides greater security for the organisation by extending its activities into another stage of its existing production.	Marks & Spencer and clothing manufacturers Breweries and pubs
Diversification	The organisation extends its range of products and its activities (Conglomerate). It therefore spreads the risks.	Rank Organisation: hotels, bread office copiers entertainment

Because the monopoly of a market distorts the market mechanism and can act against the public interest, the government prevents the development of pure monopolies. The Monopolies and Mergers Act, 1965, set up the Monopolies and Mergers Commission which investigates those mergers which are likely to operate against the consumers' interests. Any proposed amalgamation is referred to the Commission if 25% of a market would, as a result of the merger, be controlled by one supplier; or where the assets acquired in the merger exceed £5 million.

(a)   The restriction protects the public against injury.

(b)   Removal of the restriction would deny customers and clients substantial benefits. For example, the Cement Makers' Federation argued in the Court that prices were lower as a result of restrictive agreements, because the agreements reduced the degree of risk and kept many more firms in business.

(c)   Removal of the restriction would affect exports. Some firms have had long-standing agreements to cooperate in overseas markets. Such agreements may, however, be subject also to overseas legislation (for example, an Anti-Trust action brought in the United States was conceded by British book publishers, although the agreements in question were acceptable under British law).

(d)   Removal of the restriction would increase unemployment, since inefficient firms might go out of business.

(e)   The restriction does not directly or indirectly discourage competition.

Nevertheless, the main intention of many restrictive agreements has been to distort the market as a mechanism, and to attempt to gain some of the advantages of monopolistic control.

Questions on Part One

1   'In 1974 the number of births in England and Wales were the lowest since the Second World War; and in Scotland were the lowest since records have been kept.'
    Assess the main social, political and economic implications of this fact.

2   Do you think that the distinction between customers and clients is significant? Explain your answer.

3   Examine the differences between markets which are met by commercial organisations and markets served by non-commercial organisations.

4   Using the statistics in Tables 2.2 and 2.3, construct an appropriate diagram to illustrate the nature and destination of the United Kingdom's exports.

5   Explain what is meant by an 'economic resource', and describe, briefly, the nature of resource markets.

6   Distinguish between the market as a mechanism and the market as demand.

7   Explain what is meant by a 'shift in demand', and outline the main factors which can cause a shift in demand.

8   Construct a questionnaire to assess the reaction of local ratepayers to the provision of local government services.

9   Explain what is meant by 'product life cycle'. Using the concept of 'product life cycle' appraise the need of an organisation to adapt to market changes.

10 Compare and contrast methods of distributing goods, and outline the reasons why a producer chooses a particular method.

PART TWO
The Formation and Management of Organisations

Introduction: The main characteristics of organisations

This part examines the aims, formation, structure and obligations of organisations by analysing some of the main characteristics which organisations have in common. Not all characteristics are considered fully here (for example, the resources employed by organisations are examined in Part 3), but the list below provides an overview which is expanded in the following chapters.

1 Organisations have a purpose – aims. Organisations are established to meet a need in society. In meeting that need some organisations will set very definite and clear aims: for example, a manufacturing firm will want to stay in business and make a profit. Other organisations, such as hospitals or social services, will tend to react to circumstance rather than decide on clear aims (except the general aim of improving the services offered).

2 Organisations employ resources. All organisations employ people, they use consumables such as stationery and raw materials, and they have various types of plant and equipment as well as buildings.

3 Organisations have a formal structure. Each person in an organisation will be given a position in the organisational structure. The formal structure is often an hierarchical pyramid, as illustrated in the diagram overleaf.

4 Organisations have to be directed and controlled. The function of managers and supervisors in an organisation is to acquire and control the human and non-human resources in the organisation with the objective of implementing the policy of the business. Examples common to all organisations are the recruitment of staff and delegation of duties, financial control, and the purchase of equipment.

5   *Organisations are accountable.*   Most organisations are responsible for their actions and decisions to some form of authority:

> Public Companies to shareholders
> Nationalised Industries to the government minister concerned
> Civil Servants to government ministers
> Local Authority officials to elected representatives
> Governments to the electorate

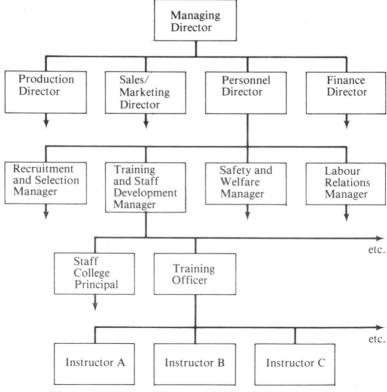

A typical formal organisational structure (pyramid) highlighting the personnel department's line management

6 Organisations have to meet legal requirements. All organisations which employ people have to comply with employment regulations dealing with recruitment, conditions of work and dismissal. Those organisations which sell goods have to meet legal requirements for consumer protection, and the actions of all private organisations are limited by company legislation.

Further characteristics of commercial organisations
Private organisations and nationalised industries in a mixed economy have some additional common characteristics:

7 Commercial organisations are subject to some form of competition. The degree of competition varies from one industry to another and some firms such as those in the Stock Exchange or a Commodity Exchange are engaged in almost pure competition. This contrasts sharply with the nationalised industries which are almost pure monopolies but still face some competition: for example, the electricity industry competes with gas, coal and oil for home heating, but has virtual monopoly in home lighting.

8 The government intervenes in commercial organisations. The extent and nature of government intervention is determined by the political party which is in power: a socialist Government is much more inclined to intervene, but all governments will impose taxes and controls.

5

Aims and Interdependence

Different contributions by organisations

Private organisations are formed mainly to provide for material wants and commercial needs in society, and so manufacturing and commerce dominate the private sector of British industry. Government organisations, on the other hand, tend to satisfy society's need for defence, law and order, management of the economy, education and social welfare. Organisations can only exist if they respond to needs and wants, and therefore their aims are primarily to satisfy the needs and wants of people, either directly or indirectly, or through meeting the needs of other organisations.

There is a distinction between an aim and an objective. *Aims* tend to be long term, they are indefinite and indicate intentions rather than specific goals. *Objectives*, however, are more specific, and generally they can be measured. The attainment of profit illustrates this difference. The best known aim of a private organisation is its desire to obtain, and possibly maximise, its profits. But this is not a clear-cut goal because (*a*) profitability is sometimes difficult to assess; and (*b*) short-term losses are sometimes incurred to bring about long-term profitability, for example price reductions which can undercut and eventually eliminate a competitor.

A company will convert the *aim* of profitability into a more specific *objective* such as to obtain a 15% return on capital during twelve months' trading.

The aims of an organisation are normally decided by the board of directors, or in the case of public organisations by government ministers, when policy decisions are made. The policies of an organisation clarify the aims and establish long-term plans. The conversion or implementation of an organisation's policy into specific objectives and tasks is the role of administrators and managers, and the process gives rise to the sequence shown in Fig. 5.1.

Set Aims ⟶ *Decide* Policy ⟶ *Organise* Tactical Action

Long-term plans ⟶ Set short-term departmental objectives

Fig. 5.1   The administrative process

Aims of private organisations

Shareholders and owners ensure that profitability is a main aim of private organisations, but the profit motive can obscure the fact that businesses are groups of people and each person in an organisation may have a desire to get prestige from the growth and size of the firm as well as satisfy a basic need for job security. The influence of employees on an organisation's aims is very strong. This final point is most important because evidence in the published literature of companies shows that most companies have several different aims which may become clear long-term goals in themselves, with profitability being a measure of success rather than an ultimate goal. Examples of these other aims are:

1   Survival.   A desire to remain in business almost at all costs is frequently illustrated by workers taking over insolvent organisations. Job security also dominates the activities of managers who, when a firm is in financial difficulties, will appeal to the Government for help and at the same time declare a belief in private enterprise.

2   Increasing the share of the market.   Expansion of the company's activities is often good for the morale of employees and shareholders, although it can lead to problems of administration and lower profitability.

3   Prestige – improving the company image.   Many companies will develop customer and public relations in the hope of creating a 'status' image. The desire to obtain a Queen's Award for Industry illustrates this aim.

4   Cash flow.   Some firms will aim to maintain a constant flow of cash into the company so that working capital is always available. Working capital is often more important than profitability, although the two are obviously interlinked.

The wide range of personal goals, expectations and decisions which exist in a firm make it very likely that the most significant aims of a private organisation will be influenced by the people within the organisation.

Aims of commercial public corporations

Public Corporations, unlike private organisations, have their aims decided by the Government. The White Papers of 1967 and 1978 which dealt with the aims of the Nationalised Industries give them two broad obligations:

1 *Commercial obligations.* Nationalised industries have to manage their resources and use various pricing policies to ensure that an adequate return on their capital is made. The target rate of return on capital varies from industry to industry, but is calculated as though the public corporation were acting as a commercial firm.
2 *Social obligations.* The commercial aims of nationalised industries are compromised by their social obligations. For example, the Post Office must provide a postal service in rural areas even when that service is unprofitable. There is conflict between the two main political parties as to the role of the nationalised sector, which adds to the confusion. A Conservative Government would stress the commercial aims more rigorously than a Socialist Government.

Aims of government departments and local authorities

The aims of government departments and local authorities are laid down by statute, and each organisation within the public sector has legal obligations to provide certain services. For example, the Department of Education and Science, through the Local Education Authorities, provides compulsory education for children between the ages of 5 and 16 years. The provision is the responsibility of the LEAs, and the maintenance of educational standards is the responsibility of the DES.

Government departments and local authorities thus have their aims much more clearly defined than private companies. They are not in business to make a profit; they acquire their funds primarily through taxation and so do not have the yardstick of profitability with which to measure success. However, techniques have been developed in recent years which enable government bodies to clarify the aims of a particular project or service. The technique of Cost-Benefit Analysis (CBA), where the costs of a project are listed and compared with the benefits, has helped to improve the analysis and understanding of the complex issues in public expenditure. CBA also provides comparisons between projects because it uses a standard measurement which is quantifiable, and by so doing it clarifies the economic and social aspects of policy decisions in the public sector. The technique is very complex, but the following list of items which were considered in comparing sites for the construction of a car park provides a simplified example of the nature of the exercise and the number of variables involved:

Costs	*Benefits*
Purchase of land	Rents from car parking
Capital building	Increase in business in locality
Maintenance	Less traffic congestion
Wages	Need for fewer car park attendants
Pollution	Fewer accidents, therefore less cost on NHS.

Some costs and returns are easy to identify, for example the purchase of the land or the rents from car parking. But the hidden benefits, such as fewer accidents, or hidden costs, such as more pollution caused by increased traffic, are not easily isolated.

Interdependence and the complementary activities of organisations

An interesting aspect of Cost-Benefit Analysis is that, although it is used in the public sector, it highlights the important fact that the aims and activities of organisations are not independent. Private organisations create hidden costs and benefits for other firms and for society in general. No organisation is isolated.

Everyone in a modern industrial society is a consumer, and most of the adult population are producers. None could exist entirely on his own efforts – even those who produce food require services and goods produced by others, such as housing, clothing and education, as well as additional types of food. The more economically advanced society becomes, the more interdependent people and organisations become, so that if one sector such as electricity fails to function then most businesses also fail to maintain output.

The activity of one business completes or complements the activity of other businesses. The extent of complementary activity or interdependence can be illustrated by several examples:

1 The need for raw materials and producer goods. One of the best examples of interdependence is the need that most organisations have for the products of other firms. Farmers need fertilizers and farm machinery; the health service needs hospitals, pharmaceuticals, complex medical equipment, as well as everyday items such as beds and linen. All organisations require basic supplies such as fuel, stationery, water and waste disposal. No organisation can exist in isolation.

2 The need for social services. Firms are dependent on one another for raw materials and producer goods. This is a fairly obvious form of interdependence. Less obvious but equally necessary is the need for educated and healthy people. All organisations depend on the education service to provide literate and numerate people, and they also depend on the health service either to prevent illness or to help sick or injured employees to return to work as soon as possible.

3 Strike action. Strikes, particularly in basic industries such as fuel and power or transport, can soon disrupt the whole of the economy. In a rail strike people cannot easily get to work, many goods are not distributed, and letters and parcels are not delivered.

4 The need for imports. The United Kingdom is heavily dependent on other countries to provide food and raw materials. Some 80% of all goods imported in the UK fall into this catagory (demand is inelastic). If supply of these products is restricted by war, political unrest, climatic catastrophe or any other factor, then organisations will be affected. A good example is the 1979 revolution in Iran, which reduced total world oil supplies by only 5% but caused severe problems for businesses and governments in the industrial world.

5   *Levels of employment.*   Mass production requires mass consumption. All goods and services which are produced have to be bought, otherwise the producing organisation will go out of business. When people become unemployed their income falls and with it their purchasing power. Unemployment caused by the failure of one firm will often lead in this way to the failure of other firms.

6   *Level of public expenditure.*   Demand for goods and services is, as we have seen, the basis for all organisational activity. The Government, through its expenditure policies on defence, housing and social services, represents the most important customer for many firms and thus, by controlling public expenditure, can influence the level of business activity. Cuts in public expenditure frequently lead to unemployment in many other organisations, as well as those directly affected.

7   *Inflation.*   Harold Wilson, when Prime Minister, said that one man's wage increase was another man's price increase. This comment illustrates the relationship between costs and prices. All wages and salaries are part of an organisation's costs, and they will be taken into account when prices are determined. Increases in wages will often lead to increased costs which will lead to increased prices: wages and prices are interdependent, though the extent to which this is so is often disputed.

6

The Formation of Organisations

Organisations function within a legal framework. The nature and extent of the framework varies from the very formal, in which public limited liability companies operate, to the less formal rules which govern the operations of a social club.

Legal rules apply to many aspects of a business from its creation and operation to its eventual dissolution. The main thread which runs through company law is the recognition that joint or corporate action is necessary for attaining business aims.

The creation of organisations

Corporate action is an important feature of institutions and consequently the formation of a corporation through an *incorporated association* is the main method organisations use to establish themselves, both in the public and private sector. By incorporation the organisation has an existence which is separate from its members: it is in effect an artificial 'person' and as such can enter into contracts and sue and be sued.*

Private corporations

Registration under the Companies Act is the most common method

---

* This basic rule applies even when the company is in practice a one-man company. For example, Salomon & Co. Ltd was run as a one-man company with six relatives having nominal shares in the company; in Salomon *v* Salomon & Co. Ltd, 1897, it was held that Salomon was an entirely separate legal person from Salomon & Co. Ltd.

whereby private firms become incorporated. The types of private company which can be created under company legislation are:

Public Limited Liability Company. Members of the general public can purchase shares in the company through the Stock Exchange. All the best known private enterprises are in this category.

Private Limited Liability Company. The shareholding of private companies is restricted: the public cannot subscribe for shares or debentures in private companies. The members of such companies tend to be families or small groups (such as 'pop' groups).

Both of these types of company have limited liability, which means that the personal liability of the owners is restricted. Unlimited liability would mean that in the event of loss all the members would be liable for all debts which have been incurred, and thus might have to sell their private possessions (houses, cars, etc.) to repay the debts. Limited liability restricts a member's loss to the amount of money he or she has invested in the company.

Unlimited liability of members was normal until the mid-nineteenth century, when limited liability was introduced. The advantages of limited liability are that it:

(*a*)   Limits the extent of an investor's risk and therefore encourages investment generally.

(*b*)   Encourages institutions such as insurance companies and trade unions to make corporate investments (institutional investment).

(*c*)   Attracts finance into high-risk ventures which under unlimited liability would not be considered.

The nature of limitation on liability varies in the following ways:

1   Company limited by share.   This is the most common type of limited liability and occurs when the extent of the members' risk is limited to the amount of shareholdings. All companies quoted on the Stock Exchange are in this category.

2   Company limited by guarantee.   In this instance shares are not purchased by members, but an incorporated association is formed and the members guarantee to provide a certain sum if the company is wound up at a loss. This type of formation is generally found in non-profit-making undertakings such as trade associations.

3 Unlimited companies. Corporations can choose not to have the advantages of limited liability. This generally occurs in organisations where any liability would be small. Such companies do not have to file accounts with the Registrar of Companies.

Public corporations

Public corporations are created either by Royal Charter or, more commonly, by special Act of Parliament (statute). The main public corporations are the nationalised industries and local government authorities. The owners of public corporations are, in effect, the general public and the question of limiting liability does not arise: in the event of loss by a public corporation the State has unlimited liability.

Rules and relationships of companies

When a limited liability company is formed, the law requires the organisation to provide details of the nature of the association between its members, and information about its external relationships with other bodies. These details are contained in two documents: the Articles of Association and the Memorandum of Association. Both of these documents are lodged with the Registrar of Companies when a new company is set up.

The Articles of Association: internal rules of companies

The nature of the association between members can vary, but the Articles will always provide details of: (*a*) the nominal capital; (*b*) when and how shareholders' meetings are to be conducted, and the voting rights of members; (*c*) how profits and losses will be distributed; (*d*) the directors' names; and (*e*) how directors will be appointed and the nature of their authority.

The Articles of Association are a contract between the company and its members in respect of their ordinary rights as members.

The Memorandum of Association: external relationships of companies

The Memorandum of Association defines the constitution and powers of the company and the scope of its activities. It is the document which ensures that the stated aims of the company are legal and proper, and must include: (*a*) the name of the company, including the word 'Limited'; (*b*) the address of the registered office; (*c*) a statement of the company's aims; (*d*) the amount of capital the company wishes to raise; and (*e*) a statement that the shareholders' liability is limited.

Unincorporated associations

Unincorporated associations are the least formal type of association and they have far fewer legal obligations than corporations. The most common form of unincorporated association in business is a partnership, although employers' associations, trades unions and social clubs are also created in this way.

The members of an organisation which is unincorporated are not separate from the organisation: unincorporated associations do not have a separate legal existence and do not enjoy limited liability.

The different types of organisations

The legal framework in which organisations are formed, described above, has led to the establishment of many different types of organisations in both public and private sectors. The following provides brief details of the legal requirements each type of organisation faces in its creation and operation.

Private ownership

1   Sole traders

These are businesses which are owned by a private person who uses his own money to run the business. Consequently the sole trader is entitled to all the profits, but he must also bear any losses which are incurred. A sole trader has no legal obligation to make his accounts publicly available; and he is responsible for the day-to-day management of the business. Examples of sole traders are small shopkeepers, jobbing builders, plumbers and hairdressers.

2 Partnerships

These are unincorporated associations and the legal rules which govern them were established in the Partnership Act of 1890. The association or partnership does not have a separate existence from its members, the numbers of which can range from 2 to 20. The partners provide the finance for the organisation, and the profits and losses will normally be shared in an agreed proportion depending on the individual's contribution to the partnership. The partners agree on the day-to-day running of the business: some members can be 'sleeping' partners, in that they do not take part in the daily operations. Partners have unlimited liability: each partner is jointly liable with the other partners for any debts. Like sole traders, there is no legal obligation for partners to publish their accounts.

Well known examples of partnerships occur in the professions, such as solicitors, accountants and estate agents. But partnerships can be formed by any group of people carrying on business with a view to making a profit, consequently partnerships are found in all types of trade and business activity.

3 Private limited companies

This type of organisation is a corporation incorporated by the Companies Acts 1948–85. The number of members can range from 2 to 50 and they provide the financial resources for the undertaking. Membership of the company is restricted to private individuals: members of the general public cannot buy shares in a private limited company. The profits are distributed to the members as dividends on their shareholding. Losses are borne by the company. The day-to-day management of the company is carried out by a board of directors. Private limited companies are often local family businesses and are common in the building, retailing and clothing industries.

4 Public limited companies

Public limited liability companies, despite their name, are the best known form of *private* company. They are corporations and obtain their share capital from members of the public. They are similar to private limited companies in that profits are distributed as dividends to shareholders and the liability of members is restricted to their shareholdings. Any losses are borne by the company. Management of the company is conducted by a board of directors who are responsible to the shareholders.

Most industries include public limited liability companies and many of them, by developing a corporate image, have become household names: Barclays, Rowntree-Mackintosh, Tate & Lyle, EMI, Beecham, Ford and Courtaulds are public limited companies.

Some public limited companies have developed into massive organisations such that a few private corporations are as large as some sovereign states. In recent years two types of large private corporation have evolved, although the distinction between the two is not clear -cut:

(*a*)   *Multi-national corporations.*   A multi-national company is a private 'holding' company with shares in many overseas subsidiary companies. The head office of a multi-national is located in a host country and its operations will be carried out by different combinations of subsidiary companies located in different countries. Each company within the holding will be subject to the company law of the country where it is located. Companies within a multi-national are connected by share ownership and by managerial control. Examples of multi-nationals which operate in Britain are:

British – BP, Dunlop and Unilever.

European – VW, Nestles and Shell.

United States – IBM, ITT, ESSO, Mars and Ford.

(*b*)   *Conglomerate companies* can have extensive overseas operations and may therefore be multi-national, but a conglomerate is strictly a company which deals with a wide range of different products. In practice the normal conglomerate is a holding company which is the major shareholder in a series of non-complementary subsidiary firms. An example of a British conglomerate is the Rank Organisation, which owns subsidiary companies trading separately in films, bread, hotels, dance halls and office copiers.

Public ownership

1   Public corporations – nationalised industries

Public corporations are created by Parliament and owned by the State, although loan stock can be issued to the general public to raise capital. Any surpluses which are obtained on trading belong to the State, but for the most part such 'profits' are mainly used to finance capital investment projects or to keep down prices. In the event of any losses the State bears unlimited liability. The government minister whose department is responsible for the industry appoints the board and its chairman, and the day-to-day running of the corporation is in the hands of these appointees.

Many of the key industries in Britain, such as coal, electricity and railways, are publicly owned. However, since 1979 the Conservative Government has pursued a policy of privatisation of the public sector, and has sold the Government's shareholdings in several nationalised industries including British Telecom, British Aerospace and the National Freight Company.

2 Public corporations – local authorities

The boundaries and functions of local authorities in England and Wales were re-defined by Act of Parliament in 1972 (Local Government Act), and re-organisation of local government took place in April 1974. The Act created three types of authority: (*a*) *Shire Counties*, such as Somerset or Wiltshire; (*b*) *Metropolitan Counties*, such as the Metropolitan County of South Yorkshire (there are seven such counties); and (*c*) *Metropolitan Boroughs*, which are part of Metropolitan Counties. The Boroughs in South Yorkshire, for example, are: Barnsley, Doncaster, Rotherham and Sheffield.

The range of services which an authority provides is determined by the type of authority. For example, the Shire Counties provide education but the Metropolitan Counties do not: instead it is provided by the Boroughs.

In Scotland, local authority services are administered by the twelve *Regional Councils* set up in May 1975.

Between them, local authorities will provide education, fire, police, ambulance and bus services as well as roads, lighting, refuse collection, baths and theatres.

The income which is required for these services comes primarily from the Government: two-thirds of local authority income is from central government block grants (rate support grant), another sixth comes from rates and the remainder is from miscellaneous receipts. Local authorities administer their services through block rather than specific grants, which means that local government officials

have some choice in how to spend their income. But since much of
what they have to provide is required by law – for example education is compulsory between 5 years and 16 years – then the extent of
an authority's discretion in expenditure is small. In addition the
central government has a system of communication and inspection
to ensure that minimum standards are maintained and that an
authority's statutory obligations are being met.

3   Central government departments

Public corporations do not employ civil servants. The Civil Service
administers Central Government Departments. Central government, like local government, provides a range of services in such
areas as trade, employment, education, social services, defence and
foreign affairs. Many of these services, such as defence or foreign
affairs, have long historical traditions, but the formation of a
government department is entirely in the hands of the government.
New departments are frequently formed and old departments
merged or even abolished to meet new problems and new pressures.
For example, in recent years departments have been formed to deal
with prices, energy, social security and the environment.

The income of central government is obtained through taxation
and government borrowing, and the level of public expenditure is
decided by the government. Profits and losses do not occur: departments underspend or overspend. The liability of a government for
its programmes is unlimited. The main sanction on public spending
is that gross mismanagement of government services will normally
mean that a government will lose office at the next election. Civil
servants, of whom there are over 750 000, help government ministers to administer their departments, but it is the minister who is
accountable to the Cabinet, to Parliament, and ultimately to the
electorate for departmental expenditure and the day-to-day running of the service.

4   QUA(N)GOs

These are quasi-autonomous (non- or national) governmental
organisations such as the Medical Research Council, the Community Relations Commission or the Water Boards. They are of
three kinds: executive bodies, advisory bodies and tribunals.

Executive bodies, such as the Water Boards, generally employ their own staff and control their own finances. Advisory bodies and tribunals, however, do not normally employ full-time staff, and their expenditure is paid by the relevant government department. In 1979 the Conservative Government established a review of non-departmental public bodies, and as a result, over 400 were abolished.

5   The National Enterprise Board

The NEB is a government-owned and government-financed holding company. It is an organisation which bridges the private and public sectors, and it was created by the Labour Government in the mid 1970s to act as a catalyst and helper to commercial organisations.

This role varies according to the government in power: the Conservatives are less interventionist and have sold off many of the shareholdings which had been acquired by the NEB. However, the Conservative Government has directed the NEB to concentrate on helping high technology companies such as those engaged in computing and biotechnology, firms in the assisted areas and small businesses.

Dissolution of organisations

Private companies which fail to achieve their aims and objectives and make successive losses are eventually wound up. This is a legal process which can take three forms:

1 *Compulsory liquidation.*   Winding-up by order of the Court usually occurs when the company is unable to pay its debts when required by its creditors. It can also occur if statutory requirements such as the holding of a shareholders' meeting are not met, or when the company fails to begin business within one year of incorporation.

2 *Voluntary liquidation.*   In this instance the members pass a 'special resolution' agreeing to dissolve the Association. If the company is unable to continue in business, then dissolution will occur when the members pass an 'extraordinary resolution'.

3 *Winding up under the supervision of the Court.*   Even when

members have passed a resolution to wind up voluntarily, the Court may still order that dissolution shall take place under the supervision of the Court and in this instance the Court may appoint a liquidator in addition to the liquidator appointed by the company.

7

Policy Formulation

Policy provides a definition of what people in organisations must or must not do. For example, the pricing policy of the nationalised industries is defined by the government. The investment policy of a public limited liability company will be decided by the board of directors. The policies of government departments are established by the Cabinet.

Policy decisions affect all aspects of an organisation. They provide a guide for further decision-making and are a framework for organisational activity. In private organisations the policy decisions will be written in the Memorandum and Articles of Association, and they will also be contained in previous decisions of the Board. In government organisations policy is mainly laid down by statute, but guidelines are also given through rules and regulations which are composed by ministers with the help of senior civil servants.

Policy decisions in organisations

There is a direct relationship between the aims and objectives of an organisation and its policy decisions. Similarly there is a direct relationship between the long-term plans of a firm and its policy framework. The formulation of policy will be integrated into long-term planning proposals.

Many firms will design corporate plans for the organisation based on a systematic study of the company's long-term objectives. In such a study the company is considered as a whole rather than as a collection of departments. Policy may be redefined to meet aims and long-term objectives.

This corporate approach can be summarised as shown in Fig. 7.1.

Set **Aims** ——▶ *Decide* **Policy**▶ *Organise* **Tactical**▶*Appraise* **the**
Long-term   Strategic   **Action**   **Process**
corporate   planning   Set short-term   Evaluate the
objectives   objectives   success of plan

Fig. 7.1   The planning process

Policy decisions: strategic planning areas
The range of policy decisions is extremely wide since, by definition, policy provides a framework for all organisational activity. The following examples illustrate this wide range:

1 Manpower policy.   People are the most important asset in an organisation, and many institutions will have a policy on manpower which will be designed to meet the long-term needs of the organisation while also meeting the requirement of employment legislation. Manpower policies deal with the selection and recruitment of people, training and promotion programmes, and dismissal procedures. For example, the policy will indicate whether the promotion of employees will primarily be from within the organisation or by recruitment from outside. Similarly policy decisions will be made as to where the education and training of staff will take place: it could be within the firm or provided by outside agencies. The main features of the policy will be the estimates of the numbers of people the organisation will need, and the type of experience and qualifications future employees will require.

2 Investment policy.   In private companies the Board of Directors will make policy decisions on investment programmes. The Cabinet and ministers will make similar decisions for public organisations. Capital expenditure decisions are the most crucial of policy decisions. Investment programmes provide new buildings or new plant and equipment, and the extent of an organisation's investment often illustrates the success or failure of previous policy decisions.

3 Marketing policy.   In private corporations the Memorandum of Association will provide a guide to the range of a company's activities, and the Board of Directors will make policy decisions on the mix of products which are to be marketed. For example, a firm might decide to diversify its interests into other fields, just as the Rank Organisation, which in the 1950s was a film distributor, made a policy decision to enter the office copying market with the Xerox Corporation of America and started to produce the market Rank-Xerox machines.

Public corporations, although they have monopoly in their own specific product, can have vigorous marketing policies to try to increase their market either at the expense of their competitors – for example gas central heating – or simply to expand their service – for example postal services.

4 Pricing policy. Commercial organisations in the public sector are given guidelines by the government with regard to their pricing policies. Nationalised industries are monopolistic and are given some discretion over the prices they charge. Their monopolistic power gives them greater freedom than private firms which face competition: the more competitive the market, the less influence an organisation will have on its own prices. There are legal restrictions in the UK on price agreements between firms, but some international producers such as the Organisation of Petroleum Exporting Countries (OPEC) make unified pricing policy decisions.

5 Distribution policy. Organisations have a choice of distributive outlets for their products as well as a choice of transport. Their distribution policy will say whether agencies should be used, where depots should be located, whether the firm should use its own fleet of lorries or subcontract to British Rail or private road hauliers.

Communication of policy decisions
Policy formulation and strategic planning is a permanent process in most organisations. Obviously during the establishment of an organisation many policy decisions will be made, but as the organisation grows further policies will be formulated. Very often these on-going policy decisions will not be written into one single document but will be scattered around in various publications. Established policy will be found in: the Memorandum of Association, the Articles of Association, Annual Reports and Company manuals. New policy

guidelines will be communicated through: internal memoranda, newsletters, notice boards and external publications.

Policy decisions in government

Organisations in the public sector which have commercial obligations will adopt very similar policy decisions to firms in the private sector. Noncommercial organisations in the public sector are subject to changes in society and in politics, and they must have policies which enable them to react to change, but generally they do not control their own policies: these are decided for them.

The main function of a government is to formulate policy. Ministers are assisted in this function by the Civil Service, which provides the administrative experience as well as information and research services to help governments decide on policy. The focus of policy formulation is the Cabinet, which is subject to control by Parliament and ultimately the electorate. It is Parliament which enacts the laws in which most public policy is embodied.

Sources of public policy

The policies of a government directly and indirectly influence all individuals and all organisations. The nature of parliamentary legislation and its effect on business will vary according to the political party in power, and as far as business is concerned will provide a framework of control with regard to employment, taxes, prices and consumer protection. These controls are implemented by government departments and are in effect their policies.

The main sources for government policy are:

1   The political manifesto.   All political parties have a philosophy which gives rise to principles and theories as to how society and therefore business should be governed. As a general rule in Britain the Conservatives prefer less legislation and interference than the Socialists.

The philosophy of a political party is influenced by public opinion as well as by members of the party. Political parties which want power must temper their philosophy to meet the wishes of the general public. Thus the pre-election policy statements which parties publish in their manifestos are frequently a compromise between their political philosophy and public opinion.

2   *Pressure groups* exist inside and outside political parties and all governments find that pressure on policy decisions comes from many sources: Trade Unions, the CBI, the large banks, professional bodies and other governments are the main sources of such pressure. The objective of a pressure group is to ensure that their interests, and the interests of their members, are considered in policy decisions.

3   *The Civil Service.*   The degree of influence on public policy formulation by the Permanent Civil Service is open to argument. The British Civil Service does attempt to provide impartial advice to ministers, but past experience as well as the nature of the information provided will have some influence on ministerial decisions.

4   *Unforeseen circumstances.*   Governments have to react to events. Society has become more complex and more interdependent and this has forced governments to be practical rather than philosophical in their policy decisions. Unforeseen circumstances mean that governments and organisations have to be flexible in policy decisions. The framework of organisational activity can never be static.

The constraints on organisations

Most organisations would prefer to operate in an environment where policy decisions could be made without any influence from internal and external agencies. However, such influence is an integral and necessary part of a free society. Democracy implies that participation will take place by people in their capacity as customers, employees and voters. Their influence may be seen by organisations as a restriction or constraint; so that, in a democracy, government ministers and company directors will try to ensure that their organisation adapts to the influence of pressure while still making autonomous policy decisions.

Internal constraints

1   *Shortage of resources – finance.*   All organisations have to allocate resources in order to produce, and the most immediate as well as long-term problems which they face are the shortage of finance or shortages in manpower and equipment. Government departments

have the perennial problem of working to cash limits; and private firms frequently have to deal with cash flow problems and the deterioration of equipment. The major task all managers face is to get the most out of existing resources. Policy decisions are frequently restricted by resource limitations.

2   Employees' attitudes – the informal organisation.   Individuals have hopes and aspirations which they will retain and show when employed by an organisation. Since the successful implementation of any policy will depend upon the cooperation of the workforce, it is unrealistic for policy-makers to ignore employees' hopes and aspirations. For example, it would be unwise to re-locate an organisation from the South East to the North East unless key members of the organisation were prepared to move. Similarly it would be unwise to introduce a new electronic data-processing system into a business unless existing operators were prepared to re-train or become redundant.

3   Bureaucracy – the formal organisation.   Organisations can become so large that their inflexibility can restrict policy decisions. Rigid and well-defined organisational structures exist in both the public and private sectors, and although bureaucracy simply means that the organisation is centrally organised, most people are familiar with the 'red tape' which is a characteristic of bureaucratic institutions. The difficulty which policy decision-makers face is that they have to recognise the limitations of central control and the problems in communication that this can cause: policy rules must be specified in great detail in an attempt to cover every case. For example, the rules which govern the administration of social security are rigid and the civil servant who implements the policy will stick to the 'rule book'. The officials do not themselves make allowances for exceptional cases even when the rules seem unfair, but such cases can usually be referred to higher authority.

External constraints
1   Changes in demand.   The ever changing nature of markets and of needs is the main external risk which an organisation faces. The political demand for a service can change overnight when an election takes place and an organisation can find that it is no longer required. For example, the Price Commission was abolished almost

as soon as the Conservatives took office in 1979. In commercial organisations, demand for their product or service can change for a variety of reasons such as changes in fashion (shorter term), or changes in demography or levels of income (longer term). Any such change can be a major constraint on an organisation's policy decisions.

2 Changes in alternative products or services. New inventions and new ideas are constantly taking place and create the need for organisations to consider new marketing strategies and new product ideas. For example, electronic data-processing is replacing manual processing, plastic drainpipes have largely replaced metal ones, nuclear submarines have replaced aircraft carriers.

3 Legal constraints. The Government, through Parliament, imposes many legal restrictions and requirements on organisations. Manpower policies are influenced by legislation in health and safety, employment protection and discrimination. Marketing policies are constrained by restrictive practice laws and consumer protection, as well as by the government's policy on prices. Wages policies may be restricted by incomes policies.

4 Government constraints. The general activity of a government will have indirect consequences on an organisation. The complex and interdependent nature of the British economy, where many firms rely on public expenditure for orders, means that the level of public expenditure will influence many organisations in the private sector. This is particularly true of the construction industry and of those companies engaged in the production of arms; but it is also true of many firms which are indirectly dependent on government spending, such as sub-contractors in the aircraft or ship-building industries.

There are more direct restrictions which can be imposed by the government in the form of taxes, overseas trade regulations and credit restrictions. When a company decides on its policies it will closely examine the influence of government controls.

5 Pressure groups. As we have seen, the whole nature of policy formulation in government is influenced by pressure groups. Although pressure groups have some constraining power on private organisations, their influence is much less on them than it is on public organisations.

Pressure groups fall into two broad categories:

(*a*)   *Permanent pressure groups*
The groups which are well established are generally the most influential. Many permanent pressure groups have become integrated into the State's policy formulation process. For example, the British Medical Association has representatives on many NHS advisory bodies; similarly the Vice-chancellors of Universities have a strong voice in the allocation of funds through the University Grants Committee. Many Trade Union and CBI officials sit on Government Economic Planning bodies. Less effective, but equally well established, are groups such as the RSPCA, NSPCC, RAC, AA and the Consumers' Association. All of these organisations exist not only to provide a direct service to their members, but also to serve their members' interests by bringing pressure to bear on other organisations.

(*b*)   *Temporary pressure groups*
Pressure groups are often formed to change a specific policy; once the change has been made, then the need for that pressure no longer exists and the group is disbanded. Such groups as those concerned with the siting of London's third airport, or with the reform of the law on abortion, are in this category.

Forms of pressure
Pressure groups can use the following techniques in their attempt to influence policy:

1   Membership of the decision-making body.   This is the most effective form of pressure. Trade Union-sponsored Members of Parliament or worker-directors are examples of this technique.

2   Use of the media.   Articles in newspapers or documentaries on television can influence organisations. For example, pressure from the *Sunday Times* was a major factor in obtaining compensation for the victims of the drug thalidomide.

3   Demonstrations and marches.   On many Sundays pressure groups hold rallies in major cities in the hope of bringing pressure on organisations. These groups range from conservationists to the Gay

Liberation Front. Marches are a very common form of action by pressure groups and some such as the Jarrow marches against unemployment in the 1930s, or the Aldermaston marches for nuclear disarmament in the 1950s, have become part of British history.

4 Strikes. Trade Unions can bring pressure to bear on the government and on individual organisations by industrial action. Almost all strikes are directed against a particular organisation and are undertaken either to remedy a grievance or to try to improve wages and conditions. However, withdrawal of labour in key industries such as energy or transport can cause such widespread inconvenience, or even chaos, that governments will reconsider their policies, especially those in relation to prices and incomes.

5 Lobby Members of Parliament. A common pressure-group technique is to try to influence Members of Parliament either directly in the lobby of the House of Commons or through petitions and letters. This form of pressure is not as effective as many other forms, but it is a recognised and traditional method of democratic action.

Pressure groups do not simply use one technique. They will adopt a variety of the above methods with the intention of changing policy decisions. This constraint on business, with the other external constraints, exists because of the interdependent nature of business activity. Everyone has an interest in public and private business, and in a democracy people can try to influence any business's policy decisions.

8

Structure and Management: Policy Implementation

Policy decisions, once made, have to be implemented and organisations have departments or functions which specialise in particular aspects of business activity. The purpose in imposing a formal organisational structure on an organisation's activities is to enable the leaders to: (*a*) define objectives for each section or department which will help the organisation achieve its corporate aims; (*b*) define the responsibilities in each department to ensure that tasks are not duplicated between functions; and (*c*) coordinate the functions within the organisation so that each department blends its activities with those of other departments to form a corporate strategy.

The functions which are found in organisations vary according to the type of organisation. Government organisations tend to have few functions, such as finance, administration and research. In business generally there are more functions, particularly in those companies which are producing a product or products rather than providing a service. The four functions which are described below are the main ones existing in most organisations.

The main functions in organisations

1 Production
The creation of a good or service is the most basic function within any organisation, and obviously the type of good or service determines the nature of the production process: coal can only be

obtained direct from nature; cereals can only be grown on arable land. It is relatively easy to define the production function in firms which are engaged in primary production or manufacturing, but for those organisations which provide a service the definition of production becomes more complex. This is because the relationship between the producer and the client is part of the production function.

The following are examples of the operation of the production function in some service industries: a doctor examining a patient, a solicitor advising a client, a shopkeeper serving a customer.

2 Marketing

In the above examples the marketing function is so strongly interrelated with the production function that the two are almost identical: the nature of the shopkeeper's service is both producing and selling, and his technique will influence his customers.

In the primary industries the marketing function is quite separate from production. Farmers, for example, use marketing boards which are outside their own business to market their products. The relationship between the marketing department and the production department in manufacturing is closer. The two departments are normally independent within the organisation but will liaise on product design (R&D) and market research, production control and sales forecasts, production costs and selling price, quality control and after-sales service, despatch/transport and packaging.

The nearer an organisation is to tertiary production the stronger is the relationship between marketing and production, so that in the pure service industries the marketing function *is* the production function.

3 Personnel

Even the smallest organisation, public or private, has a personnel function. People are an organisation's main resource and, although the links between the personnel department and other departments are not always obvious, it is important that cooperation between all departments and personnel is maintained. It is the personnel department, with the help of the other departments, which will implement any manpower policies by recruiting, selecting and training all employees. Employee development is a crucial function in organisations.

4   Finance

The use of money is common to all organisations. The financial function not only provides records of transactions such as the payment of wages or the purchase of equipment, but also it provides control techniques which show how the organisation is performing. Finance is the common yardstick whereby the use of resources is measured, consequently public and private institutions use the financial function in all departments to see how efficient each department is.

Formal organisation structures

The formal relationship between departments is defined by policies, rules and regulations and is illustrated by the familiar hierarchical organisation chart (Fig. 8.1).

This traditional form of organisation is the most common form and is found in all kinds of organisation from the army to ICI. The lines of communication within the organisation are upwards and downwards (normally downwards). In this type of organisation, where instructions are passed along lines in the hierarchy, the functions in the pyramid are called line functions and the system is referred to as *line management.* Some advisory or consultative functions such as research or legal advice often cut across departments and consequently are outside the line framework. These advisory or specialist support services are called staff functions.

Delegation: responsibility and authority

In order to carry out the policy decision, each department and each employee will be given tasks or objectives which will help the organisation to achieve its aims: this is *delegation* (Fig. 8.2).

Very often departmental objectives are achieved by routine tasks such as filing, recording or assembling. There are few tasks which will be creative or which will require exceptional skill and judgment. Those jobs which do require skill and judgment are normally accorded greater responsibility and status in the organisation. The people who are employed to lead the organisation are given the greatest responsibility and then all operation will stem from the top: tasks will have been delegated down the pyramid.

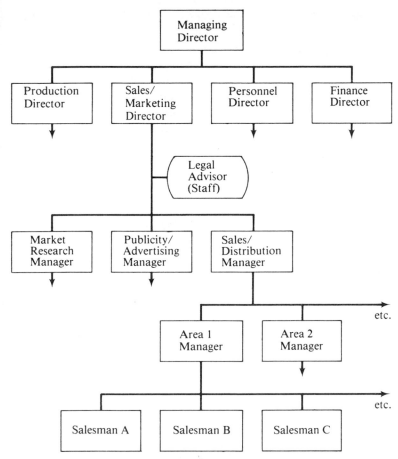

Fig. 8.1 A typical formal organisational structure (pyramid) highlighting the marketing department's line management

Responsibility for tasks cannot be delegated: a superior is always responsible for the actions of his subordinates. For example, government ministers have resigned because of mistakes made by junior civil servants – mistakes of which the minister had no personal knowledge. Superiors can assign duties and activities which naturally carry responsibility, since the subordinate with his superior will be held accountable if things go wrong. Everyone in an organisation has some responsibility, but this cannot be delegated:

Set Aims ⟶ *Decide* Policy ⟶ *Organise* Tactical ⟶ *Appraise* the
Action   Process
Set short-term
departmental objectives
and delegate tasks

Fig. 8.2   The policy implementation process

the higher a person is in the hierarchy, the more responsibility he will have.

Authority or the right to use power, on the other hand, can be delegated. In a formal structure this right is defined by the hierarchy, and no one should be given responsibilities which do not correspond to his position in the formal structure. For example, it would be unwise to send a buyer overseas with the responsibility for acquiring expensive equipment if he did not have the authority to sign orders.

To sum up, delegation is the act of assigning tasks and objectives to subordinates. Responsibility cannot be delegated, but authority can. A managing director can give his secretary the authority to organise a conference, including the right to pay for guest speakers and to purchase equipment and materials, but both of them will be responsible for its success.

The informal organisation

Delegation is an important notion in policy implementation. The departments in an organisation will assign tasks and duties down the line in order to get things done. However, this formal method of carrying out functions is questioned by a relatively new school of thought which stems from experiments carried out by Elton Mayo at the Western Electric Company factory at Hawthorne, near Chicago, between 1924 and 1932. Mayo drew attention to the fact that social groups within organisations create informal pressure because their own beliefs, objectives and aspirations could conflict with the organisation's objectives. Informal behaviour is often different from, and can be opposed to, the requirements and expectations of the formal organisation. For example, the board of directors might decide that on economic grounds the firm should be re-located from London to Liverpool, but evidence shows that informal pressure by the directors' wives to remain in London will probably have more influence on the decision than formal business arguments. In policy decisions all organisations must recognise that the implementation of the policy is a subtle and complicated process, and decision-makers should consider the nature of informal organisational pressure on policy implementation.

Management principles in policy implementation

There are principles which have evolved during the twentieth century which provide basic rules on how policy should be implemented. Managers are often experts in a particular departmental function such as finance or marketing, but nevertheless the basic principles of policy implementation will apply to each and every manager. The following list was first produced by Henri Fayol (1841–1925), who was one of the pioneers of management thought and organisation theory.

1 Planning
Policy formulation is undertaken by people who are at the top of the organisation's hierarchy. For example, in private enterprise the board of directors makes policy decisions; in government departments the ministers and senior civil servants decide on policy. The first stage in policy implementation is planning (Fig. 8.3). The managers must plan how the organisation's resources are to be used, and this involves setting targets for each department.

2 Coordinating
Departmental plans must inter-relate with those of other departments. To avoid unnecessary tasks or a duplication of departmental

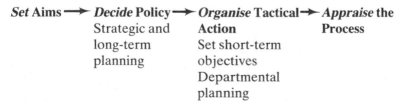

Fig. 8.3 Stages in the planning process

activity, managers must encourage communication between departments. This ensures that corporate action takes place. Communication takes place through inter-departmental committees, and coordination is one of the main reasons why managers in all types of organisation spend time in committee work.

3   Organising

In order to achieve departmental objectives a manager will delegate tasks which have been allocated to the department. Naturally these jobs will reflect the function of the department: marketing will employ salesmen, finance will employ accountants, production will employ technicians.

The main function of a manager is to get the best out of his subordinates; this implies that he must communicate with them, and communication takes time. Thus the number of subordinates any one manager can supervise is limited by the need to communicate and by the nature of the communication. In some instances where individuals can work alone for long periods, such as in research projects, then one manager or team leader can control up to fifteen or even twenty staff, but this 'span of control' is rare. Fayol devised the notion of the *scalar chain* where he recommended that the span of control or the number of subordinates reporting to one manager should not normally exceed seven or eight.

A further principle in organising people is the 'unity of command' principle. This means that subordinates should at best report to only one supervisor, and the command over one individual should not be shared between different managers.

4   Staffing

People are the most important resource in an organisation, therefore a manager must ensure through recruitment and selection procedures that the most appropriate people are engaged in the organisation. This means analysing the type of work to be done and deciding on the aptitude, experience and personality which the employee will require. The staffing function also includes schemes for improving and safeguarding the welfare of employees.

5 Directing

This does not simply mean issuing orders: once employees have been engaged, a manager must supervise and help them to maximise their potential. Directing people involves frequent communication with them to ensure that they understand the tasks for which they are responsible, and to reward them for work which they have done well. Motivation of employees through direction and guidance is one of the most important managerial functions.

6 Budgeting

Standards can be decided at policy level. For example, a production manager might have to meet a certain level of production, a college principal might have to provide a given number of courses within a cash limit, a sales manager might have to achieve a fixed level of sales. In government departments minimum standards of performance are laid down by statute. For instance, each County Council must provide a police force and an adequate fire service. On a tactical level a manager might want to reduce bad debts by 20%. A transport manager might attempt to deliver to customers within seven days instead of ten. In many instances departmental targets are expressed in, or converted to, financial terms; these budgets are a guide to managerial efficiency.

7 Reporting

The control of policy implementation requires an accurate and speedy flow of information. One function of a manager is to provide facts on his department's performance. This information is processed and the manager is subsequently given feedback on his

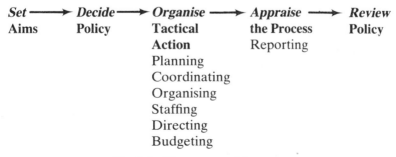

Set →	*Decide* →	*Organise* →	*Appraise* →	*Review*
Aims	**Policy**	**Tactical**	**the Process**	**Policy**
		Action	Reporting	
		Planning		
		Coordinating		
		Organising		
		Staffing		
		Directing		
		Budgeting		

Fig. 8.4 The managerial process

performance. The analysis of information (data processing) takes place in all activities: stock levels, output, sales, expenses, etc., and it provides top managers with the facts to control current policy implementation and also helps them to formulate future policy (see Fig. 8.4).

9

Accountability and Social Responsibility

Organisations do not function autonomously: managers are accountable for their actions. In public and private corporations the main duty of a manager is to satisfy those who own the company. Boards of public limited liability companies must satisfy the shareholders that their policies and performance are acceptable. Similarly the boards of the nationalized industries must satisfy the Minister and Parliament that their performance is adequate. If in each case the performance was not satisfactory, then the board or the chairman would probably be asked to resign.

This form of commercial accountability runs through all types of organisations and is an obvious requirement of profit-based institutions. Less obvious is the need for organisations to be responsible to society. Social obligations of publicly owned institutions are an integral part of their aims and objectives, and they are frequently imposed by law when the organisation is created. There are legal requirements for private organisations which impose social obligation on them – for example the Health and Safety at Work Act, 1975. However, for private organisations social duty lies beyond legal requirements, and it is the exceptional company which pursues social responsibilities at the expense of commercial considerations. Those companies which are heavily engaged in market competition will want to minimise their private costs even when their activity leads to hidden social costs.

Private organisations

The first responsibility of a private organisation is to the share-holders. The reason why people invest in business is to obtain a return on their capital, and if firms are unable to make profits then either the company will go into liquidation or the shareholders will find managers who can make a profit.

But private enterprise is an organ of society: it exists to serve society, and externalities or social costs do result from private business. Management decisions are not purely commercial but are interwoven with social implications: commercial decisions create social benefits and social costs. The following are examples arising from the interaction between firms and society:

Social benefits
1   The creation of wealth (roads, houses, energy, durable goods, etc.).
2   The provision of employment and job security.
3   The creation of social facilities in health, education and welfare.

Social costs
1   Pollution resulting from industrial activity adds to health risks and to the cost of the NHS.
2   Restrictive practices. Some firms can take advantage of events to improve their profitability at the expense of the customers. For example, increases in the price of oil during 1979 or the change to decimalisation gave some unscrupulous companies the opportunity to charge excessive prices. In all economic transactions, excessive gains are made at someone else's expense.
3   Congestion. High concentrations of business in a locality can lead to transport problems, causing delays and accidents the cost of which, although hidden, will fall on businesses and society.

The interests of society do not necessarily conflict with commercial aims. For example, increases in productivity could result from improvements in morale caused by welfare policies which make provisions over and above the legal requirements in employment protection and health and safety. The problem is to find a balance between normal commercial goals and social goals.

Nationalised industries

The nationalised industries in effect break up the traditional ownership rights, and the boards of the industries are accountable to the State represented by the minister and Parliament. The minister appoints and dismisses the board, but ultimately it is Parliament which prescribes and controls the nationalised industries. The methods of accountability are:

1   Ministerial control.   A problem for the nationalised industries is that ministers often 'interfere' with the everyday running of the corporations. Such intervention, which is often done for political and social reasons, can distort the commercial operation of the business. A common cause of intervention is the government's concern to keep down prices and wages, and the public corporations is where they have direct influence, although in theory the minister should leave the day-to-day running of the industry to the board (see Fig. 9.1).

2   Questions in the House to the Minister.   The minister who is responsible for a particular nationalised industry will be faced with questions in Parliament on the policy of the industry and its implementation. It is in this instance that ministers are held accountable for policy implementation and it is not surprising that the responsibility encourages them to interfere in the organising of the corporations.

3   Annual reports to Parliament.   Public corporations are required by law to provide detailed annual reports and accounts. Debates take place in Parliament on the reports and give MPs the opportunity to question ministers on the performance and activities of the industries.

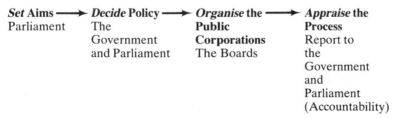

Fig. 9.1   The policy process in nationalised industries

4 Select Committee on Nationalised Industries. This parliamentary 'watchdog' carefully reviews the operations of the nationalised industries and carries out investigations into policy formulation and policy implementation. The committee has a lot of influence in setting the guidelines for the industries.

5 Consumer Councils. Each nationalised industry has a consumer council which scrutinises its operation on behalf of the users of the product or service. These councils examine the quality of the service as well as any price increases. Since the industries are almost monopolistic, the councils provide some countervailing power which in perfect competition would be provided by market forces.

The commercial and social obligations of the nationalised industries are determined by Parliament. The commercial duties are expressed in terms of (*a*) rates of return on investment, and (*b*) pricing policies. Since 1978, the Government have required nationalised industries to achieve a real rate of return of 5% on their new investment programmes. The monopolistic position of the industries means that they have some choice of pricing, and the following methods are used: average cost pricing, marginal cost pricing, and price discrimination.

The social obligations of the corporations are designed to complement government economic activity as well as optimise a monopolistic service. The social duties listed below have strong commercial implications, but are examples of the obligations of the nationalised sector which private organisations do not necessarily have to meet:

(*a*) To help the government to coordinate policies in energy and transport.
(*b*) To provide a service wherever demand exists (for example, electricity).
(*c*) To stimulate economic growth and modernise the industries through capital investment projects.
(*d*) To protect the public from monopolistic power.

These social duties of the nationalised industries do distort the attainment of commercial goals. This distortion, added to the often outdated nature of nationalised industries' plant and machinery, makes comparisons between public and private accountability complicated and difficult.

Local authorities and government departments

Non-commercial government institutions have to operate within a financial framework. The budgets or cash limits which are imposed on government organisations give them responsibilities which are not dissimilar to those of large corporate organisations. The substantial difference is of course that local authorities and government departments do not make profits: they are given funds from government revenue which they allocate to different (and competing) projects according to political policy decisions.

The social duties of a government institution are frequently laid down by statute. Most local authorities, for example, are required by law to provide services in housing, roads, education and social welfare. In the rare event of a failure to meet statutory requirement, those responsible will be compelled by law to rectify the situation.

With the development of local and central government services, a complex system of checks and balances to ensure the maintenance of standards and the elimination of corruption has evolved. The following is a list of the bodies and procedures which scrutinise government institutions.

1 The electorate. In a democracy, government organisations are accountable to the people. The electorate is the strongest pressure group in the country. During election periods the government has to explain its performance and, if the people are not satisfied, then an alternative government will be given power. In this process some government organisations can find themselves eliminated (for example, the Price Commission in 1979).

2 Parliament. The representatives of the people in Parliament systematically examine the performance of government departments. This is done both in the House and in committees. The methods of examination are: Parliamentary Questions, debates in the House, the Public Accounts Committee, the Expenditure Committee and Select Committees (non-financial).

3 Financial control. The government, in association with the Civil Service, has developed its own committees and techniques for evaluating departmental performance. The three most important are: the Public Expenditure Survey Committee (PESC), Programme Analysis and Review (PAR), and the Central Policy Review Staff (CPRS). These methods of review, and the long-established district and internal audit procedures, maintain financial control on local authorities and government departments, and they make financial accountability an integral feature of policy formulation.

4 Ombudsmen.   In recent years Commissioners have been created for Parliament, local government and the Health Service to ensure that maladministration is kept to a minimum. The Commissioners respond to complaints about a particular service and, by insisting on the examination of all relevant documents, have instituted a degree of accountability which private organisations would consider excessive.

Privatisation

The public sector accounts for more than 30% of total Gross Domestic Product, and so the public corporations, local authorities and government departments have an important influence on the economy. The Conservatives believe that this influence does not lead to increased efficiency, and that one of the best methods of improving the use of resources is to remove resource control from monopolistic public control by transferring ownership to the private sector. This process is described as 'privatisation'; and the following list shows the range of methods which the Government has adopted in its privatisation policy:

1 Public issue of shares on the Stock Exchange (e.g. British Aerospace, Cable and Wireless)
2 Sale to employees/management consortium (e.g. National Freight Company)
3 Placement with institutional investors (e.g. Government's minority shareholding in British Sugar Corporation);
4 Sale of physical assets (e.g. British Rail's hotel properties)
5 Joint ventures (e.g. merger of British Rail's hovercraft service with Hoverlloyd)
6 Contracting out of public services by central government and local authorities.

Questions on Part Two

1 Compare and contrast the aims and characteristics of public organisations with the aims and characteristics of private organisations.

2 To what extent do you think that Cost Benefit Analysis can be applied to private organisations? Explain your answer.

3 Distinguish between the different legal forms of organisation which exist in commerce, industry and government.

4 State the current objectives of the National Enterprise Board, and assess its role in modern business.

5 'Pressure groups are an essential feature of democracy.' Discuss this statement. Your answer should include examples of the strategies which pressure groups use to influence organisations.

6 Outline the factors which can constrain policy decisions in commercial organisations.

7 Using an organisational chart, explain the inter-relationship between departmental functions in a manufacturing organisation.

8 Distinguish between 'authority' and 'responsibility' and assess the importance of delegation in policy implementation.

9 Do you think that private organisations should be accountable for any social costs? Explain your answer.

10 Discuss the proposition that government organisations are subject to more rigorous control and accountability than private organisations.

PART THREE
The Organisation and its Resources

10

Money and Finance

People and organisations do not exist in isolation. They depend on other people and other organisations to produce goods or services for their own needs. In primitive economies people exchange their products for crops and goods which they need. But this is a clumsy method of exchange. It assumes that an organisation or a person will be able to find someone who not only wants the goods that the organisation has produced, but also has the product or service which the organisation could use. This primitive method of exchange is complicated and it restricted the development of business.

The creation of money made business transactions much easier. Money can be exchanged into any type of good or service, and it is therefore a *medium* of exchange: it 'lubricates' business operations.

The functions of money

1 Money is a medium of exchange

People will exchange any good or service for money. This is its most important function. In order to be a medium of exchange money must be acceptable: everyone must have confidence in the medium. Initially this confidence was created by using metals like gold and silver which in themselves were valuable. The coins, notes and cheques which are used as money today are not in themselves worth what they represent. Nevertheless they are accepted by everyone in business transactions.

2 Money measures value.

The value of goods and services is expressed in money terms so that there is no problem in comparing different products. Money provides a standard measurement in business – an employee knows how much he is worth to an employer; and he also knows the range of products and services his 'worth' will obtain. Similarly firms can use profit as a measure of success, and by using financial values they have a good idea of the range of expenditure and investment projects which they can undertake. A current problem however, which will be examined later in this chapter, is inflation. Constantly changing prices make money as a measure of value less reliable, especially for comparisons over a period of time.

3 Money can be saved

Money can be stored away and generally it will not deteriorate. Until the 1960s in Britain it was reasonable to claim that money would not lose its value. However, as we have seen, increases in the rate of inflation have made money an unreliable store of value. As a result many people now look for alternative ways of storing their wealth, by buying items which tend to maintain or even increase their value such as antiques, works of art, or land. It is unwise for a business to keep cash during inflationary periods.

4 Money can record debts

There are many transactions in business when payment is not made straight away. Money gives organisations the facility to record any deferred payments, and to receive the money either in instalments or in one payment at a later date. Inflation makes it unwise to give extended credit to customers, since the business will be losing cash as the value of the debt in real terms decreases. Conversely, most businesses will seek to defer their own payments to suppliers.

5 One-way payments can be made

Government organisations often provide a service when there is no direct exchange taking place. For example, such services as education, health, police and defence do not have to be paid for directly: they are financed out of taxation. Taxes are one-way payments which ensure that only those capable of making the payments actually do so.

Business cannot function without money. It enables all organisations to obtain resources. It enables commercial organisations to earn a reward for their product or service. It enables the government to raise revenue.

The financial needs of organisations

Revenue expenditure: short-term expenditure

The activities of an organisation are a continuous process. Money is flowing in and out of businesses all of the time. The constant demand which organisations have for resources means that they are constantly faced with expenses. In order to meet these expenses, organisations must obtain revenue from their activities – they must keep the cash flowing.

The flow of cash through commercial organisations is circular, as shown in Fig. 10.1. The money obtained from selling goods or services is used to finance further production. Although the flow of cash never ceases in a viable commercial organisation, at regular intervals the firm will produce, in a profit and loss account, details of the transactions which have taken place. The *Profit and Loss Account* is a summary of the resources a firm has acquired and how they have been allocated during the financial period (usually twelve months).

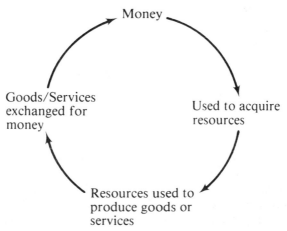

Fig. 10.1   Cash flow in an organisation

The Profit and Loss Account

Table 10.1 shows the items which are often included in a profit and loss account and illustrates the main resources which most firms would acquire. The expenses on these resources are then deducted from the income obtained from trading during the same period to give an idea of the profit (or loss) which has been made.

Table 10.1   The Profit and Loss Account and the organisation's resources

Expenditure (£)	*Type of resource (factors of production)*
Stocks of raw materials	Natural resources or producer goods
Wages and salaries	People
Directors' fees	People
Lighting and heating	Energy
Rent and rates	Land
Interest on loans	Capital finance
Hire of plant or leasing	Capital equipment

An important point is that a profit and loss account does not show whether revenue income has been fairly constant and then ensured a flow of cash to pay the immediate expenses. Any major delay in receiving money will probably cause a firm to have cash flow problems and run into financial difficulties.

Capital expenditure: the acquisition of fixed assets

The short-term expenditure of companies loses its value as soon as it is expended. Naturally it helps the firm to earn income, but the payment of rent or electricity bill is a 'one-off' exercise. Where a company spends money but does not obtain a permanent asset the expenditure is termed 'revenue expenditure'. When a company purchases plant or equipment which will be used over a long period of time, this expenditure is termed 'capital expenditure'.

The distinction between revenue and capital expenditure is not always simple. Clearly the payment of the heating bill is revenue expenditure, and the purchase of a computer is capital expenditure. But there are some items which cannot easily be categorised. For example, any transport costs when using British Rail would be a revenue expense. The purchase of a van to perform the same function, on the other hand, would be a capital expense. Similarly the leasing or hiring of equipment is revenue expenditure, whereas purchase of the same equipment is capital expenditure.

In spite of the lack of clarity it is apparent that organisations will require large sums of money to purchase long-term assets. Investment in fixed assets is necessary for three main reasons:

1 Expansion and growth. New capital resources in an organisation provide the capacity for expansion. The purchase of more aircraft by an airline, or the construction of more colleges by the government, allows the 'industry' to grow and output to increase.

2 Efficiency. The replacement of obsolete fixed assets by new machinery or new equipment can help to improve the productivity of an industry. For example, developments in computers have increased the efficiency of many administrative departments. New technology in heavy industries such as steel and ship-building has made the UK's competitors more efficient.

One of the problems with fixed assets as a resource is that their use cannot easily be changed. Once capital investment has taken place in specific plant, such as a steel rolling mill, the capital cost is so large that the plant has to be employed for many years even when it is obsolete.

3 Increased competitive power. Improved efficiency also improves competitive power. Organisations have to invest in order to be competitive. The above examples of ship-building and steel production are illustrations of the impact of technology on competition.

The need for capital investment creates five main problems for organisations:

1 How to raise the money? It is unlikely that companies will earn enough revenue to finance their initial capital projects from their own resources.
2 What balance to have between different sources of finance?
3 Which alternative investment project to choose?
4 How to build into the organisation provision for expensive purchases in the future?
5 What rate of return to try to get on the investment (pricing policy)?

Sources of commercial finance

Commercial organisations will rely on the revenue obtained from sales to pay for the day-to-day running of the firm. Surpluses will be 'ploughed back' into the organisation to finance expensive investment, so that profit can be a major source of finance. Quite frequently, however, firms will require money either in sums larger than their profits or more quickly than their profit is created. In these circumstances organisations will use additional sources of finance.

Short-term sources of finance and resources

1   Bank overdrafts are one of the most common sources of business finance and used for current rather than long-term needs. The amount borrowed varies according to need. Since interest is paid only on the amount overdrawn on the account, the cost of borrowing varies as needs change. Overdrafts provide a flexible source of short-term finance which tends to be cheaper than bank loans.

2   Bank loans.   A bank loan is a fixed sum which will be paid back during an agreed period. Firms normally take out a bank loan in order to finance a specific long-term project. Loans tend to be more expensive than overdrafts; there is very little flexibility in a loan and the interest charged is often at a higher rate than for overdrafts.

3   Hire purchase.   Like consumers, firms can acquire goods through hire purchase. In hire purchase a finance company pays for the goods, which are then obtained through a normal supplier. Ownership remains with the finance company until the end of the payment period. The cost of borrowing the money is added to the purchase price, and the debt is then paid in instalments. This is an expensive source of finance, however, and only small businesses tend to use it, mainly when other forms of credit are not available.

4   Leasing is becoming a popular method of acquiring equipment – it accounts for more than 10% of total capital expenditure in the UK in any one year. An operating lease separates the use of equipment from ownership. This contrasts with a mortgage or hire purchase agreement, where the user either owns the equipment or property from the start of the contract or has the option of acquiring it during or at the end of the payment period. Under an operating lease the leasing company will hire the equipment to another user. A finance lease, however, is similar to hire purchase in that the user has the option of purchase at the end of the leasing period.

Under a leasing arrangement the cost of the capital equipment is paid for out of revenue expenditure. The advantages of leasing compared to outright purchase are:

(*a*) No large sums of money are required to obtain capital equipment. This means that the user has a lot of flexibility in the use of fixed assets.

(*b*) The payments are fixed in advance and this enables the organisation to calculate the true cost of the asset over its expected period of use, and therefore to budget more effectively.

The popularity of leasing is illustrated by Table 10.2, which gives statistics published by the Equipment Leasing Association.

Table 10.2 Assets acquired under UK leasing arrangements (1982, £m at original cost)

	£m
Plant and machinery	957
Computer and office equipment	477
Oil exploration equipment, aircraft and ships	517
Commercial vehicles and railway stock	320
Cars	256
Consumer durables, buildings and others	213
Total	2740*

* estimated to be 13% of total capital investment in the UK.

5 *Trade Credit.* The initial capital which is acquired by paying in arrears for goods and services is important to small firms. When firms are in cash flow difficulties they can resort to acquiring short-term funds by delaying the payment of bills, by running down stocks, and by not putting income into some form of reserve. During inflation it is profitable to delay the payment of creditors, and, of course, the money acquired in this way does not bear interest. But it is a practice which has its dangers, in that creditors are suppliers and they could refuse to supply raw materials or producer goods, etc.,

unless payment is reasonably prompt. Equally, depletion of stocks as well as inadequate reserve funding are measures which could have serious consequences in the long run.

6   *Debt factoring* is an arrangement which increases the rate of flow of cash into an organisation. Under the arrangement a factoring house 'buys' a firm's (the client's) trade debts as they occur: when the client issues the invoice the factor pays up to 80% of the debt, after deducting charges. The balance of 20% is paid by the factor to the client when the customer pays the factor. By this arrangement a firm does not have to wait several weeks to obtain revenue from its sales – it can get the greater part almost immediately.

7   *Sale of existing assets.*   Some organisations purchase Government Stock or shares in public companies, and these securities are convertible into cash at quite short notice. Other assets are not necessarily as easy to convert into money, but fixed assets can be a source of finance. Such items as cars, computers and office equipment have reasonable second-hand values.

The ease with which a firm can convert its assets into cash is known as *liquidity*. That is why when a firm is wound-up it goes into liquidation: it sells its assets. The liquidity of an item varies according to its market ability. Fig. 10.2 summarises the degree of liquidity of the more common business assets.

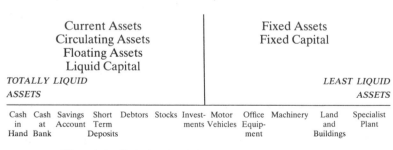

Fig. 10.2   Relative liquidity of business assets

The sale of an asset to raise finance will be influenced by the asset's liquidity. The more liquid an asset is, the more quickly it can be converted into cash.

Long-term borrowing

1 Shares. Incorporated public or private companies can issue shares in order to raise large amounts of money. The purchase of shares gives a person part-ownership in the company, with voting rights at shareholders' meetings. Because shareholders provide capital for a company, the company has a responsibility to try to earn sufficient profit to pay a dividend to shareholders. The size of any dividend varies according to the type of share:

(a) *Ordinary shares – equities.*   Ordinary shareholders have voting rights (equity) at shareholders' meetings. But they are not entitled to a fixed rate of dividend. The size of the ordinary shareholders' dividend varies according to the size of the profits and the directors' decision on the proportion to be retained by the company.

(b) *Preference shares.*   As the name implies, preference shareholders are given preference over ordinary shareholders in the payment of dividends. Preference shares always carry a fixed rate of dividend but the nature of its payment will vary according to the nature of the preference. For example, some – cumulative preference shares – can accumulate fixed dividends over time.

(c) *Deferred shares.*   Deferred shareholders are generally few in number and only receive a dividend after ordinary shareholders have been given a stated minimum. This minimum, and deferred shareholders' voting rights, depend on the terms of the issue. Deferred shares are normally held by the founders of the company and carry valuable rights.

2 Debentures – loan stock.   When a limited company borrows money it commonly does so by issuing loan certificates called debentures. A debenture certificate holder is a creditor of the company, not a member, and thus does not have voting rights. Debentures are long-term loans to companies; they bear a fixed rate of interest and will be redeemed at the end of a stated period. The interest on debentures must be paid whether the company makes a profit or a loss, so that in effect debenture interest is a fixed expense which will be shown in the Profit and Loss Account. Failure to pay the interest means that debenture holders can exercise a legal charge on the assets of the company.

3   Mortgage.   The issuing of shares and debentures are methods of raising money which are available only to incorporated associations. Sole traders and partnerships will require long-term finance to provide for large capital outlays such as the purchase of premises, and for this purpose they will sometimes take out a mortgage. A mortgage is a long-term loan against which the property is offered as security. Failure to pay the interest and capital charges means that the Building Society or mortgagor can exercise a legal charge on the property secured.

4   Finance for Industry (FFI).   The needs of smaller firms for finance are not on the same scale as large organisations, but they are just as acute. Unfortunately for small businesses, the general public are not as willing to invest in small firms as they are in large organisations. To overcome this problem specialist organisations have developed specifically to finance small business units. The Industrial and Commercial Finance Corporation is one such body, which was incorporated with the Finance Corporation for Industry to form the FFI. The commercial clearing banks own 85% of FFI and the remainder is owned by the Bank of England. It provides long-term loans to small firms and to large firms which have difficulty in raising capital, as well as to firms which wish to exploit new developments in technology.

5   Government assistance.   Successive governments have provided investment or cash incentives to certain sectors of British industry; and the following list gives examples of the type of assistance which has been provided in the 1980s:

1   Assistance for industrial innovation such as space technology and information technology
2   National Enterprise Board investment in advanced developments such as computing, biotechnology and underwater engineering
3   Industrial energy packages which are designed to assist industry with energy prices
4   Enterprise zones which are special areas of economic and physical decay which receive relief from certain taxes and rates
5   Assistance for the construction industry such as improvement grants and inner city projects

6 Enterprise packages which offer financial encouragement to small businesses and family companies

Sources of public finance

Commercial organisations in the public sector have very similar financial problems to private companies: they have to be profitable and they have to ensure that there is an adequate flow of money to acquire resources. The non-commercial organisations do not sell their services and therefore they do not have the problem of cash flow. They are given money by the government and have to work within strict cash limits.

The general philosophy in cash limits is that organisations have relative freedom to spend within the limit, but no freedom to spend beyond the limit. The central government and the local authorities are left with the problem of how to raise the money. The following measures are the main ones used:

Direct taxation

1 Personal taxation. Earned income is taxed. Income earners are able to deduct certain allowances from their gross income, and any remaining income is then taxed. The proportion of tax paid increases as taxable income increases.

2 Corporation Tax is a tax levied on company profits. Companies, like individuals, can deduct allowances from their gross profits. The allowances are in effect items of expenditure. The remaining net profit is then taxed at a standard rate.

3 Capital-Gains Tax. When individuals sell an asset it is assumed by the Inland Revenue that this is trade and consequently any profit or gain is taxed. The assets which are charged include all forms of property such as securities, works of art, and land. Exemptions are granted on certain assets such as a person's home.

4 Capital Transfer Tax. This tax applies to all gifts over a fixed sum, whether they take place during a person's lifetime or on his death. The rate of tax varies according to the sum transferred.

5 North Sea Oil. Oil production in the North Sea provides the Government with additional revenue in the form of North Sea Oil royalties and also as Petroleum revenue tax, which is a profit-related tax. Supplementary petroleum duty was abolished in 1982.

Indirect taxation

1   Value Added Tax (VAT) is imposed on products and services at every stage of production. The rate of tax remains constant and as the product increases in value (value added) the more revenue will be collected. Certain items such as food, coal and books are zero-rated, and some services – such as education and health – are exempt; but zero-rating and exemptions cause problems in collection. For example, children's clothes are zero-rated – the problem is to define 'children's clothes'.

2   Customs and Excise Duties.   Apart from goods from EEC countries, most imported goods are subject to customs duty. Excise duty is levied on home-products such as alcohol, petrol and cigarettes. The demand for these products is fairly inelastic, so the government can be fairly sure of the amount of revenue it will create.

Other forms of taxation

1   National Insurance contributions.   This is a form of direct tax which is shared between the employers and the employees. Employers pay over 50% of National Insurance contributions. Unlike other taxes, this tax is raised specifically for the National Insurance Fund, the National Health Service, and the Redundancy Fund.

2   National Insurance surcharge.   This has nothing to do with national insurance, except that employers pay it along with National Insurance contributions as an additional percentage charge on exactly the same bands of earnings. It is, in effect, a payroll tax paid by all employers except charities, on all except the very lowest paid or part-time workers. It is a means of raising revenue, like any other tax, and, because it adds to labour costs, has often been called a 'tax on jobs'.

3   Motor vehicle duty.   Ownership of a motor vehicle incurs a tax which for cars is at a standard rate regardless of the size of the car.

4   Rates.   Two-thirds of local authority income comes from the central government. The local authorities supplement these grants with income from rates, a tax based on the rateable value of properties. The value is assessed by specialists and is determined by the location of the property as well as its size and the number of rooms. The rate which is levied is decided by individual local authorities and to some extent reflects the expenditure of that authority.

The Water Authorities can also raise money on the basis of rateable value.

The importance of each source of public finance can be assessed by examining the percentages of revenue obtained by the government and local authorities from each source. Table 10.3 gives the percentages which existed in 1982/3.

Table 10.3   Sources of public finance, 1982/3.

(Total = £131.4 billion)

	% of total
Income tax	23.4
National Insurance	14.8
Local rates/rents	11.8
Value Added tax	11.2
Oil duties	3.9
Corporation tax	3.7
Interest on loans	3.7
Tobacco	2.7
National Insurance surcharge	2.6
Spirits, beer, wine	2.5
Petrol revenue tax	1.8
Supplementary petrol duty	1.5
Vehicle excise duty	1.4
North Sea Oil royalties	1.1
Other sources	6.2
Borrowing	7.7
Total revenue	100.0

Borrowing by local authorities and central government

The main sources of government borrowing are:

1   The issue of loan stock.   The local authorities and the central government issue loan stock which is similar to debentures in private corporations. Government stock is issued on the Stock

Exchange and the loan certificates can be purchased by any individuals or firms. Since the borrower is the government, such stock is termed *gilt-edged*: the lender is guaranteed a fixed rate of interest as well as repayment of the loan. Local authorities also issue loan stock to the general public, as well as borrowing directly from the government.

2   *Funds from overseas.*   Overseas investors who want to hold their money in sterling can purchase government stock.

3   *Treasury bills.*   These are used to borrow money on a short-term basis (usually 91 days). Because such loans are short-term the rate of interest is usually lower than for long-term loans.

Internal sources of finance

Internal funds are extremely important to organisations. Not only do they provide money for day-to-day operations (working capital), but they also provide finance for future investment. It has been estimated that internal funds account for more than two-thirds of funds from all sources.

Profits

The amount of profit a business makes is not always easy to calculate. One of the main problems, especially during inflation, is the valuation of a firm's assets. For example, the price of property is constantly changing and consequently the value of premises is often difficult to assess. The problems of inflation are outlined in more detail later in this chapter.

Accountants have conventionally used two definitions of profit:

Increase in assets.   Profit or loss is the increase or decrease in net assets which results from normal business activity. The sale of existing assets and long-term capital transactions are excluded from the calculation.
Revenue less expenses.   Profit or loss is the difference between total revenue from sales less any resources or assets used in the process.

Tax has to be paid on any profit and the shareholders will decide how the remainder will be allocated. Profit can be distributed as dividends to shareholders and/or be put into a reserve fund. It is the reserve fund which is the source of internal finance.

Depreciation
A second method which commercial organisations use to provide for future purchases is depreciation. The purpose of depreciation is to reduce the cost of a fixed asset to a scrap or realisable value. The amount of money used to reduce the cost is deducted from the initial capital outlay in the Balance Sheet and is also treated as a legitimate expense in the Profit and Loss Account.

There are several methods of depreciation. Two more popular ones are:

Straight-line method.   The scrap value of the asset is deducted from its initial cost and the remainder is written off over the estimated life of the project on a constant or fixed-instalment basis.*
Reducing balance method.   This method recognises that the value of an asset is higher during the first years of ownership. The depreciation charge is a fixed percentage of the remaining balance, so that each year the actual charge gradually reduces.*

Problems of inflation: falling money values

Money is not constant in its value; during inflation the cash in an organisation becomes an unreliable measure of value. Inflation distorts the calculation of profit and the valuation of assets. The following is a summary of the problems caused by falling money values:

1   Asset values.   During inflation the 'book' or recorded value of an asset tends to be inaccurate. Constantly increasing prices make many asset values on Balance Sheets too low.
2   Depreciation.   When fixed asset values are low, the depreciation charges will also be too low. A major reason for setting money on one side is to provide for future purchases. Inflation can make such provision inadequate.
3   Stock.   There is a temptation for firms to include the increased value of stocks in their profits. But a firm has to be careful not to

* For an example, see Appendix 4.

distribute such increases to shareholders because the extra value will be needed to replace stock.

4   *Cash.*   Cash resources lose their value during inflation but this loss is not shown in the accounts.

5   *Borrowing.*   It pays to be in debt during inflation because often the rate of interest does not adequately reflect inflation rates. Any 'gain' by borrowing is not shown in the accounts.

6   *Growth.*   The growth of a firm is difficult to assess because the changing value of money makes measurement difficult.

There were a series of proposals during the 1970s to try to remedy these problems. The Sandilands Report on Inflation Accounting was published in 1975, and in 1976 and 1979 the Accounting Standard Committee published proposals. Briefly, the main aims of the proposals were: (*a*) to try to calculate 'current cost operating profit' by making adjustments for inflation to depreciation, the cost of sales, and the working capital; and (*b*) to create a reserve which included any surpluses arising from revalued fixed assets or stock as well as any adjustments to working capital and gearing.

Balancing different sources of finance

Private corporations – capital gearing

Since there are many sources of finance open to large organisations, they have to make a choice on the balance between them. The choice will be influenced by three considerations:

1   The cost of the source.
2   The proportion of fixed assets to current assets. A high proportion of fixed assets in an organisation would indicate that a high proportion of 'permanent' capital is required.
3   The need for working capital. Loans from immediate cash needs are usually obtained from short-term sources, especially commercial bank borrowing.

The capital structure of a company can be assessed by various ratios. One of the most important ratios for this purpose is the *gearing* of the company. The gearing is the ratio between a company's equity (ordinary shares and dividend capital) and its permanent loan capital (preference shares and debentures). A company must pay interest on its permanent loan capital before it can decide on the dividend to award to ordinary shareholders, and therefore the ratio between the two will affect dividends. Debenture and preference shareholders have a prior charge. (Examples of how the gearing is calculated will be found in Appendix 4 along with other financial ratios.)

What is the 'right' gearing ratio depends on the degree of risk the company faces and the nature of the industry. Those firms likely to make very different amounts of profit (or even loss) from year to year should avoid having too much permanent loan capital – a high gearing. The capital market consists of a wide variety of people and institutions, and they will differ in the degree of risk they are willing to take as well as the amount of return they will expect from their investment. Companies have to take into account these differences when deciding on which source of finance to use. The cost of the source plus the company's own expected yield will ultimately influence the balance between the different sources.

Smaller businesses are less fortunate than public limited liability companies. They do not have the advantage of being able to choose between a wide variety of sources; they mainly rely on their profits and borrowing from commercial banks to finance their activities.

The balance in public finance

The government has the problem of deciding on the balance between revenue from taxation and public borrowing, as well as between direct and indirect taxation.

Revenue and borrowing

The expenditure patterns of governments are not fixed, but a high proportion of government services must be provided by law. In addition to this constraint, established patterns of spending mean established patterns of resource utilisation. These patterns are difficult to change. For example, once a hospital has been constructed it is difficult to change its use.

It is difficult, then, to change either the size or the pattern of government expenditure. Naturally, in the first instance, it is the established level of spending which will determine how much money is required by the government. But it is not the only consideration which will influence the level of government revenue and the public borrowing requirement. Another important factor is the government's assessment of the economic situation.

Budgeting for a deficit.   In budgeting for a deficit the government intends to spend more than it collects in taxes. The reason for this is the need to stimulate the economy by giving consumers more to spend, through tax reductions, and by increasing government spending on social services and capital projects. The excess in expenditure will be financed through government borrowing. The issuing of loan stock in the Capital Market will have an effect on the general supply of money: as treasury bills increase, so will the money supply increase.

Budgeting for a surplus.   The government can reduce Public Expenditure and/or increase taxation when it wants to reduce total spending in the economy. This policy is normally adopted when there is inflationary pressure in the economy and the government wants business activity to contract. A danger is that high levels of taxation might discourage effort and at the same time encourage high wage demands, both of which could lead to higher inflation.

A neutral or balanced budget occurs when the government considers that neither stimulus nor restraint is necessary. However, since there are millions of independent decisions made every day, many of which will be affected by government spending, it is extremely unlikely that a budget can in fact be wholly neutral.

Direct and indirect taxation
The raising of public revenue is more complicated than the earning of sales revenue by commercial organisations. Governments do not impose taxes simply to obtain money: it is the prime reason but not the only one. As we have seen, taxation is also used to influence the pattern of consumers' expenditure and to stimulate the economy. In addition, all British Governments in recent years have attempted to redistribute wealth by imposing higher taxes on those who can most afford it. With these three purposes in mind the government will decide on a balance between direct and indirect taxation. Table 10.4 outlines the advantages and disadvantages of direct and indirect taxation.

Table 10.4 Direct versus indirect taxation

		Advantages		*Disadvantages*
Direct Taxation	1	Relatively cheap and easy to collect.	1	Discourages hard work and enterprise.
	2	Equitable in that it falls on those who can afford to pay.	2	Increases the time and resources spent on tax avoidance.
	3	Gives the government fairly direct control over people's spending.	3	The tax on company profits tends to reduce investment.
Indirect Taxation	1	Does not discourage effort.	1	Indirect taxes are regressive: as a proportion of income they fall more heavily on the poor.
	2	Can be used for specific social policies such as reducing smoking or gambling.	2	Can be difficult and costly to collect.
	3	People have a degree of choice in whether they will pay the tax.	3	The amount of revenue to be raised by VAT cannot easily be predicted.

Deciding between investment alternatives

The two elements which an organisation will take into account in an investment decision are the *cost* of the project and the expected *benefits* which the project will bring. These two factors will be considered regardless of whether the investment is made by a public or private organisation. The cost of a project is fairly easy to estimate since the price of machinery or plant or equipment is known. Organisations can also make reliable estimates of running and maintenance costs. The benefit side of a project, however, is not so easy to predict: the degree of risk, the timing of the benefits, as well as the missed opportunity to invest the money elsewhere, make the assessment of the rewards from investment unreliable.

The degree of risk
A significant difference between commercial and non-commercial investment decisions is that commercial investment carries a degree

of risk. Competition from other organisations makes predictions of the rewards from an investment project unreliable. The risk of failure, especially in marketing new products, is high: 80% of all new products fail to become established.

The timing of the benefits

Investment is forward-looking, in that it will only produce results in the future. A major feature of investment decisions is the time lag between the initial investment and the eventual return. Money, in effect, buys the time between the initial outlay and the eventual return. To complicate the issue is the fact that money received at different times has a different value. The sooner an organisation receives a return, the sooner it can employ the money to earn further rewards. A delay in obtaining earnings from an investment decreases the value of the earnings. Tables have been devised which discount future money earnings back to a present value, as shown in Table 10.5.

From the table it can be seen that the present value of 1 which is to be received in four years time and discounted at 5% per annum is worth only £0.8227. Tables have been compiled for all rates of discount up to 48% and for periods up to fifty years.

Missed opportunities to invest – Opportunity cost

A notion which runs through all investment decisions is the one of opportunity cost. The benefits from an investment project are produced over a number of years, and during that time the money used on the project might have been used more profitably elsewhere. The true cost of an expenditure is the lost opportunity of spending the money on alternative schemes. Normally the benefits

Table 10.5   A discount table showing the present value of £1 receivable or payable in future years

	Rate of Discount	
Year	2%	5%
1	0.9804	0.9524
2	0.9612	0.9070
3	0.9423	0.8638
4	0.9238	0.8227
5	0.9057	0.7835

which would have arisen from an alternative scheme will never be known. But a common and constant indicator is the return that would have been obtained if the money had been lent to someone else – the rate of interest. If an organisation chooses to lend money rather than buy resources, it can make a reliable estimate of the reward it would obtain. When using discount tables the rates of discount vary from 1% to 48% and a problem is which rate of discount to select. A good guide is the rate of interest one would get if the money was lent.

Table 10.5 shows quite clearly that the longer returns are delayed, the lower the present value of the £1 becomes. This fall in value should not be confused with the falling value in money caused by inflation. Discount tables simply show how the value of the £1 falls at a particular rate of interest; even if the inflation rate were zero money would still lose its value over time because delay costs either income which could have been earned had the £1 been 'in the hand', or interest paid on the borrowed £1.

Techniques which incorporate the above ideas of timing and opportunity cost have been devised to help businessmen to decide between different investment alternatives. The risk element is always present in commercial ventures, and although market research and other management techniques can help to reduce the element of risk, it can never be eliminated. On the other hand, discount tables can be used to overcome the problem of timing of the returns, because estimates of the income can be discounted to present values which allows fair comparisons to be made. If the rate of interest used in the discount tables is the same as that which could be earned by lending the initial capital, then the notion of 'opportunity cost' has effectively been included in the comparison.

Pay-back
This is the crudest method of investment appraisal. The pay-back period is the time taken for an investment to generate sufficient revenue to recover the initial outlay. The investment programme which is selected is the one which repays the initial cost in the shortest possible time. Therefore the pay-back method emphasises the project which brings immediate reward.*

* For an example, see Appendix 5.

Average rate of return

The average rate of return is the ratio of profit (after depreciation) to capital outlay. Net profit is more commonly used than gross profit. The capital outlay can be the initial sum invested or the outflow of cash over the life of the project. Although the average rate of return is not as crude as the pay-back method, it ignores the timing of the cash flows and therefore is not ideal. Time is an important factor in all investment projects.*

Internal rate of return (IRR)

One of the most common investment appraisal techniques is the internal rate of return method, which uses the discount tables to compare alternative projects. The method takes into account the cost of the project as well as the timing of the inflow of cash. IRR uses the net present value of the £ to find a rate of interest which will discount the cash flows of a proposed investment to zero.*

Cost-benefit analysis (CBA)

Commercial organisations in the private and public sectors will use discounted cash flow (DCF) techniques. (In fact the nationalised industries should only undertake investment projects which promise to yield more than a minimum test discount rate which in 1967 was set at 8%.) The yardsticks for measuring commercial investment cannot, however, be used to assess investment in schools, hospitals, defence, etc. Instead *cost-benefit analysis* (CBA) is applied.

The idea of discounted cash flow is used in cost-benefit analysis, but unlike the internal rate of return method CBA takes into account all costs and all benefits which accrue to society, whether actual payments or receipts are involved or not. These costs and benefits (which will be given financial values) will be discounted to present values. This form of analysis is most often used in connection with projects which have social as well as economic implications, such as the construction of motorways, bridges, airports, dams, etc.

---

* For an example, see Appendix 5.

Social costs

The main difference between CBA and commercial methods of appraisal is that CBA takes into account social or 'hidden' costs as well as financial costs. For example, if it were proposed to build a new toll bridge across an estuary like the Severn, then the crude costs and benefits shown in Table 10.6 could be considered.

Table 10.6 Cost-benefit analysis

	Costs	*Benefits*
FINANCIAL (visible)	Construction of the bridge. Approach road construction. Repairs and maintenance. Provision of lighting. Wages of toll keepers. Administrative costs.	Income from tolls.
SOCIAL (hidden)	Noise pollution Fumes pollution Congestion at peak times. More accidents from increased traffic.	Saving of time and distance. Fewer public vehicles required. Saving of fuel. Less wear and tear on other roads. More economic activity

This example is only a simplified illustration. Evaluating the costs and benefits associated with a particular project can be very complex. In spite of this, CBA does allow public administrators to compare investment alternatives, and not only does it clarify financial considerations, but it also highlights social implications such as conservation and pollution.

Obtaining a return on investment

Non-commercial organisations allocate their services according to need. In commercial organisations, market forces – prices – determine how products or services are distributed. The price of a product also determines how much income an organisation will obtain from a capital project. It greatly influences the cash flow into an organisation, and consequently affects its acquisition of additional resources.

The pricing policy of commercial organisations can be a constantly changing process. The setting of prices requires technical understanding of market forces such as elasticity of demand as well as practical knowledge of changes in fashion, design and competitors' strategies. The degree of control a firm has over its prices depends on the competition it faces, that is, the number of other firms producing similar products.

The main factors which will influence a company's pricing policy are:

1   The cost of the product.
2   The planned return on capital investment.
3   The company's need for liquidity.
4   The supply of similar products.
5   The nature of demand and its elasticity.
6   How much of the existing market the company wants to obtain.

The pricing methods which exist are:

(*a*)   *Cost-plus pricing.*   This is probably the most common form of pricing. Firms need to have a good knowledge of their expenses, because to set the price they have to calculate the average cost of the product and then add a profit margin.

(*b*)   *Marginal-cost pricing* is a system which is adopted by organisations in imperfect competition – for example the Nationalised Industries. It is a method which in theory *maximises* the profit a company can earn.

(*c*)   *Variable pricing, Price discrimination, Price differential.* Many organisations are able to charge different prices for the same product, commonly through quantity or cash discounts. Off-peak pricing practised by British Rail, the telephone service and many hotels provide other examples. The reason for off-peak pricing is to try to switch demand to periods when capital resources such as railway stock, telephone exchanges and hotel bedrooms are lying idle.

(*d*)   *Corporate pricing.*   Organisations which produce a variety of goods sometimes have a corporate pricing strategy. This system is adopted either when the company wants to establish a reputation for stable prices or to cross-subsidise weaker products. For example, the Rank Organisation subsidised its investment in hotels with profits from Rank Xerox.

(*e*) *Bidding for tenders.* Government and local authority contracts are awarded to those organisations which *tender* the best bargain. The price, which will often be set for the one contract, and delivery times are the most important factors which are considered when bids are judged.

11

People in Organisations

Organisations employ three main resources or factors of production: *natural resources* such as land and raw materials; *man-made resources* such as buildings, machinery and equipment; and *people*. Of these, people are arguably the most important asset to any organisation.

Specialisation

Most people in organisations are specialists. The degree of special skill which is required in a job obviously varies, but it is important to realise that almost everyone in employment is a specialist to some degree. This simply means that in a job we concentrate on specific or specialised tasks – only sole traders perform all the functions in their organisations.

One of the main reasons for the growth in the economy during the nineteenth and twentieth century has been the development of specialisation. Specialisation occurs when people, regions or even countries concentrate on what they can do best. Specialisation is common in all organisations and takes place when the total operation is broken down into a series of sub-tasks. The mass production of motor cars provides a good example: in car production hundreds of different components are manufactured separately; the components are then assembled on a production line where each employee performs a repetitive specialist task.

The advantages of specialisation are:

1 People can concentrate on what they are best at. Given the ability, a person can choose to become a secretary or an engineer.

2 Repetition of the same task increases a person's skill and improves efficiency.

3 Constant employment in the same job can lead to suggestions for improved methods of operation.

4 Breaking operations into sub-routines encourages automation, so that mass production and economies of scale can take place. This advantage is double edged: automation increases productivity and wealth, but at the same time can lead to redundancy and unemployment.

There are also disadvantages which specialisation creates:

1 Many tasks are so repetitive that they are boring. Those jobs which do not require much imagination or creativity can cause boredom which leads to frustration, discontent and low morale. Such tasks tend, however, to be those which can most easily be automated.

2 Even when jobs require imagination, the total operation can be so large and so complex that employees do not understand how their work contributes to the total process. This, like boredom, can cause feelings of uselessness and frustration.

3 Specialisation creates interdependence which reduces self-reliance. People and organisations who are dependent on one another become vulnerable to strikes and similar activities by other people.

4 Specialisation can lead to poor control of people, particularly in large organisations. Communication lines become long and weak and organisation structures become complex. All this makes the job of managing people in an organisation more difficult.

The nature of labour markets

The range of occupations in business is extremely wide and it is unwise to make too many generalisations and comparisons between different occupations. One of the most basic and standard indicators of what people are worth is the amount of money an organisation is willing to pay them. Salaries and wages are the price of people in organisations, and reflect the supply of and demand for particular skills and knowledge. The difference between labour markets is the difference in people's knowledge and skills.

A person does not necessarily belong to only one labour market, but can apply for a variety of jobs. For example, almost every ablebodied person could do unskilled work, therefore the supply of people in this labour market is very large and consequently the price is relatively low. However, the more skill and knowledge a person has, the more specialised he tends to be and his 'rarity value' will give him a high price.

The factors which determine the labour market to which a person will normally belong are:

1 *Qualifications.*   Academic and professional qualifications are one of the main indicators employers use to assess people. Where an occupation requires long periods of study, then people in those markets tend to be in short supply, and therefore they command a high price. For example, it takes several years of study for architects and doctors to become qualified, but when they are qualified and experienced they are highly paid.

2 *Experience.*   Many employers are unhappy about employing 'raw recruits'. There are circumstances where a firm would like to train its own personnel from the beginning of their employment, particularly in fields which require initiative and new ideas. But advertisements for many occupations ranging from typists to sales directors state that experience is an essential requirement.

3 *Aptitude.*   Some people are fortunate to possess skills which are rare. Sports 'stars', pop 'stars' and others in the entertainment industry are paid high salaries because their skills are much in demand but short in supply. Individual talent in this category cannot easily be acquired by training and education – it is often an inherent gift. Natural gifts are not confined to jobs in entertainment, but also apply to inventors, designers, artists and so on.

4 *Social skills – Personality.*   Almost all employees in the service industries have to be able to cooperate with the general public, and some occupations put particular emphasis of certain types of social skill. The shop assistant and the salesman require the ability to

persuade. People employed in the social services require the special skill of listening to the problems of others and of suggesting remedies or solutions. Employees in the hotel and catering industry have to be able to deal with difficult customers, and even in manufacturing industry an employer will always consider how well a new recruit is likely to 'fit in' with the existing workforce. Where delegation and participation are common, *all* employees require the ability to communicate and the ability to listen.

Job description and job specification

An interesting feature of the labour markets is that many organisations do not specify the type of person they require: instead they will provide the details of a job or task in a job specification. The Department of Employment has given the following definitions of a job description and job specification:

Job Description: A *broad* statement of the purpose, scope, duties and responsibilities of a particular job.

Job Specification: A *detailed* statement of the physical and mental activities involved in the job and, when relevant, of social and physical environmental matters. The specification is usually expressed in terms of behaviour: what the worker does, what knowledge he uses in doing it, the judgments he makes and the factors he takes into account when making them.

The skills and knowledge which organisations need

The enormous variety of job specifications which exist in business illustrate the range of diversity and specialisation in occupations. It is not presumed that the five categories outlined below cover this wide range, but they do provide a guide to the role of manpower in organisations.

1 Unskilled. Many jobs do not require any training or previous experience, for example manual labour or assembly work. These occupations are often highly repetitive and boring, as well as being poorly paid. Much unskilled work could be performed by machines, but the capital cost would be too high. Almost all businesses have such jobs and they tend to be at the bottom of the organisational hierarchy.

2   Mechanical or motor skills.   There are some tasks in business which are performed by machines which require an operator. The more complicated the machine, then generally the more skilled the operator has to be. Jobs which require motor skills can range from the semi-skilled occupations, such as a machine operator in an office or factory, to highly skilled occupations, such as an airline pilot.

3   Intelligence and knowledge.   Occupations which require a high level of motor skill sometimes also demand a high level of intelligence and aptitude. An airline pilot is a good example. There are jobs in business which do not need mechanical skills but make exacting demands on people's knowledge. The professions of law, finance and insurance, and the jobs in research and design, are examples of this. They are occupations which are often staff, rather than line, functions in the organisational hierarchy.

4   Administrative or managerial skills.   The ability to organise other people is a fairly rare skill. It not only requires knowledge and understanding of the functions within an organisation, but also the ability to motivate people: to persuade them to give their best towards the aims of the organisation. In addition to this knowledge and ability to motivate, managers must be able to organise non-human resources using techniques of forecasting, planning, coordinating and controlling. These are techniques which require judgment as well as knowledge. People who possess managerial qualities tend to be near the top of an organisation's hierarchy.

5   Decision-making skills and initiative.   Decision-making is an everyday occurrence for everyone. We decide what to eat, what to wear, when to go out, and so on. Similarly decisions are part of an organisation's everyday activities. Routine tasks, by their very nature, exclude the employee from the decision-making process, but middle and top management will be using their judgment every day. The higher one goes up the hierarchy, the more necessary is the skill of decision-making. People at the top of an organisation are employed to have initiative – to make decisions. For example, boards of directors are employed to make policy decisions in investment, manpower and marketing. The risks which all organisations face mean that organisations have to be run by people who have the ability to diagnose and assess the risk, and the capacity to decide on the correct strategy. Business is constantly changing and organisations require people with enterprise and initiative in order to survive.

The five categories outlined above can be placed in a hierarchical pyramid (Fig. 11.1) which indicates the relative size of the labour markets for each catagory. The pyramid also illustrates an organisation's hierarchy.

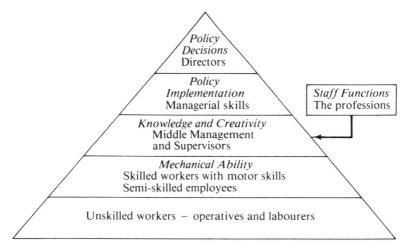

Fig. 11.1   Labour markets and the organisational pyramid

The recruitment of human resources

The recruitment of people into an organisation is normally carried out by the Personnel Department. The steps in the recruitment process are:

1   Analyse the task – job analysis
The objectives of an organisation are sub-divided into a series of separate specialist tasks or jobs. The personnel department will analyse the delegated tasks in order to find out what type of labour skills and knowledge are required. The purpose of job analysis is to produce a job description or job specification.

There are several methods which can be used to analyse a job:

(*a*)   *Observation.*   The task is observed and recorded as it is performed by an 'average' employee. The problem with this method is that it will not show the amount of thinking which is necessary.

(*b*)   *Interview.*   Interviewing an existing job holder causes problems when the employee is disinterested in or even aggressive towards the analysis.

(*c*)   *Questionnaire.*   Questionnaires can be compiled and administered to many existing employees.

(*d*)   *Equipment.*   The materials and the equipment which the job requires can be assessed.

(*e*)   *Records.*   Previous records of similar tasks can be examined.

2   Provide details of the job – job specification

The job analysis should provide the personnel department with sufficient information to compile details of the skills and knowledge which the job requires. These details normally specify:

(*a*)   *The motor skills required.*   This describes what the employee actually does, and the nature of the machinery and equipment which the work involves.

(*b*)   *The mental skills required.*   This is a description of the knowledge needed to perform the task.

(*c*)   *The decision skills required.*   This specifies the degree of judgment and initiative which the employee will have to use.

3   Advertise the job – recruit employees

Some posts are restricted to internal applicants and in these cases the job will be advertised on an organisation's notice board and in internal circulars. The reasons for internal appointments are, firstly, that promotion within a company improves morale, and secondly, that they allow an organisation to reduce its workforce if that is necessary (natural wastage).

Most employees, however, are recruited from outside the organisation from the following sources:

(*a*)   *Press advertisements.*   Many newspapers and journals display columns of 'situations vacant', which is the most popular method of advertising a post. Occasionally firms use box numbers rather than disclose the company's name. This happens when there are details such as salary policy which the organisation wishes to keep secret.

(*b*) *Government agencies, Job Centres.*   Many occupations, but particularly unskilled and semi-skilled vacancies, are advertised in Job Centres which are administered by the Department of Employment.

(*c*) *Private agencies.*   These are private firms which perform a similar function to government Job Centres except that they will help organisations to recruit in markets where labour is in short supply – that is, where the skills that jobs require are rare.

(*d*) *Further and higher education.*   Many employers approach universities and colleges directly. Higher educational institutions employ full-time careers guidance officers who liaise between employers and students and assist both in employment problems.

(*e*) *Direct applications.*   Anyone can approach an organisation at any time and ask for a job. This is true for all levels of employment. Where labour skills are rare or where a person is particularly talented it is common for organisations to approach individuals directly.

4   Interview and select the applicants

Interviewing is the most widely used method of assessing people. Normally an organisation will draw up a shortlist of those candidates whose skills and knowledge are closest to the job specification. There are legal rules in this process which an organisation should observe. The Sex Discrimination Act, 1975, and the Race Relations Act, 1976, make it illegal to discriminate in all aspects of employment.

The candidate who is selected is the one who, in the opinion of the interviewing panel, has the qualities and skills demanded by the job specification.

5   Appoint the candidate: the contract of employment

The appointment of a person is a contract between the employer and the employee. The employer makes the offer of the job and the employee accepts the offer in writing.

Conditions of employment

The employer is obliged to provide certain details of the conditions under which the job is to be performed. These obligations arise from two Acts of Parliament: the Contracts of Employment Act, 1972, and the Employment Protection Act, 1975.

According to the 1972 Act an employment contract must contain:

(*a*)   The names of the employer and employee.
(*b*)   The date when employment commenced.
(*c*)   Details of the pay or how the pay is to be calculated.
(*d*)   When the payment of wages or salaries will be made (usually weekly or monthly).
(*e*)   The terms and conditions of work (hours, holiday pay, sick pay, pension scheme).
(*f*)   The length of notice required on each side.
(*g*)   Trade Union rights.

The Employment Protection Act, 1975, adds further requirements: the contract of employment must also contain:

(*a*)   The title of the job.
(*b*)   Details of whether previous employment counts towards the period of employment for notice purposes.
(*c*)   Guidance on the rules relating to disciplinary and grievance procedures.

How organisations manage people

Induction: first impressions

Induction is the act of introducing a new employee to an organisation. Its purpose is to help new recruits to become part of the organisational structure by introducing them to their jobs and their working environment.

The methods which are commonly used are: (*a*) visits to the departments within the organisation; (*b*) lectures and talks by senior management; (*c*) films on the organisation's activities; and (*d*) introductions to colleagues and supervisors.

The content of an induction programme can include: (*a*) the organisation's rules and policies; (*b*) the organisation structure; (*c*) health and safety measures; (*d*) welfare facilities; and (*e*) the organisation's services and products.

Development of people: training and education

People are an employer's most important resource and so it is in the interests of an organisation to try to develop the skills and knowledge of its employees. The benefits which result from training and education are:

1 Increased productivity and output.
2 Improvements in the quality of output.
3 Greater flexibility of skills of the employees.
4 Greater job satisfaction.
5 Reduced turnover of labour.
6 Improved employee morale.
7 Improved promotion prospects for employees.
8 Improved safety awareness.

The initial skills and knowledge which people possess are acquired at school and college. The emphasis in education is mainly on the development of knowledge, and organisations use this basis to develop specialisms. The training and development process applies to all levels of an organisation's hierarchy – no one can consider himself fully developed.

The methods of training and education which organisations will use vary according to the type of development required. There are three broad catagories:

1 Skill training – the development of motor skills

Although the advantages of training apply to all organisations, the cost of training schemes is relatively high. Firms could make an apparent saving by ignoring employee development programmes and 'poaching' skilled employees from other organisations which ran development schemes. The unfairness which this created was remedied by the Industrial Training Act, 1964.

The Industrial Training Act, 1964, created the Industrial Training Boards (ITBs); and the Employment and Training Act, 1973, established the Manpower Services Commission (MSC). The ITBs, under the direction of the MSC, aim to improve the skills and knowledge of employees and to make them more mobile. The cost of the boards is met by a levy which employers pay according to their payroll.

The New Training Initiative (NTI), published in 1982, recognises the importance of skills training. It specified three fields which would form the basis of industrial training in the 1980s: youth training, retraining and updating, and skills training. More formalised instruction in motor skills, in such establishments as government skillcentres, has now replaced the traditional 'sitting next to Nellie' methods, where employees learned new skills by observing an experienced employee.

2   Social skills: relating to other people

The growth of the service industries, and a better understanding of how people work together, has led to an increased interest in the improvement of social skills: the ability to relate to other people. Social skills are not exclusive to the service industries: all occupations require employees to have the ability to cooperate with people. Training boards, technical colleges and the MSC have developed courses, especially for young people, which aim to improve social skills. The abilities which the courses concentrate on are:

(*a*) *The ability to communicate.*   Misunderstanding can occur between employer and employee and it often leads to conflict. The knowledge of how to present a point of view, either in written or spoken form, is vital to employer-employee relationships. An employee's willingness to participate in an organisation will often be influenced by his ability to communicate.

(*b*) *The ability to listen.*   As we have seen, many occupations comprise delegated tasks: they are small specialised parts of a total effort. In order to carry out delegated tasks and duties, an employee must understand them. The ability to listen to what has been said improves the employee's understanding.

(*c*) *Awareness of other people.*   The attitudes and perceptions of people vary according to their personality and experience. Managers in particular have to be aware of the needs of their subordinates in order to motivate them. All employees have to work with one another, and understanding of each others' needs and attitudes leads to greater cooperation and increased job satisfaction.

The methods used to develop these abilities in employees are very similar to those used in management and supervisory training, which are outlined below.

3   Supervisory and management skills

The skill which managers require above all is the ability to manage people: to motivate them to improve their performance. In addition, top managers must be able to make decisions, and this requires a knowledge of the constraints on decisions as well as the techniques which help decision-making.

Management training courses are provided by public and private institutions. Polytechnics and universities run short courses as well as full-time postgraduate courses. There are also private management colleges at Henley and Ashridge. The armed forces and the Civil Service, as well as public and private corporations, run their own staff colleges which design courses for the organisation's special staff development needs.

The methods of training and education which these bodies use are very similar. They are:

(a)   *Formal lectures.*   The purpose of formal lectures is to pass on knowledge. Normally the content of management lectures will deal with organisation and motivation theories, constraints on decisions, and management techniques.

(b)   *Case studies, simulation exercises, role playing.*   One of the problems of management training is to make the learning environment as realistic as possible. Case studies, simulation exercise and role playing give students practical awareness of the problems of managing people and of making decisions. They enable students to participate in realistic problems.

(c)   *Discussion groups.*   There are no absolute solutions to problems which occur in business. Discussion groups enable managers to exchange ideas and experiences so that they can learn that there are many aspects and different points of view on solutions to business problems.

(d)   *Business games* simulate a commercial environment. Teams of management students analyse the relationship between such variables as price, quality and output, as well as employer-employee relationships, and decide on a team strategy. The advantages of this exercise are, firstly, that students can apply theories and principles, and, secondly, that they can learn to cooperate in working groups.

The welfare of employees

The difference between development and welfare schemes is not always clear. As we have seen, employee development concentrates on improving knowledge and skills; and these will undoubtedly improve the employee's welfare. However, most welfare programmes are specifically concerned with the physical and social well-being of people rather than their abilities.

Some welfare facilities are required by law. The Health and Safety at Work Act, 1974, requires organisations to provide:

(a) *Hygiene facilities*, such as lavatories, cloakrooms and drinking water.

(b) *Safety programmes*, which must include the maintenance of safe plant and equipment as well as training and supervision in accident prevention.

(c) *Safety devices and clothing*. Some occupations are dangerous because of the high level of fumes, dust, sparks or noise. Protective clothing and equipment must be supplied by the employer.

(d) *A safe working environment* in relation to space, lighting, heating and ventilation.

Some organisations will provide welfare facilities above the legal minimum, for example:

Social and sports clubs. People enjoy social contact outside work and it helps the organisation if employees form relationships through their social and sports clubs. Such relationships strengthen the bonds between organisations and employees.

Fringe benefits. Successive governments have imposed restrictions on pay and this has led to an increased growth in alternative financial rewards such as pension schemes, sick pay, subsidised meals and company cars.

Joint consultative committees

Joint consultation provides employees with the opportunity to discuss welfare matters with their employers. It gives employers the opportunity to assess the impact of policy decisions on employees. Joint consultative committees consist of representatives from all levels of an organisation, and they discuss matters related to welfare. In some organisations joint consultation covers wider personnel problems such as training and discipline. It is important to note that these discussions are consultations, not negotiations – *collective bargaining* procedures generally cover negotiable questions such as wages and conditions of employment.

The informal organisation

The welfare facilities which are provided by the organisation are, to some extent, the formal organisation's recognition of the informal organisation. The formal organisation is symbolised by policies, rules and regulations, and above all by the hierarchical pyramid of authority. During the past fifty years it has been recognised that people in organisations have their own aims, ambitions, expectations, needs and behaviour patterns which will be different from, and sometimes in conflict with, the aims and policies of the formal organisation. The real power and influence in an organisation is not necessarily represented by the formal organisational chart.

The source of employee-employer conflict is not simply wage costs. Other sources of conflict include work which has not been recognised or personal goals which have been frustrated. People need to get satisfaction from their jobs, otherwise work alienation and poor morale will develop.

It is the realisation by managers that the performance of employees can be improved by taking account of their individual needs which is the basis of modern methods to improve employee performance. The purpose of employee motivation is not only to improve job satisfaction, but also to increase the effectiveness of people in organisations.

The Human Relations School

Modern motivation theory, and our understanding of the behaviour of working groups, stems from the research into the informal organisation by social psychologists. The most influential work has been published by four writers:

Elton Mayo

The importance of the informal organisation was first discovered by Elton Mayo at the Hawthorne factory of the Western Electric Company, near Chicago, between 1927 and 1932. Mayo and his colleagues discovered that pressure within the informal group could increase output even when the working environment was made worse. Conversely, the informal group's attitudes could serve to restrict output even when financial incentives were offered to individuals.

Up to 1930 it had been assumed that individuals were fairly isolated within organisations. After the Hawthorne experiments managers began to appreciate that people work in informal social groups; and that the pressure within informal groups frequently exceeds the strength of formal rules and regulations.

Douglas McGregor

The theory developed by McGregor questioned basic assumptions about the motivation of employees. These basic assumptions McGregor called Theory X. In Theory X it is assumed that most people dislike work, avoid responsibility and respond to authoritarian leadership. In contrast, McGregor maintained in his Theory Y that most people find work natural and pleasing, do not need external controls when motivated, enjoy responsibility and enjoy participating in solving problems.

The contrast is between work-centred management (Theory X) and people-centred management (Theory Y). Douglas McGregor advocated the latter.

A. H. Maslow

Maslow's theory is that the needs of employees are very complex and that they occur at different levels. He argued that in order to motivate people managers should understand the different needs and different levels of need of employees. The levels are in an ascending or hierarchical scale: the second level cannot be satisfied unless the first one is, and so on. Maslow classified the needs into five levels:

> *First level: Basic needs*
>> hunger
>> thirst
>> sleep
> *Second level: Security needs*
>> warmth
>> housing
>> security
> *Third level: Affection needs*
>> companionship
>> recognition
>> friendship
> *Fourth level: Status needs*
>> praise/esteem
>> possessions
>> power
> *Fifth level: Self-actualisation*
>> personal development
>> creativity
>> use of full potential

The pressure of these needs will vary within individuals and between individuals. An interesting observation is that the first, second and, to some extent, the fourth levels can be satisfied by financial reward. But such needs as recognition and personal development require managers to look for additional methods to motivate people.

Frederick Herzberg

Herzberg contrasted the factors which he found gave job satisfaction with those which created dissatisfaction. He argued that the provision of satisfying factors would motivate people. The 'motivators' include recognition of work done, responsibility for tasks, sense of achievement and promotion prospects.

On the other hand Herzberg said that there were factors which, although absolutely necessary in a job, would not motivate people. Inadequate provision of the maintenance factors – wages and salaries, fringe benefits, rules and regulations, and relationships within the organisation – would tend to cause dissatisfaction.

The satisfying factors or 'motivators' are not the opposite of dissatisfying or 'maintenance' factors. It is significant that those elements which had to be adequate to maintain a person in a job would not, according to Herzberg, motivate a person.

The findings of the industrial social psychologists (Human Relations School) show that motivation is an intricate thing. Financial reward is an important but complex method of motivating people. But money is not the only motivator: equally important are recognition and responsibility. As a result of the work of the Human Relations School new methods of motivation are being adopted by organisations. These include job rotation, job enlargement and job enrichment (see Chapter 14).

Employee/employer relationships

Although people are an organisation's most important resource, they are also a very costly resource. It is inevitable that some conflict will occur between employer and employee since an employee will want to maximise his wages, and an employer will want to minimise his wage costs.

In order to secure benefits from employers, many groups of employees have organised themselves and formed trade unions. By the 1970s there were over 450 trade unions and their combined membership exceeded 12 million. The objectives of organised labour are:

1 To increase wages and salaries.
2 To improve the conditions of employment (hours of work, overtime, shift-work, etc.).
3 To improve the working environment (space, lighting, heating, ventilation and safety).
4 To protect the employees from unfair or even illegal practices such as unfair dismissal.
5 To represent individual employees in cases of dispute.
6 To ensure that all employees receive adequate training.

Trade unions are now the most influential pressure group in business. During their development, and up to the present time, they have been subject to legal rules. The landmarks in trade union history are:

The Tolpuddle Martyrs (1834)
Trade Union Act (1871)
Taff Vale Judgment (1901)
Trade Disputes Act (1927)
Industrial Relations Act (1971)
Trade Union and Labour Relations Act (1974)

The Employment Act 1982 made important detailed changes to the existing legislation. The main changes were:

(*a*) Exclusion of the legal immunity of trade unions in certain circumstances e.g. secondary picketing;
(*b*) Extended protection for individuals from compulsion to join a closed shop;
(*c*) Tighter balloting requirements;
(*d*) Amendments to the rules affecting compensation and relief for union related dismissal;
(*e*) New provisions affecting legal proceedings against trade unions;
(*f*) Directors' reports to contain a statement on how employee participation will be developed.

Trades Union Congress (TUC)
Most trade unions are affiliated to the Trades Union Congress, which was formed in 1868. The main objective of the TUC is to act as a pressure group to influence government and business decisions. It also promotes research and publicity on behalf of organised labour.

Employers' associations
Employers have formed associations which help members in their industrial relations problems and provide assistance in trade matters. The large national associations are called Employers' Federations. Employers' Associations provide a wide range of services for their members and will:

1   Negotiate and deal with organised labour.
2   Help with technical problems.
3   Liaise with other organisations, especially the government, local authorities and professional bodies.
4   Seek to improve customer relations.
5   Encourage cooperation in research.

Confederation of British Industry (CBI)

Many Trade Associations are members of the Confederation of British Industry. The CBI was formed in 1965 under a Royal Charter, and its aims are to formulate and influence industrial and economic policy. The CBI also encourages the development of methods to improve efficiency in British industry. It is the managers' counterpart to the TUC and as such is one of the best known pressure groups in business affairs.

Collective bargaining

The parties in collective bargaining are the trade unions and the individual employer or employers' association or federation; and the bargaining is generally about wages and salaries, conditions of work and productivity arrangements. The distinction between joint consultation and collective bargaining is that in collective bargaining *negotiation* rather than *consultation* takes place, and any agreement becomes a formal agreement rather than an 'understanding'. Normally collective bargaining is held at national level, but it can take place within an organisation. Legislation such as the Health and Safety at Work Act, 1974, and the Employment Protection Act, 1975, however, has tended to put more emphasis on local rather than national agreements, and in so doing has narrowed the difference between collective bargaining and joint consultation. Disputes in collective bargaining will normally go to arbitration.

Disputes

The causes of a breakdown in employer/employee relationships can be very complex. The most common cause is pay and conditions of work. However, poor management practice such as inadequate communication, lack of consultation and no recognition of work well done, will often create low morale and lead to disputes.

In a dispute the action which employees can take against their employers are:

1 Absenteeism. Frequently employees who are dissatisfied with their job will not turn up for work. Absenteeism accounts for more working days lost than strikes do. Of course many workers absent themselves because of genuine illness or domestic difficulties. These reasons apart, it is a form of 'informal' protest many individuals use against their employers.

2 Go-slow, work-to-rule, refuse to cooperate. The specialisation which dominates human activity in organisations requires well defined rules and regulations. The rules are a flexible framework for tasks – they are open to interpretation. If employees work to rule they will rigidly interpret all rules and obey them to the letter. In addition, employees can limit their cooperation by refusing to work overtime or to attend joint consultative committees. In a work-to-rule the organisation can still function, but not without problems.

3 Strike action. Withdrawal of labour from an organisation is a drastic form of action. Not only is the organisation unable to function properly, but also the employees who are on strike will not be paid by the firm. Where the trade union agrees with the strike, then it is deemed 'official'. Unofficial strikes occur when the employees have not obtained central union approval for their action.

Conciliation and arbitration

Parliament has established several statutory bodies which help to settle industrial relations problems. Two of the most important are:

1 Industrial Tribunals deal with a variety of problems, including discrimination, equal pay, unfair dismissal and redundancy. They are similar to courts of law in that they attempt to decide what is the most reasonable case in a dispute. Appeals can be made by dissatisfied parties to a higher court, but only on a point of law. The chairman of a tribunal is an independent, legally qualified person and the other members are representatives of employers and trade unions.

2 The Advisory Conciliation and Arbitration Service (ACAS) was established by the Employment Protection Act, 1975, and is an independent body with the following powers and duties:

(*a*)   To improve employer/employee relationships.
(*b*)   To help solve disputes when requested.
(*c*)   To investigate voluntarily any industrial relations problem and publish the findings.
(*d*)   To investigate terms and conditions of employment and the recognition of trade unions.
(*e*)   To prepare codes of practice for the conduct of employer/employee relationships.

Termination of employment

Resignation, giving notice

Employment is a contract between the organisation and the employee which can be ended at any time by either party. Employees do not have to give reasons for leaving an organisation, but an employer has to be careful not to infringe the Employment Protection Act, 1975. The period of notice which either party must give is normally written into the contract of employment and varies according to the length of service. An employee may bring a case for wrongful dismissal when insufficient notice is given by an employer.

Dismissal without notice

An employee is dismissed when an employer terminates the contract of employment. Employers can legally dismiss a person without notice for serious misconduct, and examples of conduct which might warrant instant dismissal are:

1   Stealing from the employer.
2   Fighting on the employer's premises.
3   Repeated absence from work.
4   Refusal to obey a reasonable instruction.
5   Serious neglect of duties or continued inability to perform delegated tasks.

Dismissal with notice

Employees whose conduct does not warrant instant dismissal can ask the employer to give reasons for the dismissal, and to show that no discrimination has taken place and that the dismissal is fair. There are three Acts of Parliament which prevent employers from discriminating against employees: the Equal Pay Act, 1970, the Sex Discrimination Act, 1975, and the Race Relations Act, 1976. In addition, the Trade Union and Labour Relations Act, 1974, protects employees against *unfair* dismissal. Employers can legitimately dismiss an employee for only three reasons:

1 Persistent inadequate performance or conduct, after due warning.
2 The post has become redundant.
3 Statutory requirements: employment cannot continue without contravening the law. For example, if the government were to enforce strict legislation on the publication of pornographic material, then those employees who specialise in producing such material could legitimately be dismissed.

Any other reason would be classified unfair for those employees who have more than 26 weeks' service and are employed for more than 21 hours a week. Employees who have been unfairly dismissed can complain to an industrial tribunal.

Redundancy
Under the Redundancy Payments Act, 1965, an employee is considered to be redundant when his job is no longer required by the organisation. Redundancy often occurs when an organisation closes down, but can also occur when reorganisation takes place.

An employee who has two years' service and has worked for at least 21 hours a week is entitled to minimum rates of redundancy pay (which are tax free). For each year of employment: (*a*) between ages 18 and 21, half a week's pay, (*b*) between ages 22 and 40, one week's pay; and (*c*) between ages 41 and 65 (60 for women), one-and-a-half weeks' pay. Industrial Tribunals hear disputed cases of redundancy.

Retirement
Women can retire from work at 60 and men at 65; they are then entitled to a retirement pension. Some organisations prepare people for retirement by providing pre-retirement courses, reductions in the working week and longer holidays. Welfare and social facilities are sometimes available for those who have retired.

Questions on Part Three

1   Why do you think that leasing is becoming a popular method of acquiring equipment? Explain your reasons.
2   Explain the consequences for a commercial organisation of changes in the value of money.
3   Using examples, explain the nature and purpose of Discounted Cash Flow techniques with particular reference to Cost Benefit Analysis.
4   Compare the advantages and disadvantages of the various methods of depreciation.
5   In relation to the motivation of people, do you think that there is a contradiction between the theories of Maslow and Herzberg and the philosophy which says that reductions in taxation act as incentives? Explain your answer.
6   Outline the factors which determine to which labour markets a person belongs.
7   Examine the basic differences between acquiring human resources and acquiring non-human resources.
8   Compile, in report form, a training programme for newly appointed junior operatives in a medium sized manufacturing organisation. Your report should include the following headings:
    (*a*) Induction, (*b*) Training within the firm, (*c*) Day-release, and (*d*) Assessment of the operatives.
9   Explain, giving examples, what is meant by 'informal organisation'.
10 The aims and objectives of organised labour are irrelevant and counter-productive in our modern Welfare State. Discuss.

PART FOUR
Efficiency in Organisations

12

Costs

Money, as we saw in Chapter 10, is a measure of value. An organisation's efficiency, or the value it gets from its use of resources, is represented by how much money the organisation spends on different items in relation to the output it gains from its expenditure. For example, if there are two breweries producing identical amounts and types of beer, the brewery with the lower costs of production would be considered to be more efficient. Efficiency, then, is the relationship between costs (use of resources) and output.

Types of costs

Costs are the expenses which are incurred in producing and distributing either goods or services, and there are two types of costs in all organisations:

Fixed costs are those which an organisation would have to pay even when production is not taking place – for example, rent for the premises (land and buildings); rates paid to the local authority (land and buildings); interest paid on loans (capital equipment); and depreciation (capital equipment).

These examples illustrate the fairly obvious fact that money which is spent on fixed assets such as plant and equipment is a permanent or fixed cost. Fixed costs are those expenses which are primarily used to provide long-term capital resources, and additional expenses, such as staff salaries, which will be incurred regardless of the level of production.

Variable costs are those which vary with output, and any costs which are not fixed are considered to be variable – for example, expenditure on raw materials, fuel, lighting and heating, and the wages of those directly engaged in production.

Difficulties in the classification of costs

In practical terms it is not always easy to differentiate between fixed and variable costs. For example, some administrative costs – such as telephone bills or postage expenses – will have a tendency to vary with output, although the relationship between them and output is not as strong as it is between raw material costs and output. On the other hand, some administrative costs are fairly fixed: the salaries of managers and staff have to be paid regardless of output. But salaries are not as fixed as capital costs, because managers can be made redundant when production remains low for a long time.

A second difficulty occurs in relation to capital costs. The provision for depreciation is classified as a fixed cost, but the actual deterioration of a machine is related to how frequently it is used. Production does create a cost of capital equipment through wear and tear. Equally, time makes equipment obsolete and leads to a deterioration in plant and buildings. In effect, therefore, all costs are variable in the long term. Fig. 12.1 illustrates the degree of permanence of various costs in the short term.

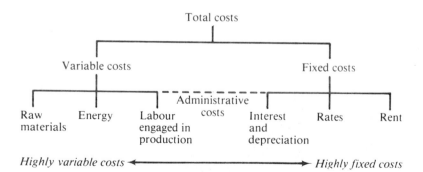

Fig. 12.1   The short-term variability of costs

Unit costs

The total costs of production are made up by variable costs and fixed costs. An organisation, however, is not necessarily interested in total costs but in how much each *unit* of production costs. This is particularly true if a firm is confident that it can sell every unit at a certain price. It is the unit costs rather than the total costs which give a better representation of the efficiency of organisations.

For example, consider two companies which are producing very similar bicycles which sell at £80.00 each. Company ABC produces 5 000 at a cost of £60.00 each: total cost = £0.3m. Company XYZ produces 20 000 at a cost of £55.00 each: total cost = £1.1m. Company XYZ incurs greater total costs than Company ABC, but produces the bicycles at a lower unit cost. Company XYZ is therefore more efficient than Company ABC.

In practice it is unlikely that two such firms would charge the same price. Company XYZ would probably use its efficiency to charge a lower price than Company ABC, thereby boosting XYZ sales.

There is a relationship between unit costs and the unit price:

$$\text{unit cost} + \% \text{ profit} = \text{unit price}$$

The relationship between output and costs

Time has an important effect on costs, in that all costs will eventually vary. Equally, output itself has an effect on the unit costs of an organisation: unit costs can never remain constant. Assuming that everything else remains constant as production increases, then unit costs will fall. A simple example illustrates this point:

Units produced	Fixed costs £		Variable costs £		Total costs £	Unit costs £
0	400	+	0	=	400	∞
1	400	+	1	=	401	401.00
10	400	+	10	=	410	41.00
50	400	+	50	=	450	9.00
100	400	+	100	=	500	5.00
250	400	+	250	=	650	2.60
500	400	+	500	=	900	1.80
1 000	400	+	1 000	=	1 400	1.40

Unit costs get nearer and nearer to variable costs, but of course they can never become equal to variable costs.

Assume that Company Toy produces jigsaw puzzles for which the fixed costs are £400, and the variable costs £1.00 per puzzle. As production increases so total costs will increase (Fig. 12.2a), but unit costs will fall (Fig. 12.2b).

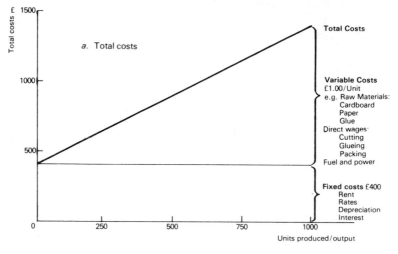

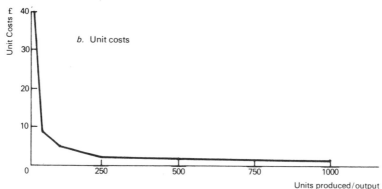

Fig. 12.2   Behaviour of costs

The reason for the fall in unit costs is that, as output increases, the fixed cost element becomes a smaller and smaller proportion of total costs. In the initial stages of production, however, the impact of fixed costs on total costs, and therefore on unit costs, is very great.

Economies of scale

All organisations, particularly those with high fixed costs, will benefit from producing on a large scale, because increased output reduces the percentage of fixed costs to total costs. The reductions in unit costs which result from increases in output are known as the 'economies of scale'. The following are examples:

1   Set-up costs.   The motor car industry has to spend large sums of money to establish or 'set up' a production and assembly line. Similarly the printing industry 'sets up' presses to produce newspapers or books. The long production runs which this type of industry can then undertake reduces the fixed costs to a smaller and smaller proportion of total costs; and unit costs become lower at each stage of output.

2   Marketing costs.   Advertising expenditure is not directly related to production. The more units a firm produces, the smaller advertising expenditure becomes as a proportion of total costs.

3   Administrative costs.   A complex computer installation or a research and development team are relatively expensive administrative costs which are fixed. Large firms can afford such costs only when they form a small percentage of total costs.

Efficiency, productivity and scale

We have seen that increased output automatically makes fixed costs a smaller proportion of total costs and therefore reduces unit costs. So large-scale production does create some savings or economies, but these economies are not increases in efficiency or productivity. The real test of efficiency is to reduce *in absolute terms* either the variable costs or the fixed costs.

An increase in productivity can occur in two ways:

When output increases and costs remain constant.   Costs represent factors of production or resources, so a test of efficiency is to get more out of existing resources.

When output remains constant and costs fall.   If an organisation can use fewer resources – raw materials, energy, people – and yet maintain production levels, then productivity has increased.

The expansion of output not only reduces the percentage of fixed costs to total costs, but also provides organisations with opportunities for increasing productivity. For example, other economies of scale are:

1   Capital cost saving.   The capital cost of some fixed assets does not increase in direct proportion to size. This is primarily because volume increases at a greater rate than surface area. For example, the design size of oil tankers can be doubled from 100 000 tons to 200 000 tons, but the materials which are required do not double: the costs increase from about £6m to £10m. Jumbo jets do not cost twice as much as other passenger jets to build and yet they can carry twice the number of passengers.

2   Improved purchasing power.   Large firms can benefit from reduced purchasing costs because they can obtain their supplies in bulk. They can often afford to purchase expensive new equipment. For example, word processors are more efficient for some tasks than copy typists, but only fairly large firms can afford such equipment while the investment cost remains high.

3   Savings in finance.   Large organisations can attract investors and are able to 'shop around' for the cheaper sources of finance. Not only do their funds tend to cost less, but finance is easier to obtain and therefore borrowing requires less effort and less time.

4   People.   Large organisations can afford to employ specialists who are skilled in such management techniques as work study or organisation and methods which will help to improve the efficiency of the organisation. They can also afford to train their own management staff in motivation and similar skills which will improve the performance of employees.

It would be wrong to assume that only large organisations can improve productivity. Increases in output and size provide organisations with the above opportunities for reducing fixed and variable costs; but there are techniques for improving efficiency which *any* organisation can use, regardless of its size.

Techniques for improving efficiency

1 Improved methods of work and operation: work study
An organisation can systematically analyse its existing procedures by:

(*a*) Identifying the goals of particular tasks.
(*b*) Recording in a systematic manner (using a flow chart) how a task is performed.
(*c*) Examining the record made in (*b*) with the intention of eliminating duplicated and wasted effort.
(*d*) Designing and introducing a revised and improved method.
(*e*) Making periodic checks to ensure that the new procedures operate as planned.

Work study can improve the performance of many employees, particularly those who are engaged in repetitive tasks such as assembly work. It can also be used to improve the layout of a factory, hospital ward, office, etc., so that space is used more effectively.

2 Organisation & Method (O&M)
O&M originated in the Civil Service during the 1940s, and is particularly useful in administrative departments. O&M is in effect the application of work study ideas to the office. It uses the same type of systematic analysis, with the objective of simplifying and improving office methods. The benefits which can result from O&M are:

(*a*) Improved flow and speed of information (e.g. accounting records).
(*b*) Better records and easier access to information (e.g. staff records).
(*c*) Closer control of operations (e.g. quicker response to customer complaints).
(*d*) Avoidance of bottle-necks caused by delays (e.g. the processing of customers' orders).
(*e*) Improved security procedures (e.g. handling cash and confidential documents).

3   Standardisation

A common approach is useful in all areas of business activity – tools, equipment, procedures, forms, etc. Conversion from one system to another either costs time and money or is impossible. Standardisation eliminates conversion problems and reduces obsolescence of equipment.

The following are examples of standardisation from which the whole of business can benefit:

(*a*)   Standard basic components, such as the threads on nuts and bolts.

(*b*)   Standard measurements, such as metric.

(*c*)   Standard terminology and procedures, such as airport procedures.

(*d*)   Standard equipment, such as containers for lorries and ships.

Organisations can benefit too from internal standardisation. For example:

(*a*)   Standard packaging which makes the storage and transport of finished goods cheaper and easier.

(*b*)   Standard methods of production and the interchangeability of parts (e.g. when the tools used in the production of one car are used again in the production of another model).

(*c*)   Standard communication procedures (e.g. standard forms and reports make recording and filing much simpler).

A danger in standardisation is that it can make organisations inflexible because of 'red tape', and it can make the reaction to change slow.

4   Statistical techniques/Operational Research (OR)

Because change and risk are so prevalent in business, the application of probability theory can help organisations to predict when events might go wrong; and it can help them to select the best course of action – to decide on the best alternative. OR describes a series of techniques which can assist managers in planning and decision-making. All of the techniques have a mathematical basis, and their practical application is complex. The main OR techniques are:

(*a*)   *Critical Path Analysis (CPA)* can shorten the time of projects, especially construction projects such as bridges, roads, buildings and ships. The technique can be refined to indicate the best time to allocate resources.

(*b*) *Simulation/queuing theory.* In simulation techniques a mathematical model is constructed to represent the many variables which exist in a real system. Different combinations of variables are tested to find the most efficient allocation of resources or to find the solution to a problem. For example, it helps to solve queuing problems such as aircraft waiting to land, goods waiting to be processed, customers waiting for buses, or customers waiting for telephone calls.

(*c*) *Game theory: competitive strategies.* This technique is used by the armed forces to test different battle strategies. Its commercial application is in marketing, where the reaction of competitors to different marketing strategies is predicted.

(*d*) *Quality control.* The quality of products can be controlled by using statistical techniques which help human or machine errors to be detected quickly.

(*e*) *Stock control.* Stocks (of raw materials, stationery, spare parts, etc.) are kept by all types of organisation and techniques have been developed which help organisations to keep sufficient stock without running out, and at the same time to minimise the cost of holding stock.

5 Productivity/incentive schemes

Productivity agreements enable employees to become more effective and so reduce wages costs. The terms which can be included in a productivity agreement are:

(*a*) Payment by results, bonuses, fringe benefits.
(*b*) Reduction in overtime. Wage costs are more expensive when overtime is worked.
(*c*) Flexible working hours.
(*d*) Elimination of rigid demarcation between different jobs.
(*e*) Elimination of time-wasting.

Financial reward does motivate people, but it is limited in its capacity to act as an incentive. In the long run, employees have to be given other rewards as well as recognition and responsibility if they are to maximise their contribution to an organisation.

6   **Technology and automation**
Improved efficiency is often achieved by developments in machinery and equipment. A most revolutionary impact has been made, and is being made, on business by developments in microelectronics. Silicon-chip technology will affect all organisations, for example stock control in retailing, data processing in the small business, word processing in administration, and so on. (See also Part Six.)

Costs and geographical location

The efficiency of an organisation is not decided simply by its size and its management practices. The geographical location of an organisation will affect its costs. For example, office accommodation is more expensive in central London than in Aberystwyth. On the other hand there are advantages in being located in London, such as the speed of communication or the large market of office employees, which can offset the high rents and cause offices to be London-based. These advantages are called *external economies*. When deciding on its location an organisation will try to get maximum savings and incur minimum costs from the immediate environment. But not all organisations have a choice of where they will be situated – coal mining can only take place where there is coal, docks can only be located in sheltered waters – so the location decision of an organisation cannot always be in terms of costs. The factors which influence the location of organisations are:

1   Historical reasons: industrial inertia.   Many industries became established in particular areas because of the nearness of certain supplies, especially energy. For example, the manufacture of wool was established in Yorkshire because of the availability of water power in the Pennine valleys. Steel production was located in Sheffield because of the availability of coal as well as iron ore and limestone. Even though the initial advantage has declined, many industries have remained in their first locations because of 'industrial inertia'. Other advantages, such as a skilled workforce, have replaced the initial attraction.

2   The distribution of 'nature's gifts'.   Extractive industries have very little choice of location: mining, quarrying and oil drilling must be based at the source of the product. Similarly the location and type of farm is influenced by topography and climate. The fishing industry is located near to harbours and fishing grounds.

3 The current availability of resources. Manufacturing industry requires raw materials, energy and labour in order to produce, and will often be located close to an essential resource. The Ford Motor Company was established in Dagenham, Essex, because of the supply of labour. Modern steel production is located close to ports where iron ore can be imported.

4 Closeness to a market. The service industries have very little choice in location decisions – they must be situated where the demand for their service exists. Thus insurance and banking are located in commercial centres; hairdressing salons, restaurants, retail outlets, and central and local government services are located in populated areas. Those firms which produce finished products which are fragile or valuable will also want to be located near to a market, to minimise the cost of damage or loss during transit.

5 Cost of transport. Those organisations which manufacture a product must choose either to be located near to the supply of raw materials or near to their market. The decision will be influenced by the costs of transport. If the finished product is bulkier and heavier than the raw materials, then the production will be situated near to the market. Generally speaking, raw materials are cheaper to transport than finished goods, so that industries which produce furniture, clothes and durable goods tend to be located close to the supplies of labour which are also consumer markets.

Nature's gifts	Raw materials	Transport costs	Working population	Customers and clients
Primary industries have little choice		Secondary industries can choose		Service industries have little choice

Fig. 12.3 Factors determining location of primary, secondary and tertiary sectors

As we can see from Fig. 12.3, the two sectors of business which have very little choice in location are the primary and tertiary industries. The manufacturing sector has much greater choice, and it is the cost of transport which will influence most firms' decisions on location. They will balance the cost of transporting the raw materials against the cost of transporting the finished product.

External economies

Once an industry becomes established in a particular location there are advantages which accrue. It is these advantages which cause 'inertia' or lack of mobility in the system. The benefits are:

1   Local authority and central government services.   The National Health Service, Education and Housing become established wherever people are. Some of these services, such as courses at the local technical college, can become specifically geared to the needs of local organisations.

2   Commercial facilities.   Banking, insurance, and security organisations will adapt their services to meet the needs of a local industry. They become familiar with the particular problems of local organisations and provide a specialised service. In addition, local Chambers of Trade and Employers' Associations develop, and then provide, specialised assistance in research and cooperation.

3   Marketing and distribution facilities.   An established industry will encourage the provision of specialised haulage and warehousing facilities, as well as the creation of local mailing agencies.

4   Ancillary/support industries.   Interdependence, which is a dominant feature of modern business, means that ancillary organisations will develop around established producers. For example, car production in the Midlands has encouraged the siting of hundreds of car component manufacturers in that area.

Organisations and production systems

The nature of an organisation's product or service will greatly influence its location; similarly it will also determine the type of 'system' through which the organisation will achieve its aims. Because of the nature of their product/service, most organisations do not have any choice in the type of system they will adopt. For example, mining has to be carried on in an 'extractive' system. Although one system will dominate the business of an organisation, it will generally use more than one system. All industrial organisations, for example, have a production function which forms part of the manufacturing system, a financial function in the administrative system, and a marketing function in the service system.

The systems which are described below are general illustrations of the types of arrangement which can dominate the activities of an organisation, and which will influence the organisation's efficiency. It would be wrong to believe that every organisation fits neatly into one particular category.

1 The extractive system. Mining, quarrying, fishing and farming are engaged in the extraction of products and produce from nature. Developments in technology have made the extractive industries more capital-intensive, but traditionally they require a high proportion of their total costs to be spent on labour in order to produce.

2 The manufacturing system: flow production. In manufacturing it is common for the operations to be broken down into a series of repetitive tasks where componenets are assembled to form a finished product such as a car. The mass production of durable goods such as radios, vacuum cleaners, refrigerators, etc., requires high capital investment in fixed assets to set up the production process. The people employed in assembly or flow production tend to be unskilled or semi-skilled.

3 The construction system. There are products which cannot be created on a 'massive' scale. Some, like power stations, roads or bridges, can only be produced once. Others, such as aircraft, ships and houses, are normally produced in batches. The organisations in a construction system tend to be more flexible than those in manufacturing because their investment in fixed assets tends to be a smaller proportion of total assets. On the other hand, they will employ highly skilled people who can adapt to different work situations.

4 The communications system. The transport industries and the post and telecommunications services provide a communications system; they produce the facilities for people and organisations to make contact. The industries in this system require both high capital investment in advanced technology, and a large number of employees, many of whom are highly skilled.

5   *The service system.*   Most organisations have a relationship with the service system; for example, the marketing function is part of distribution. The service system includes commercial industries such as retailing, hotels and catering, and hairdressing, as well as the public services such as health, education and social welfare. A significant feature of the service system is that the organisations which use it are dispersed throughout the country in direct relation to the population. The system is labour intensive.

6   *The administrative system.*   Organisations are dominated by the administrative system when their main aim is to control and produce information. Naturally administrative systems exist in all organisations, but the activities of some institutions, such as the Civil Service, the commercial banks, the building societies and insurance companies, are primarily administrative – they manage information. The developments in computers and electronic data-processing are making these organisations more capital-intensive, but they remain large employers of people.

The different methods of efficiency which the various systems create can be summarised in chart form (Table 12.1).

The law of diminishing returns and the diseconomies of scale

The efficiency of a business is influenced by the way it is managed; and by organisational features such as system, location and scale of operations. Set against these influences there are two important principles regarding inefficiency which apply to all organisations, particularly those which expand. The two principles are: the law of diminishing returns, and the diseconomies of scale.

The law of diminishing returns
The law of diminishing returns states that as more and more resources are allocated to a fixed asset, then eventually output will diminish (Fig. 12.4).

Fixed resources have a finite capacity. For example, there is a

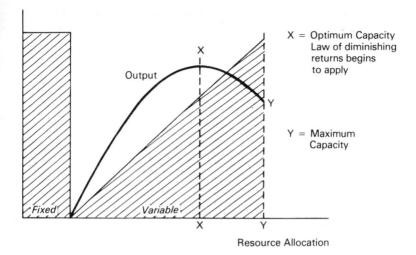

X = Optimum Capacity
Law of diminishing
returns begins
to apply

Y = Maximum
Capacity

Resource Allocation

Fig. 12.4 Optimum and maximum capacities – the law of diminishing returns

limit to the number of animals which can graze in a field, or to the number of tables which can be placed in a restaurant. There are some assets, however, where it is difficult to assess their capacity. What, for example, is the maximum capacity of the road system? Although it is efficient to use resources as much as possible, it is a mistake to believe that a resource is always most effective when it is worked at maximum capacity. Employment to maximum capacity of most resources will result in delays, bottlenecks, breakdowns, congestion and all the other factors which cause inefficiency.

In all systems there is an *optimum* mix of resources which will maximise output, and this mix can often be assessed by OR techniques. Since it is rare for the optimum capacity to be the same as maximum capacity, then managers, when they want to allocate resources most effectively, should use management techniques to assess the optimum use of their resources and so avoid the onset of the law of diminishing returns.

The diseconomies of scale
One of the problems of large organisations is that, although increased size brings the benefits of large-scale operations, they will probably run into the diseconomies of scale. For example:

Table 12.1 Organisations and production systems

Type of system	Examples	Nature of the fixed assets	Nature of the labour
Extractive	Mining Quarrying Fishing Farming Oil Gas	Has become more capital intensive using highly specialised capital equipment	Employs a small % of working population Dangerous work
Manufacturing	Durable goods Vehicles Food processing Printing Chemicals	High 'set up' costs	Large number of employees. Low-skilled assembly work
Construction	Roads Bridges Aircraft Ships Houses	Equipment has to be adaptable as well as highly specialised	High technical and motor skills required. Labour has to be mobile in some cases.
Communications	Rail Road Sea Air Post Telecommunications	Highly expensive fixed assets required. Assets soon obsolete	Labour intensive industries. Employ all types of labour
Service	Retailing Hotel & catering Health Education Social welfare	Premises tend to be the main capital asset	Labour intensive industry. Social skills important
Administration	Civil services Banking Insurance Local govt.	The main capital assets are premises and data-processing equipment	Becoming less labour intensive. Employs mainly 'professional' people

Position regarding the economics of scale	Location decision	Efficiency Methods used	Comments
Growth limited by 'Nature's Gifts'	No choice in location	Productivity and incentive schemes	Coal, gas and some oil production are nationalised. Farming controlled by EEC policy
Long production runs and high output Economies of scale	Choice between raw materials and labour supply	Standardisation Quality control Stock control	Traditionally known as 'flow production'. Includes many well known corporations: ICI, BL, Unilever
Short production runs and high-cost products	Apart from 'batch' production very little choice in location	Standardisation Critical path analysis Simulation models	Design plays a very important part in the system. Very competitive system
Organisations tend to be monopolistic and large-scale	Provides a communications service for almost all the population	Research and development Queuing theory	Most organisations are nationalised. Social obligation to provide a service for total population
There are many small units in the commercial sector	Can be situated any-where near to population (market)	Stock control Queuing theory	Competition in the commercial sector is high. The public organisations are the most expensive govt. services
Problems of coordination and communica-tion. decentralisation common	Main organisa-tions are based in London. Exist in all areas of population	Organisation & Methods	Administration is a function found in all organisations

1 Communication problems. Large organisations can have problems with internal and external communication. The lines of communication become extended and 'red tape' develops. For example, customers find it difficult to complain when organisations are large, and employees feel that the firm is impersonal.

2 Poor coordination and control. Central control can become difficult. The skills and knowledge which are needed to control and coordinate large organisations are rare. A lack of control might allow managers to develop their own aims and objectives so that they build up their department at the expense of other departments in order to get increased status or more power.

3 Slow reaction to change. The need for standardised procedures in large organisations can make them so inflexible that they reject good ideas and plans which do not fit into the standard pattern. Highly centralised organisations can be slow to adapt to change.

4 Obsolescent equipment. The purchase of expensive fixed assets is easier in large organisations but it can be costly and create inflexibility. Some of the nationalised industries provide good examples of capital equipment which is obsolescent – rail stock, telephone exchanges, power stations, steel plants. Although such equipment is less efficient than contemporary equipment, once it is installed it is too costly to change for a long time.

13

Financial Information

Financial information in an organisation enables managers to perform three functions:

1 To record. The money values of resources and of transactions in any organisation can be recorded using accounting techniques. The records enable companies to produce periodic statements of the value of assets, liabilities and capital.

2 To analyse. The presentation of financial information is required by law for many organisations, and so accounting conventions have developed as to how financial information should be presented. The standardised or conventional methods of accounting enable organisations to analyse financial information; and to make comparisons of performance between one year and another (intra-firm comparisons), and between similar organisations (inter-firm comparisons).

3 To control. Organisations can maintain a degree of control over departments by examining and regulating their expenditure. Accountancy provides reliable technique for the internal management of organisations.

Recording transactions

There are three reasons why organisations should record their transactions.

Firstly, the Companies Acts impose statutory requirements on companies to publish their accounts. Public limited companies, the nationalised industries, and non-exempt private companies must keep and publish a proper record of transactions with respect to (*a*) receipts and expenses, (*b*) sales and purchases, and (*c*) assets and liabilities. The accounts must give a 'true and fair view' of a company's affairs.

	Trading Account	£
add	Income from sales	+ sales
deduct	Costs directly related to production	− direct
	e.g. cost of raw materials	costs
	wages of operatives	
	fuel to drive machines	
gives	the Gross Profit on trading	= gross profit
add	Gross Profit on trading	+ gross profit
add	any Income other than from sales	+ additional
		income
deduct	any Expenses not directly incurred in	− indirect
	trading/manufacturing	costs
	e.g. depreciation of fixed assets	
	debenture interest	
	directors' fees	
	salaries	
	rent and rates	
gives	the Net Profit (loss) before taxation	= net profit

Appropriation Account

Taxation

add	Net Profit	+ net profit
deduct	Taxation	− taxation
gives	the Net Profit after Taxation	= net profit
		after tax

Other Appropriations

add	Net Profit after Tax	+ net profit
		after tax
add	Balance carried forward from previous year	+ previous
		balance
deduct	Gross Dividends paid or proposed to be paid	− dividends
deduct	Redemption of debentures or other loans	− redemptions
deduct	Transfers to reserve (plough-back)	− reserves
gives	the Balance on the Profit and Loss Account	
	which will be shown in the Balance Sheet	= balance

Fig. 13.1 Profit and Loss Account of XYZ Ltd for the year ending—19...

Secondly, private commercial organisations have to pay tax on any surpluses which are earned through trading. Consequently they must keep proper books of accounts which represent in a fair way all transactions. These books will be examined by the Inland Revenue authorities.

Finally, it is in the interests of a public company to publish its financial information in a form which is readily understood. Public limited companies require long-term finance from the general public, and the shareholders' and potential investors' assessment of a company is normally obtained through its published financial record.

The recording and presentation of financial information is carried out according to accounting conventions. The two most important standard documents are the Profit and Loss Account, and the Balance Sheet.

The Profit and Loss Account

The Profit and Loss Account records what has happened during a particular period (normally the financial year), and the conventional presentation is shown in Fig. 13.1. (See also Appendix 4.)

The Profit and Loss Account is a summary of a firm's activities during a financial period: it does not show that income and expenditure are constantly taking place. Every working day sales will be made and resources will be acquired.

Profit performs two important functions. As the Profit and Loss Account shows, if a firm makes sufficient profit after tax then some money can be 'ploughed back' into the organisation through a reserve fund. Profit enables a company to grow. Equally important is the second function of profit: it provides short-term funds (working capital) to meet day-to-day expenses. So profit provides both long-term and short-term finance.

In spite of the development of standards in the presentation of the Profit and Loss Account, there are problems in assessing and measuring profit.

1 Profit is a relative measure. Profit has more meaning when it is seen in relation to the amount of capital employed in its creation. For example, if Company ABC has assets of £2 000m and makes

£2m net profit, and Company XYZ has assets of £200m and makes £2m net profit, it would be unreasonable to conclude that both companies were equally successful. Net profit is a relative figure. It needs some qualification if it is to be used as a test of efficiency.

2   Timing.   Profits can fluctuate from year to year, and therefore annual Profit and Loss Accounts describe the fortunes of a company only for a limited period. For example, compare the profit performance of the two companies in Table 13.1. Investors and directors would generally prefer the consistent profits of Company XYZ rather than the erratic performance of Company ABC. The Profit and Loss Account for one year does not show these fluctuations.

Table 13.1   Profit and losses after tax (£m)

Year	1	2	3	4	5	Total
Company ABC	+19	+3	+11	−5	+14	42
Company XYZ	+10	+9	+ 7	+8	+ 8	42

3   Inflation.   Money as a measure of value is not reliable during periods of inflation. Consequently organisations have problems in valuing stocks or in deciding on the amount to set aside for the depreciation of fixed assets (see Chapter 10). Since there is an element of choice regarding the presentation of certain money values in the Profit and Loss Account, the accounts do not always give a 'true and fair view' of the performance of a firm.

4   Allocation of costs in large organisations.   In large organisations the cost of some items is not easy to apportion to particular trading activities. For example, where a large corporation spends money on corporate advertising, or on centralised research and development, the cost of these activities is not easy to allocate. Poor allocation of costs could hide unprofitable ventures and distort profit figures.

The Balance Sheet

The Balance Sheet is a statement of the financial position of a company at a certain date. It provides details on the assets, liabilities and owners' equity; and is required by law to be produced once during a financial year. Some companies produce 'interim' statements to show the position at a quarter or half year.

The purposes of a Balance Sheet are:

(*a*) To show, at a specified time, the total capital employed in the business (share capital, loans and amounts due to creditors).

(*b*) To show how the organisation has converted money into 'real' or 'productive' assets.

(*c*) To provide a record which allows auditors and owners to keep a check on the assets of a company.

(*d*) To provide a record which can be analysed to show how the organisation is performing. The Balance Sheet shows the gearing of the company, the balance between fixed assets and current assets, and the balance between current assets and current liabilities.

The fixed and current assets of a company are the resources which the company employs in addition to people in order to produce goods and services. Assets are acquired by incurring liabilities and by using shareholders' equity. Therefore the fixed and current assets should equal the equity (which includes any reserves and retained profit) and liabilities of a company. If a company's books are correctly kept, then both sides of the Balance Sheet should balance:

Assets = Liabilities + Owner's Equity

The apparent precision of a Balance Sheet is misleading. The techniques of accounting, if they are carried out correctly, will ensure that a Balance Sheet will always balance. But the information which is disclosed can be deceptive. The problems of inflation and changing money values (see Chapter 10) affect the accuracy of Balance Sheets. Fixed Assets, such as premises, do not necessarily represent their actual values. Similarly the value of stocks and the allowance for bad debts can only be estimated. It would be unwise to assume that the guesses of accountants are always accurate. A Balance Sheet represents the accountant's fairest view of the position of a company and, like a Profit and Loss Account, it is not an absolute record. (See also Appendix 4.)

Schedule 4 of the Companies Act, 1985, requires firms to disclose financial information in a specified format, and Fig. 13.2 shows the minimum headings which are required to be included in a Balance Sheet presented in vertical format 1.

	£	£
Called-up Share Capital Not Paid		0000
Fixed Assets		
Intangible assets	000	
Tangible assets	000	
Investments	000	0000
Current Assets		
Stocks	000	
Debtors	000	
Investments	000	
Cash	000	0000
Prepayments and Accrued Income		0000
Creditors: Amounts falling due		
within one year		(0000)
Net Current Assets (Liabilities)		0000
Total Assets *less* Current Liabilities		0000
Creditors: Amounts falling due		
after more than one year		(0000)
Provisions for Liabilities and Charges		(0000)
Accruals and Deferred Income		(0000)
Net Worth of the Company		
The above is financed by:		
Capital and Reserves		
Called-up share capital	000	
Share premium account	000	
Revaluation reserve	000	
Other reserves	000	
		0000
Profit and Loss Account		0000

Note: Items shown in brackets () are minus figures.

Fig. 13.2 Balance Sheet of XYZ Ltd as at __19. . .-vertical format 1

The presentation of the Balance Sheet in a vertical format is a relatively recent practice. The traditional form of presentation is a horizontal format; and a simplified example of the layout is given in Fig. 13.3. The information which is included in both the vertical and the horizontal formats is similar: it is customary in both formats to show assets and liabilities in order of liquidity – the least liquid item is shown first and the most liquid last. The two advantages of the vertical format are that, firstly, it is generally easier to understand. For example, the horizontal layout shows shareholders' capital as a liability and this can cause confusion. Secondly, it emphasises important features such as the working capital and the net worth of a company.

	£		£
Share Capital	0000	Fixed Assets	0000
		shown at cost *less*	
Reserves	0000	depreciation to give	
		written-down value	
Liabilities and Provisions	0000		
Current Liabilities	0000	Current Assets	0000
	£		£

Fig. 13.3   Balance Sheet of XYZ Ltd as at ___ 19 . . .-horizontal format

Analysis of financial information: measures of efficiency

In spite of the defects which financial records have, they do give the best indication of the efficiency of an organisation. Several techniques have evolved which enable businessmen to compare the performance of an organisation from year to year, and to compare similar organisations. The following are three important methods of financial analysis.

1   Working capital

Without finance, a business cannot obtain resources and therefore it cannot operate. The fixed assets in an organisation need to be used as frequently as possible – it is very costly and inefficient to have plant and machinery lying idle. There are many necessities which are required before fixed assets can operate, the most important being people, raw materials and energy. Money and other highly liquid assets (those assets which can quickly be turned into cash) are the lifeblood of business activity because they help an organisation to acquire these three important resources on a continuous and current basis. Liquid assets are the capital which help to lubricate the fixed assets in an organisation.

It is not surprising that one of the most important areas of financial analysis is that which is concerned with this 'working capital'. Working capital is the current assets minus current claims which could be made on those assets (Fig. 13.4).

Current assets

Cash in hand
Cash at bank
Payments in advance
Debtors
Stock of raw materials
Stock of finished goods

less

Current liabilities

Trade creditors (for goods supplied)
Expense creditors (for services)
Taxation payable
Dividends recommended
Debenture interest due
Bank overdrafts

Fig. 13.4   The composition of working capital

It is important to remember that the flow of money through an organisation is a continuous process. The current assets, or circulating capital, are constantly providing the resources which the fixed assets employ.

If the working capital is insufficient, then it is likely that the organisation will run into difficulties. Fig. 13.5 illustrates the flow of circulating capital through an organisation, but it also indicates some of the difficulties which could occur. For example:

(*a*) Insufficient cash to pay creditors means that the organisation is unable to purchase raw materials, fuel, etc., and is unable to pay wages.

(*b*) Holding too much cash is an expensive and inefficient practice, especially during periods of high inflation. Money has to be employed if it is to generate profit.

(*c*) If stocks of raw materials are low, then production could be held up and the delivery of finished goods delayed.

(*d*) Holding too much stock can cause deterioration and obsolescence.

By analysing its working capital on a regular basis, an organisation can attempt to avoid these problems.

2 Ratio analysis

The relationship between items on the Profit and Loss Account and the Balance Sheet can be clarified by using financial ratios. Their main use is that they provide additional information over and above single items in the recorded accounts.

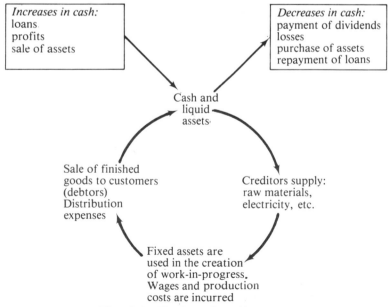

Fig. 13.5 The flow of working capital

A ratio, like any statistic, is useful only when it is compared with the same ratio from a previous year or from a similar organisation. There are more than one hundred ratios which *could* be calculated, but the most useful ones are described below (see also Appendix 4).

Tests of liquidity
These ratios help the organisation to analyse the flow of cash through an organisation.   ability to turn
                                                        something into
                                                                   cash
(*a*)   *Current ratio*
        current assets: current liabilities
The current ratio is a way of quickly assessing the nature of the working capital. If the ratio is less than 2:1 then the firm could be running into liquidity problems and might find it difficult to pay its way.
(*b*)   *Acid test ratio*
        current assets *less* stock: current liabilities
The current ratio includes stock, but stocks are not easily converted into cash. The acid test ratio excludes stock, and illustrates the relationship between highly liquid current assets and all current liabilities. Analysts would normally look for an acid test ratio of 1:1 – the ability to meet immediately all current liabilities.
(*c*)   *The average period of the collection of trade debts*
        debtors: annual sales
This ratio shows how quickly an organisation could convert the money owed by the debtors into cash in hand. For example, a ratio of 1:4 would indicate that the average period is three months, 1:2 is six months, and so on. The longer the period, the less liquid the debts are.

Tests of profitability

(*d*)   *Rate of return on capital*
        net profit: capital employed (fixed assets *plus* working capital)
A company would hope to obtain a consistent return on capital which, if the organisation is successful, is higher than that achieved by similar organisations.
(*e*)   *Profit to sales*
        net profit: sales *or* gross profit: sales
This ratio illustrates the relationship between profitability and

turnover. It is sometimes used in conjunction with break-even analysis.

Ratios in themselves have only a limited value if they are used purely for intra-firm comparisons. Firms can increase the value of such ratios by subscribing to the Centre for Inter-firm Comparisons. This body provides a confidential service and helps companies to compare their own ratios, costs, sales, output, etc., with other similar (but unidentified) organisations. If the comparisons are unfavourable, then it is a sign that the management of the organisation could be inefficient.

3 Break-even analysis

A firm breaks even when its total costs equal total sales revenue. Once the total sales revenue exceeds total costs then the firm is making a profit. This relationship between revenue and costs can be illustrated diagrammatically with a break-even chart (Fig. 13.6). The volume of production/sales is plotted on the horizontal axis, and the revenue and costs on the vertical axis. The chart illustrates the amount of profit or loss at various volumes of sales/production.

There are three assumptions in the construction of break-even charts which could be unrealistic. The diagrams show the effect if the assumptions are *not* realised.

(*a*) All of the goods which are produced will be sold (Fig. 13.7).
(*b*) Costs, selling price and product mix remain constant (Fig. 13.8).
(*c*) The capacity, technology and the fixed assets of the organisation remain unchanged (Fig. 13.9).

The effects of changes in the many variables of price, costs and technology can be incorporated in break-even analysis, however. A chart which does take account of these will be complicated but more realistic and therefore more useful. The main advantages of break-even analysis are that it enables businessmen to:

(*a*) assess the impact of changes in turnover on profitability.
(*b*) predict the effect of changes in price and forecast the percentage change in turnover which would occur when the selling price changed.
(*c*) analyse the relationship between fixed and variable costs.

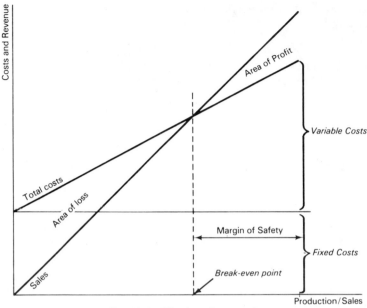

Fig. 13.6   The break-even chart

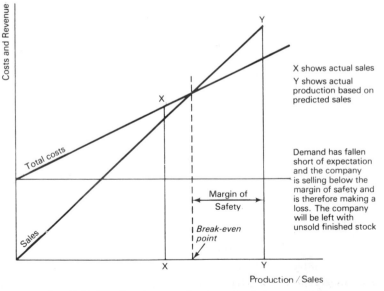

Fig. 13.7   The break-even chart – sales below production

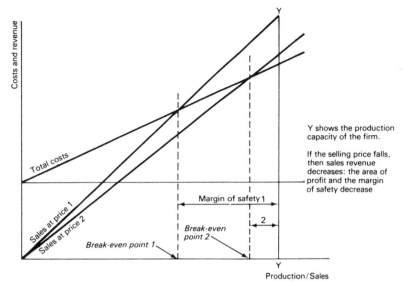

Fig. 13.8 The break-even chart – selling price falls

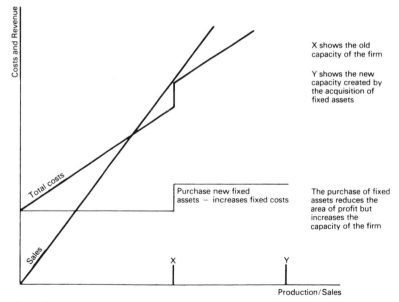

Fig. 13.9 The break-even chart – capacity increases by acquisition of extra fixed assets

(*d*)   predict the effect on profitability of changes in efficiency or changes in costs.

(*e*)   assess the effect of changes in the capacity of the plant brought about by investment in new fixed assets. (See Appendix 3.)

Financial control

Since money represents the allocation of resources in any organisation, the best method of controlling the efficiency of a business is by watching and directing expenditure. Financial control is exercised internally by accountants and managers, and externally by auditors.

Internal control-budgeting

A budget is a plan which is based on estimates of future revenue and spending. It establishes the allocation of costs and expenses in relation to a given objective over a defined period of time. A budget can include the employment of capital, as well as plans related to daily income and expenditure. The procedure for budgeting (Fig. 13.10) is to:

1   Define departmental goals and allocate expenditure to specific programmes.

2   Set, in consultation with the departments, standards of operation of programmes in relation to costs.

3   Obtain the information on actual spending in a systematic manner.

4   Compare the actual performance (spending) with the set standard. These comparisons will take place at different times according to the nature of an organisation's operations. A government department or a manufacturing organisation will probably set targets annually and analyse them every six, or even three, months. A retail outlet might set its standards every six months, to coincide with seasonal variations in demand, and analyse them every month.

5   Take action when marked variations occur between the actual and the planned spending, then either the plan is revised or the operation and the efficiency of the department are examined in detail. This is the stage in the budgeting process when organisations can attempt to become more efficient, by questioning the

validity of departmental objectives and by considering alternative methods of operation.

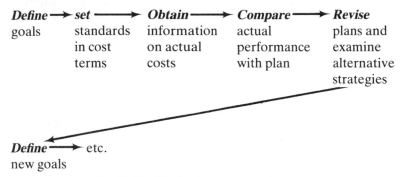

Define → **set** → **Obtain** → **Compare** → **Revise**
goals   standards   information   actual   plans and
             in cost   on actual   performance   examine
             terms   costs   with plan   alternative
                                                       strategies

Define ← → etc.
new goals

Fig. 13.10   The budgetary control process

The recording and analysis of the Profit and Loss Account and the Balance Sheet is an operation which is restricted to commercial organisations. Budgeting, however, is practised by all types of public bodies as well as by private organisations. For example, 'Output Budgeting' or 'PPBS' (planning–programming–budgeting–systems) is carried out by government departments in consultation with the Treasury. In PPBS, departmental objectives are defined and funds allocated to broad areas. Then on a regular, and on an *ad hoc* basis, systematic review of particular sectors of expenditure takes place.

The advantages of budgetary control are that it:

1 Clarifies the aims and policies of organisations in relation to specific departments, and helps the organisation to translate its policies into departmental programmes.
2 Clarifies departmental objectives and helps managers to define lines of authority and responsibility.
3 Helps the development of corporate strategies and stimulates departmental cooperation.
4 Improves central control. Actual performance can be compared with planned or budgeted performance.
5 Helps to improve efficiency. It shows which resources are used in relation to specific activities, and how well they are being used.

Auditing

External auditors provide a means of control which is required by law. The Companies Act, 1976, codified in some detail the appointment and resignation of the external auditor, and strengthened the auditor's position in relation to the disclosure of information by company officials and access to company records. The auditor performs these functions by systematically examining on a sample basis all relevant documents.

The functions of an external auditor are to:

1   Examine documents such as invoices, receipts and contracts in order to verify their accuracy.
2   Examine administrative procedures to prevent and discourage fraud and embezzlement.
3   Certify that proper records have been kept and that the recorded accounts agree with the details of transactions in the organisation's books.
4   Certify and report that the accounts give a 'true and fair view' of the company's affairs.

The external auditors who check the accounts of companies will report to the shareholders at the Annual General Meeting. A similar reporting function is carried out by District Auditors in local and Central government. District Auditors not only perform similar duties to private auditors: they check the accuracy of the financial records of government bodies and local authorities; but they also assess whether public expenditure has been within the law (*ultra vires*). Local authorities and government organisations cannot spend money outside their statutory authority. For example, at one stage councillors in Clay Cross refused to obey the law and increase council house rents; in effect they subsidised rent payers by £6 985. The District Auditor surcharged the members of the council for the £6 985.

Many organisations in the public and private sectors have their own system of internal auditing. Although by law the internal auditors cannot replace external auditors, they perform similar functions. Internal auditors also help to improve the efficiency of organisations by:

1 Helping to maintain the policies and procedures within an organisation.
2 Promoting accuracy in record keeping, and helping to reduce errors.
3 Guarding against misappropriations such as theft, fraud and embezzlement.

14

Communication

Communication between people is common to all jobs and is one of the most important activities in any organisation. Organisations are able to improve their efficiency by controlling operations, coordinating functions and motivating employees through communication.

All forms of communication have four basic elements:

1 The message. People communicate in order to pass on a message. The variety in the content of business messages is enormous: messages range from simple signs, such as 'Enquiries', through verbal requests or instructions, to complex financial or technical reports.

2 A source – the transmittor. All messages arise from a source. Communication can only take place when a message is transmitted. Communication is not taking place if facts, opinions and ideas are never expressed.

3 A medium – transmission. There are many formal methods which a person can choose to transmit information in business – letters, memos, reports, etc. Equally important are the informal methods, such as facial expression, posture and other forms of 'body language'.

4 A receiver. Communication only becomes complete when the message is received. People in business receive orders, instructions, reports, etc., which often require them to perform some action. However, it is not realistic to assume that a receiver will always respond to a message or, if a response does occur, that it will be performed in the way the transmittor intended. Messages can be misunderstood, and are frequently misinterpreted.

Communication within the organisation

The purpose of internal communication

It is important for business efficiency that internal messages are understood. The purpose of most formal internal communication is to initiate action, and the performance and efficiency of an employee will be influenced by the effectiveness of internal communication. Messages are transmitted for a variety of reasons, the following being some of the most important:

1 Informing – presenting facts. A lot of business communication occurs because people have to be kept informed. Managers have to be given information on all aspects of an organisation to enable them to control the organisation's activities. Employees have to be informed of changes which will directly affect their working environment, such as changes in safety procedures or the introduction of new technology. They will also have to be informed of changes in the conditions of employment, such as wage rates, fringe benefits and pension schemes.

2 Commanding – giving instructions. If an employer wants full cooperation from an employee it is unwise to issue direct commands. Cooperation has to be encouraged rather than commanded. Nevertheless, when tasks are delegated, orders and instructions have to be issued. If the transmittor – who is generally the supervisor – wants cooperation, then instructions have to be communicated in a considerate manner.

3 Negotiating – presenting a case. Differences in opinion are common in all human activity. A person's responsibilities, experience, knowledge, attitude and personality will colour his opinions and make conflict an inevitable part of an organisation's activities. Sectional interests, for example, create conflict and make negotiation a common form of business communication: departmental heads have to argue a case for more resources, trade union leaders have to negotiate for increased wages, government ministers have to persuade their cabinet colleagues to approve changes in policy.

4 Reporting – presenting findings.   Reports can be routine daily statements on such things as sales, absenteeism, costs and so on; or they can be used to present the findings of an investigation such as an auditing or market research exercise. In many instances a report will include recommendations or suggested solutions.

5 Coordinating – organising people.   In order to coordinate activity it is necessary to keep people and departments fully informed about plans and policies. For example, if an organisation is planning to hold an exhibition, then all the departments involved should be given details of what is expected from them in terms of time, personnel and equipment. Communication is used to clarify responsibilities and improve coordination.

6 Cooperating – improving teamwork.   Coordination between different sectors of an organisation will be effective only if the sectors cooperate. Cooperation is improved when participants in a joint exercise agree with the goals and objectives. To achieve agreement most organisations have developed systems of committees where different members of a team can learn about corporate goals and strategies, and at the same time contribute to the plans. Communication improves planning and teamwork.

7 Motivating and influencing attitudes.   Committees can help departmental managers to become more committed to an organisation's plans, but the success of any exercise is ultimately dependent on the participants. Communication can be used to increase the involvement of people in an organisation's activities. Managers, by talking to employees and by taking notice of their needs, can attempt to encourage and enthuse them and so improve their performance.

It is likely that communication will take place for more than one reason: a supervisor could be instructing a subordinate and at the same time motivating him. Whatever the reason for messages, organisations will be more efficient if communication is effective. The effectiveness of communication can be improved in the first instance by selecting the most appropriate route and the most appropriate method.

The routes of internal messages

1 Downwards. The formal information in an organisation generally flows from the higher to the lower levels. Commands, instructions, decisions, plans and delegated tasks are passed down the line management system through supervisors and managers to subordinates (Fig. 14.1).

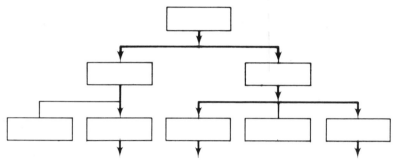

Fig. 14.1 Downward flow of communication

2 Upwards. Apart from reporting, it is rare for formal information to flow from a lower level to a higher level. Some organisations, however, have developed formal systems such as staff development interviews and joint consultative committees to encourage the upward flow of ideas and opinions.

3 Horizontal. The need for coordination between different departments means that communication between people at the same level in an organisation's hierarchy is common. This is particularly true of departmental heads who frequently meet in committees in all organisations.

4 Multi-directional. Informal communication such as gossip and rumour flow in all directions. A grapevine flourishes on misunderstanding, and concentrates on sensational and often distorted interpretations of a message. Where formal methods of communication are not effective, then generally informal methods are strong and often lead to misinterpretation and inefficiency.

The flow of information and the extent of rumour and gossip provides some guide to the effectiveness of an organisation's communication. Organisations can improve their efficiency by analysing the flow and attempting to make formal methods more effective. The formal organisational chart is important in this respect because it shows employees where formal messages *should* be sent. Financial reports go to the accounts manager and the chief executive. Production plans go from the production manager down the line to the factory operatives. Absenteeism is reported to the supervisor.

Communication is made more effective if it is transmitted to the appropriate person. In addition, it is important to select the most suitable method. The selection will depend on:

(*a*)   The content of the message. Is it confidential?

(*b*)   How quickly the message has to be sent. Can the telephone be used?

(*c*)   To whom the message is to be sent. Is there more than one appropriate receiver? If there is, then copies will be required.

(*d*)   Is a permanent record of the message required? If it is, then oral methods cannot be used.

The methods which can be selected are:

Oral

(*a*)   *Spoken instructions.*   Face-to-face contact between supervisor and subordinate is the most common method of communicating instructions. If the organisation is authoritarian, like the armed forces, then the communication is almost always downwards through the line of command.

(*b*)   *Interviews* are very common when employees are selected. They also take place when a person is considered for promotion or is being disciplined. Interviews give the interviewee the opportunity to ask questions and to state a point of view. They thus provide a means of upward communication.

(*c*)   *Committee meetings.*   Committees exist in all types of organisation. The range of committee work generally is very wide and includes library committees in colleges, finance committees in commercial organisations, and Select Committees in the House of Commons. Committee work in business can be a major part of a manager's and administrator's work and provides the best opportunity for inter-departmental (horizontal) communication.

(*d*)   *Telephones* have the advantage of speed and availability. The existence of the telephone encourages communication and facilitates coordination and cooperation.

(*e*)   *Casual conversation* is predominant in the informal structure of an organisation. It is important for the formal structure in that it gives managers the opportunity to try out ideas and plans in an informal environment.

Body language

Messages can be passed without the use of spoken language: a nod, wink, shrug, frown or glance can convey its own special meaning. The attitudes of people are frequently indicated by gestures, facial expressions and bearing rather than by the spoken word. The ability to observe these 'body signs' is an important part of communication: it is a social skill.

Written

(*a*)   *Letters* are not usually used as an internal method of communication. They are used to inform people about employment matters such as appointment or promotion, and they are therefore common in the personnel department. But other departments will tend to use memos and standard forms rather than personal letters.

(*b*)   *Memoranda.*   Internal memos provide a written record of communication between people in an organisation. It is common for several copies to be made so that those involved in a decision or activity can be kept informed. The content of a memo is varied: they are often used to initiate action or to summarise an agreed course of action.

(*c*)   *Manuals.*   The established practices of an organisation are sometimes written in manuals or similar instruction documents. Manuals provide a reference for employees, and the information in them can range from broad policy decisions to detailed instructions on routine tasks.

(*d*)   *Reports.*   Reporting is a common activity in organisations. There are technical reports, financial reports, research reports, personnel reports, marketing reports and so on. It is usual for most reports to present a collection of facts, to describe alternative solutions to a problem, to state conclusions and to submit recommendations.

(*e*)   *Minutes* are formal written records of meetings. They record what has been agreed and summarise the main points of any discussion.

(*f*)   *Notice boards/circulars.* Organisations sometimes use impersonal methods to communicate general information. Notices on safety and welfare are often transmitted by circulars or notice boards.

Feedback – response to a message

Messages which are received will normally create a response in the recipient. The response may not be what the transmittor intended, in that it could be a frown or a shrug, but any response to a message is called 'feedback'. Feedback indicates whether the message has been understood and accepted. A recipient can respond with informal gestures or he can choose some of the methods of communication which are listed above, such as conversation, letter, report, etc.

One-way communication: authoritarian-style leadership

One-way communication takes place when the transmittor does not expect, and does not get, a response from the receiver (Fig. 14.2). This type of communication is prevalent in organisations which are authoritarian in the way they deal with employees. In an authoritarian system managers issue commands, supervisors order subordinates to perform tasks, and foremen give direct instructions to operatives.

In one-way communication there is no guarantee that the message has been received, and consequently inefficient action through misunderstanding can occur.

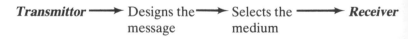

Transmittor ⟶ Designs the ⟶ Selects the ⟶ *Receiver*
message   medium

Fig. 14.2   One-way communication

Two-way communication: democratic-style leadership

Those organisations which want to avoid misunderstanding and to make communication more effective will encourage feedback. By examining the response to a message a manager can assess whether the message has been understood, and at the same time he can gauge the extent of an employee's motivation (Fig. 14.3). The desire for feedback – that is, consultation – will in itself help to encourage an employee. This type of participative or people-centred management is found when there is democratic-style leadership.

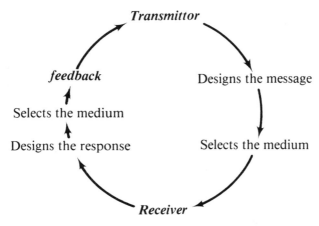

Fig. 14.3 Two-way communication

Organisations are traditionally authoritarian in the way they communicate with employees. However, people-centred management is growing slowly, and feedback and participation are being encouraged.

The problems of internal communication

Feedback helps the transmittor to learn whether the message has been understood. But the communication process is complicated: messages and responses are not always what they seem and feedback is no guarantee of effective communication. At each stage of transmission the message or response can be distorted (Fig. 14.4).

Some common causes of distortion or breakdown in communication are:

1 Perception.   Differences in perception are a major cause of distortion. People are different and it is common for messages to be

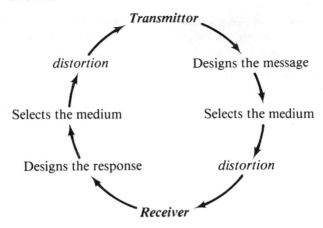

Fig. 14.4 Distortion in communication

perceived in different ways. We all interpret messages according to our experience, motives and state of mind. For example, suspicion, anger, frustration, shyness and confusion can distort our ability to communicate and to respond to messages.

2 Language problems. Careless use of language is a common cause of misunderstanding. Technical language, jargon and abbreviations, as well as ambiguity, can confuse the receiver. A common example is the use of legal jargon in government publications. Further problems can arise in communicating with those for whom English is not the first language.

3 Vague purpose. Communication can be ineffective when the transmittor has not clearly thought out why, or for whom, the message is being transmitted – for example, issuing a command when consultation is necessary, or sending a report on education standards to the housing department in a local authority.

4 Inappropriate medium. Messages can be delayed by selecting an inappropriate medium – written messages are obviously slower than oral messages. In addition, selection of the wrong medium can cause other problems, for example using casual conversation, which could be overheard, to pass on confidential information.

5 Failure to communicate. A breakdown in communication sometimes occurs because an employee informs some, but not all, appropriate recipients. This often happens when the chain of command is by-passed and a subordinate ignores his immediate superior and sends messages directly to a higher authority.

6 Status, social distance. There are occasions when communication becomes distorted because of the different status of the participants. For example, when a managing director is discussing a problem with a new recruit or an operative, there can be a degree of stiffness and formality which impairs the discussion.

7 Red tape, bureaucracy. Communication often breaks down in large organisations because of the number of employees involved. Messages in highly centralised organisations can be impersonal, inflexible and ineffective because bureaucracy creates 'red tape': many internal messages are not specifically designed for the individuals who will receive them.

8 Location. Geographical distance between participants can cause distortions in communication. It is more difficult to communicate with people overseas, for example, and with salesmen or with government inspectors who spend much of their time out of the office.

9 Distraction of the receiver. Communication can be made ineffective when the receiver does not give his full attention to the message. An employee might be distracted by family problems, ill health, or even noise, which affect his ability to interpret a message.

10 Hostility between the participants. A poor relationship between two people will tend to distort their communication. An employee who has not been promoted, or a supervisor who feels let down by a subordinate, will generally find it difficult to communicate effectively while the feeling of grievance persists.

11 Stress or frustration. The work in organisations can cause tension and stress in people. Repetitive and boring work, or the failure to have good work recognised, will tend to cause frustration and strain which will affect an employee's performance and distort his ability to communicate. Conflict in organisations is often a result of misunderstanding caused by stress.

12 The grapevine. The grapevine, or informal methods of communication, can establish opinions which formal communication is unable to change. Rumour thrives on distorted and sensational interpretations of information, and it can distort an employee's ability to perceive the true situation.

Improvements in communication

The efficiency of an organisation depends on the effectiveness of internal communication. Because people are different, communication between employees will always be a problem. The twelve sources of misunderstanding which are outlined above illustrate the extent of the difficulties in creating effective communication. Organisations can meet this problem in the following ways:

1 Improve communication skills

Courses have been designed which will help to improve an employee's understanding of communication. The two parts of such courses are:

(*a*) *Social skills.* Awareness of other people is an essential requirement for effective communication. If employees are more sensitive to the different attitudes and motivations of others, then relationships will improve and the distorting effect of different perceptions will be reduced.

(*b*) *Technical knowledge.* An employee can learn to improve his technical ability to communicate by understanding (*i*) the different roles in organisations and who should receive a particular message; (*ii*) the most appropriate medium for a particular message (letter, memo, telephone, etc.); (*iii*) when messages should be communicated; and (*iv*) the need for feedback, and the need to recognise signs in body language (nods, frowns, winks, etc.).

2 Decentralisation

Red tape and long lines of communications are common in highly centralised organisations. Government departments are notorious for their bureaucratic, formal methods of communication. However, it is unavoidable that the central government should have an elaborate system of rules and regulations: the government has to have a standard approach to the provision of services to ensure fairness and equity. It is a mistake to believe that bureaucracies are necessarily inefficient – all organisations exhibit some characteristics of bureaucracy. The problem is that centralisation can lead to ineffective communication and poor control.

Large organisations can attempt to overcome this by decentralisation – that is, by greater delegation. In decentralisation the organisation is divided into several autonomous units and each unit is responsible for its own performance. BL, for example, has several different divisions each producing a different type of car. The divisions are treated as though they are independent companies; and their performance is judged in relation to one another as well as to outside competitors. Communication between such divisions, however, is generally poor.

3 Motivation and participation

Organisations can use the grapevine as a source of feedback rather than as a source of rumour and misunderstanding. The formal organisation can also use informal relationships to induce greater commitment from employees. The theories of McGregor, Maslow and Herzberg (see Chapter 11) can help organisations to improve their internal communication. Communication can be made more effective by praising effort and encouraging employees to perform better, by recognising work which is well done, and by giving people more responsibility for their own tasks.

The problems of hostility, stress and frustration can be reduced by increased employee participation. For example:

(*a*) *Job enlargement* means that the employee carries out a series of different tasks where the level of difficulty and responsibility remains the same (horizontal move in the hierarchy). For example, a shop assistant could move from one department to another. The different working environments relieve monotony, boredom and frustration, and improve communication.

(*b*) *Job enrichment.* In job enrichment the employee is given a greater variety of tasks which differ in difficulty and the level of responsibility (vertical move in the hierarchy). For example, office workers could be given a range of jobs from dealing with the incoming post to helping the personnel department recruit a new colleague. The increased responsibility provided by job enrichment gives greater job satisfaction and reduces stress and hostility.

(c) *Job rotation.* There are several problems which are associated with job enlargement and job enrichment: the employees might not have the skill and knowledge to transfer from one job to another, the trade unions might object, the employee could demand more pay for increased responsibility, and so on. These problems can be avoided by job rotation where employees learn several minor skills which form a complete process. A team is formed and the team members can rotate the jobs democratically.

Job rotation occurs in all types of employment. For example, Volvo and Saab apply the technique to the production of cars; the Halifax Building Society rotate a team in their Head Office.

Job rotation increases individual responsibility, reduces boredom and improves understanding. It also increases employee cooperation and breaks down barriers to effective communication.

The external communications of companies

The image of an organisation is determined to a large extent by its external communication, whether with shareholders, suppliers, customers or the general public. Depending on the intended recipient, a business can use several different methods of communication.

1 Annual reports and accounts

Every company is required to send a directors' report to its shareholders each year, and the Companies Acts 1948–85 require the following information to be included:

(a) *The Profit and Loss Account.* Companies must disclose items of expenditure and income as well as any appropriations from profits. The intention is that the directors should provide a 'true and fair view' of the financial position of the company, and any material item which is unusual and significant, or arises from a change in the basis of accounting, should be disclosed.

(b) *The Balance Sheet.* The published Balance Sheet must show the share capital and the reserves, any liabilities and provisions such as loans and taxation, and the fixed and current assets. Since the valuation of assets and the quantification of liabilities relies on the judgement of the directors, then the Balance Sheet should be read in conjunction with additional notes made by the directors and the auditors.

(*c*) *Source and Application of Funds Statement.* All companies with a turnover in excess of £25,000 per annum are required to produce a funds flow statement which should show the sources from which money has come into the company and the way the money has been used in the operations of the business.

(*d*) *Report of the Auditors.* Since the directors use their judgement when calculating such items as the value of assets and liabilities, depreciation charges and the value of stock, then the auditors' report must contain explanation of the methods which have been used. Very often the auditors' report contains far more detail than the other financial statements.

In addition to financial matters, the directors' report is required to highlight details of other types of information such as political and charitable donations, the earnings of individual directors where they exceed £60,000 a year, and the value of exports.

2 Non-financial reports

The concern which is currently expressed about the social costs and social responsibilities of private organisations has led to an increased demand for information other than financial to be publicly disclosed. The following list illustrates some of the items of 'non-financial' information which companies could produce: (*a*) An outline of social objectives; (*b*) An environmental report; (*c*) A statement on the company's commitment to racial and sex equality; (*d*) A declaration on industrial relations policy; (*e*) An analysis of productivity per employee.

3 Advertising and other communication with customers and clients

The public image of a company is influenced by its advertising and its relationship with customers/clients. Companies have a wide choice of advertising media: television, posters, newspapers, direct mail, exhibitions and displays. Advertising agencies will advise companies on the best media to use.

Dealing with customer complaints and enquiries requires a degree of sensitivity and understanding which is characteristic of good internal communication. Prompt and sympathetic replies to complaints, as well as accurate invoices and statements, not only promote sales but also enhance a company's image.

4   Reports to journalists

The image of a company depends on its formal public reports and its communication with customers. In addition, communication with the press, radio and television has become an important aspect of public relations. The methods of communication include special reports, briefing groups and question and answer sessions, all of which are designed to improve public understanding of business as well as to increase a firm's prestige.

Government communication

Government ministers and local authority councillors communicate with the press, radio and television even more than private enterprise does: government policy requires public understanding if it is to succeed. The problem which faces the government is that there are many different messages required and many different recipients. The many different messages arise from changes in policies which can affect such diverse groups as pensioners, school leavers, tax payers, the disabled, the unemployed, other governments, and so on.

The main methods of communication which the government uses are:

1   Green and White Papers.   Changes in legislation must be approved by Parliament. The government sometimes publishes its ideas about proposed changes in policy in a *Green Paper*. This is a discussion document which provides feedback to ministers and civil servants; analysis of the reaction to its proposals helps the government to formulate policy in a more realistic light. A *White Paper* is a formal government report which will generally deal with one specific issue such as unemployment or education. Some are published on a routine basis, such as the White Paper on Public Expenditure which is published annually. Others are issued only when changes in policy are to be reported, for example the White Paper on the Nationalised Industries, 1967.

2 Popular media. As with commercial organisations, the government uses television, posters and newspapers to inform – either the total electorate or special groups such as tax payers. Apart from election material, the content of government communication is mainly either social (for example, health warnings) or it seeks to explain and give details of changes in policies.

3 Official publications. Government policy is so extensive and complicated, and affects so many different groups, that the government issues many hundreds of different explanatory leaflets on changes in policy. In addition, the Central Statistical Office and the government departments provide a statistical information service. The information which they publish covers all aspects of business activity: population, labour, production, prices, finance, exports and so on.

Questions on Part Four
1 Do you think that it is realistic and useful to distinguish between fixed costs and variable costs? Explain your answer.
2 'It no longer matters where an organisation is situated, since improvements in transport and communications mean that an organisation can be located anywhere at no extra cost.' Discuss.
3 Distinguish between the functions and purposes of different types of organisation.
4 Define 'productivity', and explain how a small manufacturing organisation might attempt to increase its productivity.
5 Assess the limitations of the accounting concepts and conventions which are used to measure profit and value assets.
6 Define 'Working Capital', and assess the importance of cash flow in private organisations.
7 Explain, using examples, the significance and limitations of basic financial ratios.
8 A firm which produces bicycles sells all the units it produces at £45.00 each. The firm's fixed costs are £135 000, and the variable cost for each bicycle is £15.00. The production capacity of the plant is 60 000 units. Using this information:
   (*a*) Draw a chart to show the break-even point.
   (*b*) Express the break-even point as a percentage of the firm's capacity, and outline the actions which the firm could take to change this percentage.
9 'It is unrealistic to develop training programmes to improve an em-

ployee's social skills because such skills are part of a person's basic personality and cannot be changed.' Discuss.

10   Do you think that private organisations should devise and publish social objectives? Explain your answer.

PART FIVE
Organisations and the State

Introduction

During the twentieth century the spread of economic power has led to increased interdependence in society. This in turn has led to increased conflict between different interest groups. As a result the government has played an ever-increasing role in the affairs of business, through the public institutions which are described in Chapter 15. The two spheres where governmental power has the most effect on business is in economic policy and in the enforcement of legal rules, and these are examined in Chapters 16 and 17 respectively.

15

Public Institutions

Central government departments

The implementation and administration of the government's policies is carried out by a wide variety of institutions which, as we have seen, are similar in many respects to private organisations, and which are themselves affected by the policies they implement. For example, the central government departments have to comply with employment legislation and the requirements of the Health and Safety at Work Act. In addition, they are far more likely to be directly affected by changing levels of public expenditure than organisations in private enterprise.

Separation of power
The framework in which government departments operate provides some clue to their nature. The power of the State is in three separate divisions:

1 The Legislature. Legislation is the primary element in state activity. The policies of elected governments are translated into laws which prescribe the activities of organisations and citizens, and help to resolve disputes between parties. The function of Parliament (the Legislature) is to approve or reject the proposals which will make policy legal. Members of the House of Commons and the House of Lords may debate and amend, reject or enact the legislative proposals of the government; but the two Houses do not formulate policy.

2　The Executive.　Policy is formulated by the government (the Executive), assisted by civil servants in the central government departments. The Cabinet, which is the focal point of the Executive, does not make laws but puts Bills before Parliament for approval. Once the policies of a government become law, they are implemented by the central government departments.

3　The Judiciary.　The administration of justice is separate from the administration of public policy. Judges (the Judiciary) interpret the laws passed by Parliament, and the courts provide the framework for the enforcement of legal rules.

The three 'powers' in the State are not entirely separate. The government is very active in the legislative process, and the development of quasi-judicial bodies such as Administrative Tribunals is an example of the Executive's infringement of the autonomy of the Judiciary. The central government departments are not part of the Legislature or the Judiciary; they play a vital role in the Executive's administration of policy.

Characteristics of central government departments

1　Impartiality.　Although civil servants are the secretariat of the government and work very closely with politicians, it is a tradition that the advice which they give to ministers is as objective and impartial as possible. Civil servants should not allow their own judgment to be affected by political considerations: it is the elected politician's role to inject political philosophy into policy formulation. The characteristic of impartiality means that civil servants can assist and advise any type of government, regardless of its politics.

2　Anonymity.　The Cabinet has ultimate responsibility for government policy. Civil servants give advice, but policy decisions are collectively made by ministers. It is a custom that civil servants will not be individually identified with particular proposals: they remain anonymous.

3　Continuity.　An important feature of government departments is that they provide continuity in the system of government, and in the administration of policies. It would be wrong to assume that the impartial and anonymous nature of civil service advice reduces its value. Government departments bring knowledge, experience and continuity to the policy-making process.

4 Methodology. The factors which determine the government's policies are varied: the political philosophy of ministers, and the knowledge and experience of administrators, are extremely important. Equally important is the reaction of interested groups. The civil service has evolved a system of consultation with advisory bodies and pressure groups which is an indispensable part of public policy formulation.

Functions of central government departments

The characteristics of the civil service provide an indication of the functions of government departments. The following brief summary of the functions of central government departments illustrates this relationship.

1 Policy formulation

The translation of political ideas into practical proposals is a process which requires considerable skill. An important function of government departments is to assist ministers in this process. Civil servants provide facts and ideas, they help ministers to assess alternative strategies; they provide a system of consultation with advisory bodies; they evaluate previous strategies; and they help to translate policy into legislation by drafting government Bills. Civil servants bring impartiality, knowledge and experience into the process of policy formulation. Only those employed in the top echelons of the civil service (the Administrative Class) directly advise ministers on policy, and competition to become a member of the Administrative Class is very high. In spite of the technical nature of government policy, civil servants at this level tend to be generalists rather than specialists: they are expected to be able to contribute to the work of any government department, and to give impartial advice which is based on a wide knowledge and understanding of the system.

2 Policy implementation

The implementation of policy requires that the *internal* management of central government resources must be efficient. There are approximately ¾ million civil servants in government departments, and the management of such a large number of employees, as well as the management of resources of government departments, requires skills which are similar to those required of the management of any large organisation. Civil service administrators have to possess organisational skills and knowledge in planning, budgeting, recruiting, purchasing, accounting, and so on. In order to improve the efficiency of departments the civil service runs its own staff college which aims to improve management skills and technical knowledge.

The task of most civil servants, however, is to implement and control public policy. This is achieved in two main ways:

(*a*)   *Provision of services.*   Some government services, such as those relating to employment and social security, are provided *directly* to the public. For example, local offices such as 'Job Centres' are found in every major town. Specialist services, such as the Information and Advisory Service of the Ministry of Agriculture, are provided on a regional or even a national rather than a local basis.

Much of the machinery of government is highly centralised, but it would be impossible to administer all government services directly from central government. Consequently many government services are *decentralised*, or delegated to outside bodies. The government still retains some control over standards of provision, and the amount of resources to be employed. Local authorities, for example, provide commercial services, and semi-autonomous bodies such as area water boards and the BBC provide a diverse range of commercial and non-commercial services.

(*b*)   *Regulation.*   A major function of government departments is to ensure that public policy is operated correctly, and they use the following techniques of regulation to control the activities of individuals and organisations:

(*i*)   *Inspection.*   For example, the provision of education and the health and safety of employees is examined by inspectors.

(*ii*)   *Rules and regulations.*   Government departments provide rules and regulations on how certain functions should be performed (for example, Building Regulations).

(*iii*)   *Registration and licensing.*   Certain acts, ranging from birth to the purchase of a car, have to be registered, and some activities cannot be carried out until the operator has a licence – for example, if a person wants to drive a car on the public highway, or if an organisation wants to offer credit facilities.

(*iv*) *Public inquiries.* Central government departments carry out public Inquiries into a wide range of matters which affect the public interest, such as accidents, disasters and planning decisions.

(*v*) *Financial controls.* The operations of many delegated services are regulated by the imposition of strict cash controls, and by district audit investigations.

Delegated legislation

The functions outlined above are supported by subordinate or delegated legislation, which is the power to make subordinate laws. The formulation of policy and its approval by the Legislature forms a major part of the work of the Government and Parliament. However, it is impossible in modern times for Parliament to make laws which cover every detail of complex technical operations such as aviation or architectural design. The problem has been solved by delegating the power to government departments and to local authorities to make their own subordinate laws. These laws have to be made within the constraints of statutes passed by Parliament; and they take the form either of a regulation or statutory instrument published by a government department, or a by-law passed by a local authority.

Government departments and business

The number of government departments which exists at any one time varies according to the nature of the Cabinet, which is formed by the Prime Minister. Since the Second World War there have been many amalgamations and creations of government departments to ensure that the State is able to meet the ever-changing economic and social needs of society.

The names of the departments provide a guide to the nature of the work in which they are involved. The departments which have a direct influence on business are the Department of Trade and Industry, the Department of Energy, the Department of Employment and the Deparment of the Environment. All of these departments have either been created or reorganised since 1960.

The Treasury

A very important department which is not listed above is the Treasury. It is a department which has existed since the seventeenth century, and, because its origins are so distant, there are no statutes governing its structure and powers. The powers of most other departments have been created by statute rather than custom. Through custom the Treasury has become the 'Ministry of Finance': it controls national finances as well as the internal machinery of government.

The main functions of the Treasury are to:

1   forecast movements in the economy, and to assist the government in planning its economic strategy.
2   administer fiscal policy by implementing the government's policies on taxation and public expenditure.
3   help other departments in the administration of economic policies with particular reference to prices and incomes, monopolies and mergers, capital investment, and employer/employee relationships.
4   control the expenditure of government departments by such techniques as planning-programming-budgeting-systems (PPBS), and Programme Analysis and Review (PAR). The Treasury coordinates the control of public expenditure through the Public Expenditure Survey Committee (PESC), a top-level finance committee which has representatives from each department and is chaired by an official from the Treasury.

Quasi-governmental bodies (QUA(N)GOs)

Government departments exist primarily to implement and influence the policies of the Executive. But there are governmental functions which are so specialised or so technical that central government departments have neither the resources nor the expertise to administer them. As a result quasi-autonomous bodies have been established to provide specialised services. There is no coherent principle which accounts for the establishment of these bodies, and the following list of functions illustrates the diversity of services which they provide.

1 Basic services. Public boards and public corporations have been established to provide essential services such as energy, transport, and broadcasting. This category includes Water Boards, Gas Boards, Electricity Boards, the National Coal Board and the BBC.

2 Marketing services. Marketing Boards were established between the two World Wars. They are producers' organisations which include a minority of independent members appointed by the agriculture minister. The Boards have statutory powers to regulate the marketing of milk, hops, wool and potatoes.

3 Employment and training services. The Industrial Training Act, 1964, established Industrial Training Boards such as the Engineering Industry Training Board (EITB) and the Local Government Training Board (LGTB). The number of ITBs was reduced in 1982, and the remaining Boards are directly responsible for training within their respective industries. However, the Manpower Services Commission (MSC), which was established by the Employment and Training Act, 1973, has overall control of industrial training.

4 Regulation. The growth of delegated legislation has meant that the activities of some individuals and organisations are regulated by quasi-autonomous bodies. For example, the licences for those who want to practise chiropody are issued by the Board for the Professions supplementary to Medicine; the licences of those who wish to operate airline routes, both public and private, are issued by the Air Transport Licensing Board.

5 Research. The government sponsors research into the environment, technology, science and the social sciences through research councils. The purpose of the councils is to vet applications for research funds, and to promote research into fields of public interest.

The power of a minister in relation to semi-autonomous governmental bodies is exercised in two areas: the appointment of board members, and the control of their income. However, the degree of ministerial control varies according to the nature of the organisation's operation. For example, the nationalised industries complain of too much control, whereas the BBC, on the other hand, suffers from very little political interference in its operations.

The Bank of England

The Bank of England is one of the most important semi-autonomous governmental organisations. The Bank, which has had a long relationship with the government, was nationalised in 1946. It performs a two-way role: it acts like a government department, and in co-operation with the Treasury helps to control the government's economic policy; and it is the City's representative in government. The Bank of England has close links with commercial banks, the Stock Exchange, and other commercial organisations; and it is able to represent their views when policy is formulated.

The Bank of England has two main functions:

1   Monetary Policy
(a)   The Bank liaises with the Treasury on economic forecasts, and advises the government on the supply of money.
(b)   It controls short-term and long-term government loans.
(c)   It controls the level of interest rates through the Minimum Lending Rate (MLR) and advises the government on the need for adjustment.
(d)   The Bank manages the gold and foreign currency reserves, and helps to regulate the price of sterling.

2   Banker
(a)   The Bank of England is the banker to the government, to the commercial banks and to other central banks.
(b)   It manages and controls the issue of bank notes in the UK.
(c)   The Bank issues loan stock, and manages the National Debt.

Local Government

Local authorities provide specific public services within a statutory framework: they are obliged by law to provide certain services, and can spend money only on those activities which have been authorised by Acts of Parliament. Any expenditure outside this statutory authority is *ultra vires*, and those who sanction such spending are likely to be surcharged by the District Auditor.

The reasons for local rather than central provision are:

1 Those who have local knowledge and experience are more able to organise services which suit local variations.
2 Central government is a series of large organisations, and, because of its size, it has problems in internal and external communication. The decentralisation of many public services helps to improve the administration of the services; and gives the clients the opportunity to communicate directly with the providers.
3 Local government councillors have powers of discretion on expenditure within the cash limits set by central government, and this devolved local power can be scrutinised more directly by the electorate. Such direct inspection increases democratic participation in the provision of public services.

The Local Government Act, 1972

The nature and functions of local government was redefined by the Local Government Act, 1972. The country is divided into 'areas', each with elected part-time councillors and full-time officials. These 'areas' of local government vary. There are fifty-three *counties* in England and Wales. Scotland has twelve *regions* which were established in May 1975 by the Local Government (Scotland) Act, 1973. Each county and region is subdivided into *districts*, which have their own separate councils.

There are six *Metropolitan counties* which were created by the 1972 Act to manage the local services for the dense concentration of people in Greater Manchester, Merseyside, Tyne and Wear, West Yorkshire, South Yorkshire, and the West Midlands. These Metropolitan counties are divided into thirty-four *Metropolitan boroughs* which provide similar services to County Councils. Greater London is separated into thirty-two *London boroughs*.

The services which are provided by local authorities differ according to the type of local government area (see Table 15.1).

The services listed in the table can be summarised under four headings:

Table 15.1   Types of local authorities and the main services they provide

Type of local authority	Examples of services provided
Metropolitan county	Police and fire services Food and drugs control Public transport Roads and building maintenance
Non-metropolitan county	Social services Education Libraries Police and fire services Roads and building maintenance Food and drugs control
Metropolitan borough	Local planning, building regulations Housing Social services Education Rates collection Environmental health Libraries Licensing
Non-metropolitan district	Local planning, building regulations Housing Rates collection Environmental health

1   Education and recreation.   Local authorities administer almost all the public money which is spent on education, which forms the largest single item of local government's *revenue expenditure* budget (46%). In addition, local authorities provide finance for museums, art galleries and libraries, as well as recreational facilities such as parks, gardens and leisure centres.

2   Environment and conservation.   The nature of the environment is influenced by the decisions of local councillors. Local councils control most private building, and design their own schemes for housing and urban development. Municipal housing accounts for almost sixty per cent of *capital expenditure* by local government. In addition, local authorities are responsible for such environmental services as slum clearance, drainage and refuse collection.

3 Communications. Where it is necessary, local authorities subsidise public bus services; they are responsible for the maintenance of roads (except motorways), and administer traffic control systems.

4 Guardianship. Protection of the public is an important duty of local government. Almost ten per cent of revenue expenditure is spent on the Police, the Fire Service and the administration of justice. Local authorities are directly involved in consumer protection: they employ Trading Standards Officers and Environmental Health Officers. 'Protection' in a wider sense is also part of local government services: they provide the Social Services, and take care of the homeless and orphans.

Institutions in international trade

The International Monetary Fund (IMF)
The United Kingdom is a founder member of the IMF, which was established in 1944. The IMF's functions are to:

1 Ensure that world trade expands in a balanced way. The surpluses of foreign earnings by one country will create deficits in other countries. The IMF helps to bring about equilibrium in trading nations' Balance of Payments in the long term.
2 Promote harmony in international monetary relations, by discouraging erratic movements in exchange rates, and by promoting communication between member states.
3 Stabilise exchange rates by providing short-term credit for those trading countries which run into Balance of Payments difficulties.

There are over 100 member countries, and each pays a contribution (25% in gold, and 75% in its own currency), to the Fund, the amount depending on the country's GNP. Members can use the Fund to exchange their own currency for other currencies, so that a trading state can draw foreign currency to solve short-term Balance of Payments problems.

The General Agreement on Tariffs and Trade (GATT)

The United Kingdom subscribes, along with 82 other contracting members, to the General Agreement on Tariffs and Trade which came into existence in 1948. The aims of the Agreement are to:

1 Eliminate quotas (limits on imports).
2 Regulate trading disputes between member states.
3 Reduce tariffs (taxes) on imported goods.

The attainment of these three aims rests on four basic principles: (*a*) signatories should treat each other on an equal basis, and should not restrict trade concessions to favoured countries; (*b*) all existing trade agreements should be observed; (*c*) all limits (quotas) on trade should be prohibited; and (*d*) special trade concessions should be made for developing countries.

The European Economic Community (EEC)

The European Economic Community was established in 1957 by France, Germany, Italy, Belgium, Netherlands and Luxembourg. The United Kingdom became a member in 1973, at the same time as Denmark and Eire. The objectives of the EEC are:

1 The development of a full customs union, with free trade between member states in agricultural and industrial products, and common tariffs on goods imported into the Community. The variable nature of agricultural production has led to the development of a common agricultural policy (CAP) to control the price and distribution of produce within the Community.
2 To develop a common market for labour and capital, so that resources can move, without restriction, throughout the Community.
3 The long-term integration of social and economic policies. The aim is to eliminate differences in approach to monopolies and mergers, to prices and incomes policy, and to fiscal and monetary policy.
4 To unite member states in a common political union. The establishment of the European Parliament is the first step in this long-term aim.

The executive body of the Community is the *European Commission*. The Commission administers the policies of the *Council of*

Ministers, which is made up of representatives from member states. The decisions of the Council and the Commission are enforced by the *European Court of Justice*.

16

Effects of Government Economic Policy

Investment and wealth

The wealth of a country is determined by the nature of its resources, and by how efficiently resources are allocated. Investment is the key to the growth of wealth in a country, as in individual organisations. Capital expenditure enables organisations to expand and so increase production, but more important, it helps them to improve productivity by acquiring modern and more efficient plant and equipment. If organisations are not willing to invest in improved methods of allocating resources, then the amount of wealth which is created will decrease.

As we have seen, however, the investment decisions of organisations are influenced by many external factors. The interdependent nature of business means that organisations can never act in isolation: the investment decisions of one organisation will affect the level of activity in other organisations. For example, a decision by a steel company to invest in a large new plant which will employ over 1000 new employees will affect firms in the construction industry, the commercial service industries such as telecommunications and electricity, the social service sector such as housing and education, the local employment service, and local authority planning officers. Once the plant has been constructed, then the income which the extra workforce will receive will be spent in the locality, bringing increased revenue to organisations in the region, and eventually to organisations in the whole country. Investment by one firm thus creates extra wealth throughout the economy.

The circular flow of income

All spending, either by organisations or by people, is someone's income. There is a balance between the level of expenditure in the economy and the level of income.

The amount of money which is available for investment is determined by the level of spending on finished goods and services. If organisations and people spend *all* of their income on the immediate 'consumption' of wealth, then there will be no finance or 'ploughback' available for capital expenditure. Investment can take place only when people and organisations save some of their income.

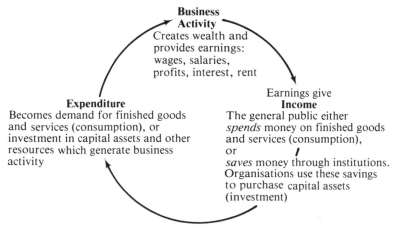

Fig. 16.1 The circular flow of income

National Income

The circular flow of a nation's income and expenditure can be counted during a period (usually one year) to give a measurement of a country's wealth. The measurement of the National Income is important for three reasons:

1 It provides information on how income and spending are distributed; and highlights the relationship between variables such as savings and investment.
2 It provides a means of comparing the growth or decrease in the standard of living in a country over a number of years.
3 It enables the wealth of different countries to be compared.

The wealth of a country provides housing, food and material goods; in addition, it gives the government the resources to improve the welfare of the people by providing services such as education and health. Consequently governments take a keen interest in the National Income and its component variables; and they try to ensure that wealth is created by business.

Increases in wealth occur only when investment and increases in productivity take place. Although the government can attempt to stimulate the level of investment, an important factor which influences investment decisions is the level of confidence of businessmen: if organisations are confident that they will obtain a 'reasonable' return on their capital expenditure then they will invest. The confidence of businessmen is greatly influenced by the activities of other organisations, and by the government's economic policy. But no government in a free country can control the overall level of business activity, although it can influence it.

The aims of government economic policy

In an attempt to improve the material well-being of the people, successive British governments have had the following aims in economic policy:

1   To promote economic growth.   A major aim of British governments has been to make the economy grow, and since the Second World War the standard of living of people in Britain has doubled. Increases in living standards provide material benefits such as houses, roads and durable goods; and bring about improvements in health, education and other welfare benefits. Therefore it is not surprising that all governments would like to see real increases in the National Income. However, increases in wealth occur only when there is an increase in the production of goods and commercial services. Hospitals, schools, museums and libraries improve the well-being of people, and they are signs of economic growth; but most public expenditure does not directly create wealth. Economic growth requires private capital investment, which is influenced by many factors, including the government's economic strategies.

2   To improve people's welfare.   An aim of economic policy is to reduce or even eliminate deprivation, and to improve the welfare of

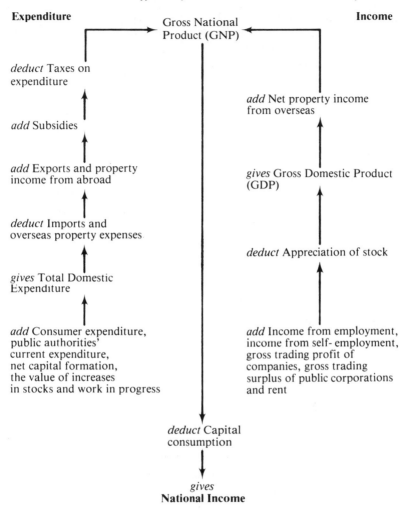

Fig. 16.2 The calculation of National Income

all citizens. This aim requires both an increase in prosperity, and a redistribution of wealth from the rich to the more needy such as the homeless, pensioners, the disabled and the sick. The system of income tax, which is used by all British governments, is progressive: it falls more heavily on the higher income earners. The intention in using progressive taxation is to redistribute wealth.

3   To curb inflation.   The stability of business activity depends on money retaining its value. Changing money values create distortions in the distribution of wealth, and seriously suppress business confidence. All governments want to reduce inflation, but although many strategies in prices and incomes policies have been tried, no successful formula for permanently reducing inflation has yet been devised.

4   To reduce unemployment.   Unemployment is measured by dividing the number who are registered as unemployed by the total working population, and multiplying by 100. This gives the percentage who are unemployed. A certain proportion of the working population will always be unemployed at any one time; the government's concern increases once this proportion exceeds 1.5%.

5   To stimulate exports.   The UK is a trading nation and requires gold and foreign currency in order to purchase food and raw materials from overseas. Gold and foreign currency has to be earned by selling British Goods and services overseas; and the government's aim is to ensure that overseas earnings are sufficient to pay for imports.

These five aims of economic policy have been pursued by all British governments regardless of their political philosophy: the difference between governments has been on *how* to achieve the five aims. A major problem is that the strategies which are used can be contradictory. For example, the encouragement of investment to relieve unemployment might increase the rate of inflation. The management of the economy is a complex technical process, and there are no obvious solutions. Economic policies affect all types of organisation, and require the cooperation of the many sectors of business if they are to succeed.

Monetary policy

The government can control the supply of money which is circulating in the economy. Many economists and politicians argue that close control of the supply of money is the key to controlling the rate of inflation: if people have more money (either wages or credit) to spend, then unless productivity improves, prices will rise. Some economists, such as Professor Friedmann, go even further and argue that there is a consistent relationship between the quantity of money in the economy and the monetary value of the National Income.

Whatever the merits of the monetarists' views, it is important to understand that there is a relationship between the level of business activity and the supply of money, and that the government can control the quantity of money in the economy. This control has a direct effect on business: the supply of money affects a firm's working capital and long-term capital, and generally influences industry's attitude to investment.

The supply of money

The supply of money is the total stock of money in the UK, and it can be measured in two ways:

1 The amount of money people and organisations have for immediate expenditure: notes, coins and cash in current accounts. This amount is known as 'M1'.
2 The amount of M1 money available plus other assets which are highly liquid. These other assets include money in private deposit accounts, money in bank accounts held by government, local authorities and the nationalised industries, and foreign currency deposits in the UK which are held by British residents. This amount is known as 'Sterling M3'.

Changes in the supply of money

Over 90% of all financial transactions, according to value, are made by cheque; and the money in the banking system is the most important part of the money supply. A remarkable feature of the banking system is that it creates money by what is known as *credit creation*. Any deposit in a bank will generate credit, and the following example illustrates the process.

Since 1971 commercial banks have been obliged to keep a *minimum reserve ratio* of 12½% of all eligible liabilities. Bankers know from experience that it is rare for depositors to demand more than 8% of total deposits at any one time. Let us assume that bank ABC plays very safe and maintains a reserve ratio of 20%, and on receipt of a deposit from Mr Y of £100, lends £80 to other people and to businesses.

The £80 will be spent on goods and services, and will thus become someone's income. The recipients will deposit this income in a bank which, like bank ABC, retains 20% for withdrawals and lends 80%, i.e. £64. This process repeats itself so that from the initial deposit of £100 by Mr Y the banking system can generate £500, while maintaining a 20% reserve ratio. The lower the reserve ratio, the more credit is generated, because more money is allowed into the system.

In reality the *minimum reserve ratio* of 12½% which all commercial banks must retain means that the British Banking system creates £800 for every £100 which is deposited! Having fixed the minimum reserve ratio, the government can control the creation of credit by controlling or regulating the *actual minimum reserves* of the commercial banks. If the minimum reserves are reduced, then there is less credit created; conversely, any increase in commercial bank reserves increases the supply of money.

Fig. 16.3 shows the structure of the commercial banks' assets; and highlights those assets which the government can regulate.

The government can control the supply of money by:

1   Open market operations.   The government, through the Bank of England, can issue gilt-edged stock which will be purchased by institutions and by the general public in the open market. The purchase of stock will cause a fall in the level of bank deposits, and so reduce the amount of credit which the banks can create. Conversely, the government can buy back loan stock, and this will release money which will be deposited in the banking system, and will generate more money. The Bank of England may also issue Treasury Bills on the open market to alter the position of the reserve assets of commercial banks.

2   Special deposits.   The government can control the amount of money created by having the Bank of England call in special deposits from the commercial banks. By calling in these cash deposits, which are part of the banks' cash reserves, the Bank of England can effectively reduce the amount of money which the banks can lend.

3   Changing the Minimum Lending Rate.   MLR is the rate of interest to which the rates of interest of bank deposits, and other

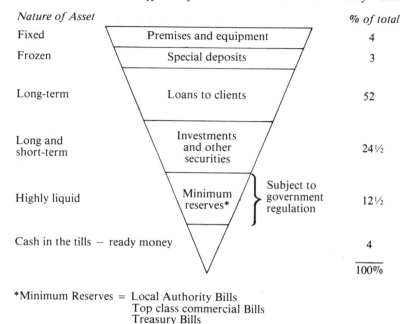

Nature of Asset | | % of total
Fixed — Premises and equipment — 4
Frozen — Special deposits — 3
Long-term — Loans to clients — 52
Long and short-term — Investments and other securities — 24½
Highly liquid — Minimum reserves* — Subject to government regulation — 12½
Cash in the tills — ready money — 4
100%

*Minimum Reserves = Local Authority Bills
Top class commercial Bills
Treasury Bills
Money at call with the London Money Market
Balances with the Bank of England

Contraction or expansion of the actual amount of assets in this 12½% leads to contraction or expansion of the remainder, since the minimum reserves must always form 12½% of the total assets

Fig. 16.3   The structure of banks' assets

lending rates, are directly linked: the commercial banks pay 2% less than MLR to most of their depositors, and charge more than the MLR to their borrowers. MLR is in fact the minimum rate of interest at which the Bank of England will provide money to the commercial banks. By changing the MLR the Bank of England, in effect, changes interest rates throughout the economy, and directly influences the cost of all borrowing.

Although the government can control the supply of money, the monetarists do not maintain that there is a precise relationship between the money supply and the creation of real wealth, or that the control of money will enable the government to control all the variables in the economy. The reason why monetary policy is advocated is that it is felt that when governments produce money without considering the state of the market, they are causing distortions in the allocation of resources, and that these distortions lead to inflation, unemployment and low investment.

Fiscal policy

Unemployment was the most crucial economic problem in the 1920s and 1930s. During that period J. M. Keynes devised a theory which helped governments, after the Second World War, to resolve some of the problems of mass unemployment. A simple explanation of Keynsian theory is that there is a relationship between the level of demand for goods and services, and the level of resource utilisation (employment of factors). Keynes said that governments are in a position to influence the level of demand in the economy because public expenditure is a large part of total (aggregate) demand. If total demand is falling, causing unemployment to increase, then the government can spend more than it receives in revenue and stimulate business activity. Equally the level of demand can be influenced by taxation policies. For example, increases or decreases in income tax will reduce or increase personal expenditure (and personal savings), and influence total demand in the economy.

The Budget

As a result of Keynsian theory the Budget has become a major form of strategy in economic policy. The Budget has two functions:

1 It is a statement of how the Chancellor intends to raise revenue to meet planned public expenditure.
2 It is an instrument which will enable the government to try to achieve a balance between demand in the economy and resource utilisation.

If economic forecasts show that demand will exceed the capacity of resource allocation, then high rates of inflation become more likely; the government can curb excess demand by increasing taxation and/or reducing public expenditure to give a *Budget surplus*. Conversely, if forecasts show that total demand will be lower than productive capacity, then unemployment is almost certain to increase; and in this instance the government can reduce taxation and/or increase public expenditure to give a *Budget deficit.*

There are many factors which the government will consider when deciding on budget strategy. Unfortunately, as we have seen, some of the aims of government economic policy require conflicting strategies. Thus, when inflation is increasing and high unemployment occurs at the same time, a budget surplus will aggravate the problem of unemployment. Conversely, a budget deficit will make the problem of inflation worse.

Revenue policies and their effect on business

1 Changes in personal taxation. There are two main ways in which the government can alter the level of personal taxation: it can change the rates, or it can alter the allowances. Changes in personal income will have a direct effect on business: if taxation is increased people will buy fewer goods and save less, firms will require fewer productive resources, and the level of business activity will decline. On the other hand, if direct taxation is reduced not only does this stimulate demand, but it could also stimulate productivity by encouraging people to work harder.

2 Corporation tax. For purposes of taxation the government distinguishes between a company and its shareholders: companies pay corporation tax on profits, while shareholders pay income tax on dividends received. This distinction can cause distortions in the distribution of dividends, since it might encourage companies to retain profits rather than distribute them. In addition, a high level of corporation tax could affect growth in the economy because companies would have less finance for private capital investment.

3 Value-added tax (VAT). Increases in indirect taxation generally reduce the turnover of businesses. The most common indirect tax – VAT – is levied on all goods and services, apart from those which are either zero-rated or exempt. Examples of goods which are zero-rated are food, coal, gas and electricity; those services which are exempt are postal services, small traders, education and health. The effect of VAT is to increase the price of all other goods and services; and increases in price generally lead to reductions in demand.

Expenditure policies and their effect on business

Fig. 16.4 shows how general government expenditure, as a percentage of GDP, increased from 36 to 47% between 1961 and 1981; so that now public expenditure accounts for almost half of the economic activity in the UK. Naturally this level of expenditure has repercussions throughout the whole economy.

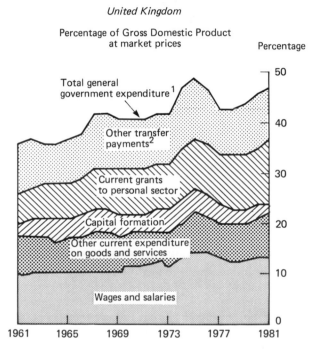

United Kingdom

Percentage of Gross Domestic Product at market prices

Percentage

Total general government expenditure [1]

Other transfer payments [2]

Current grants to personal sector

Capital formation

Other current expenditure on goods and services

Wages and salaries

[1]Combined central government and local authority sector
[2]Consists mainly of current grants to the personal sector (social security payments, educational grants etc). Also includes subsidies, debt interest and other central government and local authority grants and loans

Fig. 16.4   Total general government expenditure: by economic category
Source: *Social Trends*, 1983

1   Transfer payments.   A major element in the growth of government expenditure has been the growth in transfer payments. A transfer payment occurs when money which is contributed by taxpayers is transferred to other sections of the community. For example, subsidies on council rents, unemployment benefit, sickness benefit, child benefit and retirement pensions are all transfer payments. Although most transfer payments are made for social reasons, there are certain firms which receive direct assistance from the government in the form of subsidies – for example, some of those engaged in housebuilding and agriculture, and those firms in the regions which are eligible for employment premiums and other incentive payments. These industrial subsidies in effect re-allocate the costs of production from the firms to the taxpayer, and in doing so interfere with market forces.

2 Wages and salaries. Public organisations are labour intensive and, as we can see from Fig. 16.4, wages and salaries form a large part of total government expenditure. Wage inflation in the 1970s led to large increases in public expenditure so that it reached a level which many thought was extravagant. Consequently when the Conservatives gained power in 1979 they took action to reduce the number of civil servants and curtail local authority spending. The resultant savings in public expenditure were passed on to taxpayers in an attempt to encourage them to work harder (but see Chapter 11). In addition to controlling expenditure levels, the government, as an extremely important employer, can influence the pattern of income distribution; and interpose in labour markets.

3 Current expenditure. Public organisations are similar to private organisations in that they have to acquire resources on a day-to-day basis in order to function. Different public services require different items: schools want books, the armed forces require fuel, hospitals need food, and all public offices use stationery and office equipment. In addition, all public organisations use commercial services such as electricity, transport, telephones, post and insurance. These items, and many thousands more, come under the heading of 'current expenditure', and they have to be acquired from many different types of organisation. The government is an important customer to many private organisations; so that changes in public expenditure can also have a direct effect on the private sector.

4 Capital formation includes public expenditure on new fixed assets, the purchase of land and buildings, and the stocks of government trading enterprises. It includes the construction of schools, hospitals, roads and bridges, as well as the purchase of aircraft, ships, and transport and communication facilities. Public capital investment thus has a direct effect on such industries as construction, shipbuilding and aerospace. Changes in the level of expenditure will also leak into other sectors of the economy and affect private capital investment.

Analysis of public expenditure by percentage of total spent on each programme during 1982/3 reveals that four programmes accounted for over 70% of total government expenditure (Table 16.1):

Table 16.1 Public expenditure by programme 1982/3 (£110 billion)

Programme	% of total	
Social security	29.1	
Health and Welfare	14.9	
Defence and Overseas Aid	14.7	
Education	13.0	
		71.7%
Roads	4.5	
Law and Order	4.1	
Housing	4.0	
Environmental services	4.0	
Employment services	2.3	
Others	9.4	
		100.0%

It is interesting to reflect that only three items – roads, housing and environmental services – contribute directly to the creation of wealth. On the whole, public programmes tend to be the products, rather than the producers, of affluence.

Investment incentives

The government can encourage the purchase of capital assets by allowing depreciation to be treated as an expense on the Profit and Loss Account. In addition to this type of non-specific allowance, however, governments have attempted to stimulate private investment by various kinds of incentive, such as cash grants and low-cost loans to encourage businesses to invest in areas of high unemployment.

Employment policy

The government can attempt to solve the problem of unemployment by influencing total demand in the economy. However, unemployment tends to occur in specific locations rather than be distributed evenly throughout the country.

The main types of unemployment are:

1 Casual unemployment. People who are changing jobs, and people with seasonal jobs (for example, those employed in tourism and agriculture), can be temporarily unemployed during part of the year.

2 Structural unemployment. The changing nature of business means that some employees become redundant because their type of industry, and its associated skills, are no longer needed (for example, the decline in shipbuilding has reduced the demand for labour on Tyneside and on the Clyde; changes in coal production have resulted in miners becoming redundant in Wales and South Yorkshire). So structural unemployment is high in those regions where basic industries have changed or declined. It also occurs in industries where improved methods of operation are introduced (for example, the introduction of containerisation has reduced the demand for dock workers).

3 Cyclical unemployment. Booms and slumps are a common feature of industrialised market economies. During a slump (now more usually called a recession) business activity is low, the general demand for labour is also low, and so unemployment increases.

The demand for labour is directly associated with the level of economic activity. If governments can stimulate business investment by increasing public expenditure or through other fiscal or monetary measures, then unemployment will be reduced. However, in addition to these main policies, British governments have tried specific measures to increase employment:

(a) Retraining. The MSC (a QUANGO) is responsible for industrial training, and it controls a variety of agencies which man-

age training schemes for the unemployed. For example, courses are provided under the Training Opportunities Scheme (TOPS) and the Youth Training Scheme (YTS), where the unemployed participants are paid an allowance by the MSC during the time they attend the training course.

(*b*)　*Grants.*　Various cash grant schemes as well as subsidies are used by the Government to encourage employment. For instance the Community Programme, and the Job Splitting and Job Release schemes are designed to provide a local stimulus to employment. In addition the Government has declared certain areas of 'economic and physical decay' to be Enterprise Zones where employment is encouraged through tax and rates relief.

(*c*)　*Information.*　The government hopes to reduce unemployment and improve the mobility of labour by providing information about alternative employment. The establishment of 'Job Centres' in main shopping areas makes the information accessible for most people.

Prices and incomes policy

Since the early 1960s successive governments have implemented some form of control on prices and incomes. The aim of such a policy is to curb inflation and to avoid unemployment. Those who advocate a prices and incomes policy maintain that, without it, higher pay would lead to higher prices (inflation); it would also lead to some people 'pricing' themselves out of the labour market and becoming unemployed; and in the free collective bargaining atmosphere strikes and disruptions to production would be common.

In spite of the many types of prices and incomes policy which have been tried, there is no hard evidence that they have worked. The most successful implementation was between August 1975 and June 1978, when the rate of inflation fell from 27% to below 10%. But not everyone is convinced that this reduction was because of the prices and incomes policy: some argue that other factors, such as the price of sterling and monetary policy, caused the rate of inflation to fall.

The problem with a prices and incomes policy is that setting pay norms and enforcing wage freezes causes distortions in the labour markets. Price controls reduce profitability, and trade union power means that wage controls cannot be operated permanently; prices and incomes policies so often end in a prices and wages 'explosion'. However, abandonment of any form of control also creates problems. The main difficulty is that free collective bargaining can lead to disruptions and strikes; and those employed in the public sector might feel, because their wages are controlled by public expenditure policies, that they are unfairly treated in a 'free for all'.

Public ownership policy

Monetary and fiscal policies are viewed by all governments as a necessary intervention into free market forces. The difference between governments is in the extent of such intervention. On the other hand the public ownership of commercial organisations, which has developed since the Second World War, is controversial. The type of industry which was nationalised in 1947–8 was either a 'natural' monopoly, such as gas or electricity, or a basic industry vital to the economy, like coal. Since then, however, the steel industry has been nationalised; and holdings in private national corporations, such as Rolls Royce and British Leyland, have been acquired by the State. So there is no coherent pattern in the growth of public enterprise.

The constantly changing economic environment has meant that governments have had to react to circumstance rather than apply rigid policies based on political philosophy. Direct intervention into private business has become an established feature of British economic policy, yet it remains controversial.

The arguments for public ownership are:

1 Monopoly power. Some industries are 'natural' monopolies. For example, it would be a waste of resources if such services as gas and electricity were to be provided by competing firms: they are natural commercial monopolies. If such monopolies were left in private hands then the owners could charge excessive prices and make considerable profits. Public ownership prevents such an abuse of monopoly power since any surpluses made by the nationalised industries become part of public revenue.

2 Rationalisation. Central ownership can help to make some industries more efficient. For example, the private companies in the steel industry, between themselves, duplicated some steel production processes. After nationalisation these processes were streamlined to provide more efficient production methods.

3　Social obligations.　Some industries are more vital to society than others. The provision of a postal service, or electricity, is essential to almost everyone, wherever they live. The cost of providing these services to areas like the north of Scotland or west Wales would be too high for commercial firms. So the State, through public ownership, is able to guarantee such provision.

4　Basic industries.　The communications and the energy industries are fundamental components in the structure of British industry; and some feel that control of the economy requires the control of these basic industries. Public ownership encourages the development of joint polices both in energy and transport.

5　Defence and security.　The government is the main customer in the aircraft and shipbuilding industries. It is argued that, since the products of these two industries are vital for the long-term defence of the United Kingdom, they should be publicly owned.

A special case was made for the formation of the British National Oil Corporation (BNOC), which was established in May 1976, to help the government obtain commercial benefits from North Sea Oil. It was felt that such a rich natural resource should be exploited by the State. Therefore BNOC has the power to explore for and produce oil, and to carry out other associated activities.

Another special case was made for the National Enterprise Board (NEB) which was created by the Industry Act, 1975. The NEB's main functions are to (*a*) establish, maintain, or develop industrial undertakings; (*b*) promote the re-organisation of industries; (*c*) take over and manage publicly owned securities (for example, BL Cars and Rolls Royce); and (*d*) extend public ownership into profitable manufacturing areas. These functions will probably be modified by successive governments, however.

The range of business activities which the NEB has become involved in is very wide, including word processors, computers, plastics and machine tools. This range reflects the concern which the Labour Government of the day had about private enterprise's response to rapid developments in new technology such as microelectronics. This Government felt that private firms had been too slow or were inadequately financed to respond to rapid technological change, and that the State ought to show enterprise and initiative.

Arguments against public ownership are:

1 Monopoly power.   The degree of competition which the public corporations face varies: the Post Office is almost a pure monopoly, while the corporations in the transport and energy industries compete with one another. However, all public corporations have monopolistic control over the supply of their particular product or service. Many argue that this control creates inefficiency in the operations of the nationalised industries, and fosters indifference to the needs of the consumer.

2 Diseconomies of scale.   Although large-scale units, such as public corporations, have the advantage of large-scale production, many of them have problems in administrative control and coordination. It is argued that the lack of competition in the public sector means that there is no incentive to solve these problems.

3 No profit motive.   The lack of profit motive could create inefficiencies because of the lack of incentive to improve. However, the nationalised industries are able to measure the return on their capital, and since 1967 have had to meet a test discount return on investment. So, although they do not suffer the private sector consequences of a series of losses, they do have a yardstick of 'profitability' to measure their performance.

4 Ministerial control.   The existence of public corporations has allowed governments to interfere directly in the day-to-day running of commercial organisations, for example, by controlling prices and wages in the public corporations. Such political interference can distort the commercial operations of the nationalised sector.

In the special case of the National Enterprise Board, some critics argue that carrying out enterprise in new ventures where there is a high degree of risk is both foolish and misguided; and that high risk investment should be left to private companies.

International trade policy

Imports

Overseas *visible trade* (the import and export of goods) in the UK amounts to almost one-third of the Gross National Product. This proportion of GNP gives some idea of the importance of overseas trade to British business.

Britain is dependent on imported goods for three main reasons:

1   Natural resources.   'Nature's gifts' are not distributed evenly throughout the world. The UK has oil and coal, but lacks raw materials such as timber, furs, copper, aluminium, rubber, lead and zinc, all of which have to be purchased from countries overseas.

2   Climatic conditions.   The ability to grow food depends on climatic conditions and the amount of suitable land. Britain is able to produce only half of its own foodstuffs; the rest – such as dairy products, cereals, sugar, coffee and tea – have to be imported.

3   Surplus demand.   In spite of Britain's ability to produce manufactured goods, UK producers cannot meet the total demand in the home markets. In order to satisfy demand, therefore, the United Kingdom imports cars, watches, footwear, clothes and many other kinds of finished goods.

In addition to these imported goods there are items of *invisible trade*, such as the British government's expenditure on armed forces in Europe and on embassies around the world, and the expenditure of British tourists who travel overseas.

Exports

The United Kingdom's visible and invisible imports have to be paid for out of gold and foreign currency reserves – either the currency of the exporting country or in some other acceptable currency, such as US dollars or deutschmarks. The only way in which Britain can earn this foreign currency is to export visible goods and invisible services. The United Kingdom's main visible exports are manufactured goods, chemicals, fuel and machinery. However, these visible exports do not earn enough foreign currency, and invisible earnings in banking, insurance, tourism and shipping help to make up the balance.

The Balance of Payments

Fig. 16.5 shows the items on the Balance of Payments. The goods and services which are acquired from overseas are recorded as debit

Current Account

Visible Trade items:

(*a*)   *Imports*
Food, Beverages, Tobacco
Basic materials

(*b*)   *Exports*
Fuels
Manufactures

Imports *less* exports *gives* the *Balance of Trade.*

Invisible Trade items:

(*a*)   *Government Transfers and Services*
Military services
Diplomatic services
Economic grants
Payments to international organisations

(*b*)   *Interest, Profits and Dividends*

(*c*)   *Commercial Services*
Banking
Insurance
Shipping

(*d*)   *Tourism*

Capital Account (long-term transactions)
(*a*)   Private long-term investment
(*b*)   Long-term government loans
(*c*)   Transactions with overseas monetary authorities (e.g. IMF)

Balancing Item Shows a surplus or credit on the Balance of Payments.

Fig. 16.5   The main components of the UK Balance of Payments

items; and the goods and services purchased by foreign countries are recorded as credit transactions.

The Balance of Payments is similar to a balance sheet in financial accounts in that it always balances, and the 'balancing item' shows whether a surplus or deficit in foreign earnings has occurred. A surplus means that the United Kingdom's gold and foreign currency reserves have increased; a deficit means that the reserves have decreased.

Deficits on the Balance of Payments have been a recurrent problem in the British economy, and many technical measures have been used to try to redress the balance. As far as business is concerned, the most direct measures have been import controls, encouragement to exporters, and the manipulation of exchange rates.

Import controls
Since most of the United Kingdom's imports are essential raw materials and vital foodstuffs, it is unwise to restrict, on a general basis, the import of goods, either by *tariffs* (taxes on imports) or by *quotas* (limits on the amount of imports). Both of these measures would tend to increase the price of vital supplies, and would therefore add to inflation while also reducing consumer choice. The control of specific items, such as cars from Japan, could assist the home producer, but it might lead to retaliation on British exports by the country concerned. Therefore import controls are opposed by GATT and by many economists as a means of improving the Balance of Payments position. However, the United Kingdom is a member of the EEC, and the Community's policy is to have completely free trade within the Community, and to have 'common' barriers to imports. Thus the EEC's policy is to have free trade in food between the member states, and to use tariffs to discourage the import of food from non-member states such as Australia and New Zealand.

Encouraging exports
The Export Credits Guarantee Department (ECGD) of the Department of Trade assists exporters by providing insurance cover against the risk of default by a foreign buyer. In addition, exporters

are given encouragement by such schemes as honours awards, overseas trade exhibitions and free information on the nature of overseas markets. Many people feel that, although these 'incentives' and services help the exporter, the real solution is for British business to improve the quality, reliability and availability of products; and to sell them at competitive prices.

Exchange controls

The price of sterling (its exchange rate with other currencies) will affect the price of imports and exports. If the exchange rate is low, then imports are more expensive and exports become comparatively cheaper. If the exchange rate is high, then imports are cheaper and exports become more expensive. One way to restrict imports is to impose a low rate of exchange (*devaluation*). Until 1972 the exchange rate between sterling and the dollar was fixed, and any changes in the rate required direct government decisions. Since 1972, however, the price of the pound has been determined by the supply and demand for sterling. Nevertheless, the Bank of England can influence the exchange rate by selling sterling when the government want the rate to go down, and by using foreign currency reserves to buy sterling when the government wants the exchange rate to increase.

Movements in the price of sterling will affect all those businesses which import and export goods and services, and will have repercussions throughout the economy. Government intervention normally occurs when stability is required, because instability in the exchange rate creates uncertainty and can lead to a decline in overseas trade and in business activity generally.

17

The Legal Environment

Legal rules govern the relationship between people and organisations, between people and people, and between organisations and organisations. For example, rules apply to the establishment of an organisation, to an organisation's relationship with employees, and to an organisation's relationship with customers/clients. Although the influence of law is present in all business activity, the rules are mainly applied when conflict or uncertainty occur.

Sources of law

1   Statutes – Acts of Parliament
Legal rules are created by Parliament, primarily at the instigation of the government. Acts of Parliament or Statutes have to be approved by the House of Commons, the House of Lords and the Queen. The government translates its policies into Bills (Public Bills), and because most governments have a majority in the House of Commons, the Executive dominates the introduction of legislation into Parliament. However, individual Members of Parliament are allowed time to introduce their own Public Bills (Private Members' Bills) into the process, and outside bodies such as local authorities can have private legislation (Private Bills) introduced.

2   Delegated legislation
The process of creating law can be complicated and difficult, especially when technical and detailed rules are required. Parlia-

ment does not have the time, nor even the expertise, to design some complex rules – for example, building regulations or flying regulations. In such instances Parliament provides the principles and framework of legal rules but delegates the power to draft the more technical rules and regulations to local authorities and government departments. The local authorities produce by-laws, and the government departments issue statutory instruments.

This subordinate or delegated legislation has become a major feature of the legal constraints which are imposed on business.

3 The decisions of judges: judicial precedent

Although the parliamentary process is rigorous, and every attempt is made to ensure that the language in statutes is unambiguous, all legislation requires interpretation. The interpretation of Acts is made by judges. The decisions of judges in higher courts on interpretation must be followed by the lower courts, and decisions made by courts of equal rank are taken into account by one another. The procedure is that judges explain the legal principles on which they have based their interpretation (known as *ratio decidendi*), and the decision becomes a judicial precedent. This process, although it is slow, creates certainty and fairness in the application of legal rules.

4 Custom

General customs laid the foundation for many legal rules when law was becoming established. But custom is not now as important as Statutes as a source of law. However, regular practice will become law if it is recognised by a valid court. Such recognition occurs when the custom is not unreasonable, has existed for as long as anyone can remember, and the court can clearly identify who benefits.

The classification of law

Legal rules can be classified into two distinct groups: Public Law and Private or Civil Law. The distinction is important in that Public Law provides the rules for behaviour in the community at large; and Private Law provides the legal framework for relationships between individuals and organisations.

Public law

1   Constitutional law. The United Kingdom does not have a written constitution, and many of the rules which govern the activities of constitutional bodies are based on custom and convention rather than legal rules. For example, the collective responsibility of the Cabinet is an unwritten convention. However, the powers of government ministers and of local authorities are primarily governed by Statute Law.

2   Criminal law. The behaviour of some people is anti-social; in business, for example, fraud, misrepresentation and misappropriation of funds occur. The purpose of criminal law is to suppress behaviour which either disturbs the peace or disrupts the well-being of others. In effect the criminal law allows the State to protect the property of persons and organisations, and to protect persons from others, by punishing the offenders.

Private (civil) law

Private Law provides legal rules on a much wider basis than Public Law – rules which relate to marriage, the family, inheritance and trusts. In effect the Civil Law clarifies the rights and duties of people and organisations towards each other. The two main aspects of Civil Law which directly affect business are:

1   Law of Contract. Agreements or contracts are the most common form of relationship in business. There are contracts of employment, contracts of sale, contracts of work, and so on. The Law of Contract provides the rules and conditions on agreements between people and/or organisations.

2   Law of Torts. The Law of Torts (wrongs) clarifies the position of organisations and individuals when they have suffered injury or an infringement of their rights. Thus when a person or an organisation has been negligent, has trespassed, caused a nuisance or defamed a person's character, the Law of Torts provides the rules under which damages can be recovered for any injury which has been sustained. In order to recover damages the injured party must prove that the defendant has done something he should not have done, or has failed to do something he should have done; and has intentionally or negligently caused injury, and that the 'injured' party has suffered loss.

Liability

When a dispute occurs, the courts decide which person or organisation represented in the case is liable for any wrongful act. Wrongful acts can be both criminal and civil, and they can be regulated at the same time by criminal and civil actions. This is known as *double liability*. For example, if a trader gives a false description of an article which he is selling, he is liable to criminal prosecution under the Trades Description Act, 1968; and at the same time, if any person has suffered loss as a result of the misrepresentation, that person could sue the trader for damages in the civil courts under the Misrepresentation Act 1967.

Vicarious liability

Liability can be *strict* in that the specific party which commits the tort can be held liable, even when that party is unaware of his/her negligence or nuisance. In addition, organisations have to be careful in the way in which they operate, because they can be held vicariously liable for the actions of their employees. For example, employers can be vicariously liable for any torts (negligence, nuisance, etc.) committed by an employee when the employer is in charge of the employee's operations. Similarly, members of a partnership can be held to be vicariously liable for the torts of other members which are committed during the course of business.

The law on contracts

A contract is a legal agreement. Bargains and agreements are the essential ingredients of commercial activity, and any form of trade implies that agreements or 'contracts' have been made. Consequently the law relating to contracts has been evolving over several hundred years, and in some aspects is still being refined. Basically the legal rule in contract is that if an agreement is not carried out, or not performed correctly, then the 'injured' party has the legal right to claim some form of redress.

The essential features of an agreement – all of which have to be satisfied to make a contract legally valid – are:

1 Offer and acceptance. To make an agreement legally valid one party must make an offer to perform some function or to pay a particular price, and the other party to the agreement must unconditionally accept that offer. It is important that all the terms in the offer are accepted. For example, if an employer offers to engage someone at £10 000 per annum, and the person writes to accept the offer but says in his letter that he requires a salary of £11 000 per annum, then there is no contract of employment.

An interesting feature of the sale of goods is that it is the *purchaser* who makes the offer to buy at a particular price. The price on an article is *not* an offer, but is an invitation to offer. The retailer can accept or reject the purchaser's offer – obviously he invariably accepts.

2   Consideration.   Another important element of a contract is consideration, which is something performed, given or suffered, in return for the benefits received. Both parties to a contract must show consideration. The most common example of consideration is money exchanged for goods or services; as well as goods exchanged for goods, or goods exchanged for services, and so on.

3   Intention.   Parties to a contract must intend to create a legally binding relationship. Arrangements where offer, acceptance and consideration have been made, for example social arrangements, will not be legally binding unless the parties intended that it should be so. It is assumed in business agreements that there is an intention to enter a legally binding relationship, unless it is formally stated that the agreement is 'binding in honour only'.

4   Capacity to contract.   The law is designed to protect persons who might not be fit to enter a legally binding agreement. People who are under 18 years (minors), those who are mentally disabled, and drunken persons, do not have the capacity to enter a contract. With a few exceptions, contracts made by such persons are void or voidable.

It is a legal rule that the unauthorised use of a statutory power (*ultra vires*) is void and ineffective. Since governmental powers, and the powers of commercial corporations, are created by statute then this rule is important for almost all organisations. It means that statutory corporations such as local authorities and the nationalised industries cannot enter into contracts which are not authorised by statute. For example, a public corporation cannot sell a diversified range of products. Similarly private corporations, which are registered under the Companies Acts, cannot make contracts which are not authorised by the Memorandum of Association. For example, a firm would be acting *ultra vires* if the Memorandum had only 'retailing' listed as the firm's activity, and then it made contracts to drill for oil; such contracts would not be valid.

5 *Validity.* Sometimes a contract will meet the four essential requirements which are given above, but will become invalid because of some other factors such as:

(*a*) *Mistake.* People are not infallible: error is common in all human activity. Error in a contract may make the agreement invalid. The most common error is mistaken identity, either of the parties or of the substance of the contract. However, this rule does not allow people to be careless or casual in business agreements: the mistake must be of a genuine and significant nature, otherwise the rule is 'caveat emptor' – 'let the buyer beware, or be alert'.

(*b*) *Misrepresentation.* Some unscrupulous people make false statements to try to induce an agreement. Legislation such as the Trades Descriptions Act, 1968, makes misrepresentation a criminal offence. Any contract entered into because of misrepresentation can be voidable, and the injured party can claim damages in a civil action.

(*c*) *Uberrimae fidei.* It is important in some contracts that all facts which are material to the agreement should be declared, otherwise the contract is voidable. This is particularly true of insurance contracts. For example, life insurance contracts can require details of all previous illness and a family history of illness. Similarly, motor insurance contracts can require details of any previous accidents. Failure to provide the information at the time when the contract is drawn up can make the contract void.

(*d*) *Unlawful intent.* Some contracts are not enforceable because they are not lawful. Illegal contracts are invalid, and so too are any lawful contracts which require the performance of an illegal act. For example, contracts to misappropriate funds or to commit a public nuisance might satisfy the four essentials of a valid contract, but, because they are unlawful, are not valid.

Some contracts are void by statute. For example, contracts to restrict competition, which contravene the Restrictive Trade Practices Act, 1976, are not valid.

Inequality of bargaining power in contracts

The law will not enforce a contract against a party if the agreement was unduly influenced by the other party. This does not mean that if a person strikes a bad bargain through ignorance, miscalculation or economic weakness that the courts will interfere. Obviously threats and other forms of duress would be regarded as 'unequal bargaining power' and the weaker party is protected. But what constitutes 'undue influence' is not always clear, and so Parliament has intervened into many different kinds of contracts, and passed legislation to protect the weaker party. Examples of such 'protection' occur in the legislation which controls rents, and that which controls hire purchase agreements. An example of legislative intervention is in the field of exclusion clauses in contracts. The Unfair Contract Terms Act, 1977, clarified the position of exclusion clauses and established that:

1 An exclusion clause can only apply in a contract if it is fair and reasonable.*
2 Exclusion for liability for injury or death is void.
3 Guarantees can never exclude or restrict liability for loss or damage caused by goods which are defective, or for services which are negligently performed.

Employment legislation

Contracts of employment
Between 1972 and 1982 several Acts of Parliament were passed

---

* An example which illustrates an exclusion clause which was considered to be unfair is Levinson *v* Patent Steam Carpet Cleaning Co. Ltd (1977). Mr L. sent a carpet, worth £900, to be cleaned by the PSCC Co. Ltd. The carpet was lost, and when Mr L. claimed £900 damages the Company maintained that a clause in the contract, which said that the carpet would be cleaned at the owner's risk, limited their liability to £40. Lord Denning decided that the exclusion clause was unreasonable – i.e. it was the use of unequal bargaining power – and the Company were required to pay £900 to Mr L. for the loss of the carpet.

which dealt with the rights and obligations of employees and employers in relation to contracts of employment. The main rules are:

1 Offer of a job. The offer of a job is made by the employer, and the consideration shown by him, for the work performed by the employee, is the payment of wages/salary. In return the employee accepts that he will put himself at the disposal of the employer during agreed periods. At the time of the contract the employee must guarantee that he is fit and competent to do the work which is required, and, in some cases, declare any conflict of interest. For example, public employees are not allowed to advance their private interests when working in the public service.

The law requires the following details in the contract of employment: the names of the employer and employee; the date when employment began; pay, or the method of calculating pay; when payment is to be made (weekly, monthly, etc); and the title of the job.

2 Conditions of employment. The conditions of service are often combined with the offer of work. The employer, once the employee starts work, has the right to supervise the employee's duties, and the right to decide how the work should be performed. In relation to the conditions of service the contract of employment should give details of the hours of work, holiday pay, sick pay, fringe benefits, the grievance procedure and disciplinary rules.

3 Termination of the contract. The employment legislation requires an employer to give an employee details of how the contract of employment can be terminated. These details should include the period of notice which the employer is entitled to give and receive, and an indication of how much previous employment with another employer counts towards the period of notice.

Discrimination in employment
The three Acts which relate to discrimination in employment are the Equal Pay Act, 1970, the Sex Discrimination Act, 1975, and the Race Relations Act, 1976. Discrimination occurs under these Acts

when an employee, or an applicant, is treated less favourably than others because of his or her sex, colour or race. The rules apply to all aspects of employment and have far-reaching effects. For example:

(*a*) *Job advertisements* must not specify the sex of the applicants sought. Many advertisements now use 'person' in place of 'man' or 'woman' – for example, 'herdsperson' and 'Person Friday'.

(*b*) *Selection, promotion and training.* When an organisation draws up a shortlist of internal employees or external candidates it is illegal to exclude people because of their sex, colour or race.

(*c*) *Terms of employment.* The law does not allow people to be given more favourable terms of employment than those of the opposite sex who are doing the same job.

(*d*) *Dismissal.* It would be illegal for a company to make only women redundant simply because it was felt that the men had more pressing family commitments.

(*e*) *Equal pay.* Both sexes should obtain equal pay for work of a similar and comparable nature.

Liability for discrimination is not restricted to the person who makes the decision to discriminate: employers are vicariously liable if their subordinates perform discriminatory acts. Individuals who feel that they have a grievance because of discrimination can complain to an *industrial tribunal.* If the tribunal finds in favour of the complainant it may award an order declaring the rights of both parties, or award damages to be paid by the employer.

The Acts of 1975 and 1976 established Commissions to investigate discrimination in employment. The Sex Discrimination Act set up the Equal Opportunities Commission, and the Race Relations Act established the Commission for Racial Equality. Both bodies can institute legal proceedings against persistent offenders; and they have an obligation to promote equal opportunity and eliminate discrimination.

Health and safety in employment
The legislation on health and safety applies to all working people, and to any of the general public who might be affected. The three statutes which relate to health and safety are the Factories Act, 1961, the Offices, Shops and Railway Premises Act, 1963, and the Health and Safety at Work Act, 1974.

The Acts of 1961 and 1963 laid down specific conditions which must exist in work places. These legal requirements still apply – for example, the temperature in offices should not be less than 16 degrees centigrade, there must be adequate ventilation and lighting in all places of work, premises should be kept clean, and so on. Legal rules also apply to the guarding of machinery, the maintenance of hoists and lifts, the maintenance of stairs, and the provision of fire escapes, drinking water, conveniences, protective clothing and first aid equipment.

The 1974 Act, in laying down the principles relating to health and safety, clarified the duties of the employer and employees, and provided the framework in which a Health and Safety Commission could operate.

The employer's duties under the Act are to maintain safe plant, equipment and systems; provide training and safety measures, and supervision in safety matters; produce a Safety Policy Statement, and communicate the Policy to all employees.

The employee's duties are to take reasonable care at all times and to cooperate with the employer on all safety matters.

Enforcement

The 1974 Act established the Health and Safety Commission which consists of representatives of employers, trade unions, local authorities and professional bodies. The Commission drafts detailed rules and regulations on health and safety (delegated legislation), and enforces them through an inspectorate. If the Commission's inspectors discover practices which are outside the legal rules, they can (*a*) stop the operation by serving a prohibition notice, (*b*) make the operation safer by serving an improvement notice, (*c*) or destroy any dangerous materials or substances, and (*d*) prosecute the offenders. The offenders could either be the management or individual employees. In addition to criminal prosecution, the offenders could face a civil action for negligence by any party who has suffered damage or injury.

Consumer legislation

The statutes which relate to consumer protection are many and varied, and establish legal rules covering prices, hygiene, false descriptions, dangerous goods, faulty services and restrictions on competition. Consumer legislation provides good examples of the distinction between public and private law. For example, it is a *criminal offence to*:

1 Sell food or drugs which are unfit for consumption, such as food which has been kept beyond its life date (Food and Drugs Act, 1955).
2 Sell goods which do not meet safety standards, such as electrical equipment or toys (Consumer Protection Act, 1961).
3 Give a false or misleading description of goods or services which are for sale (Trade Descriptions Act, 1968).
4 Demand payment for unsolicited goods (Unsolicited Goods and Services Act, 1971).
5 Restrict trade. For example, manufacturers cannot compel retailers to charge a certain price (Resale Prices Act, 1976).

In certain instances the law leaves it to the discretion of the individual to take *civil* action. A person can claim against, or sue, an organisation/individual when loss occurs as a result of:

1 goods being sold which are not of 'merchantable quality' (Sale of Goods Act, 1893).
2 the person being induced to enter a contract by a false or misleading statement (Misrepresentation Act, 1967).
3 the person being deprived of his rights by unfair bargaining, such as unfair exclusion clauses (Supply of Goods (Implied Terms) Act, 1973).

Some of the most important statutes are:

1 The Sale of Goods Act, 1893, which states that when goods are bought it is automatically implied that they correspond to their descriptions – for example, a garment described as 100% pure wool must not contain any other types of fibre. The Act also states that goods should be fit for the purpose for which they have been sold. A lawnmower, for example, should not break down the first time it is used. If goods do not meet these requirements the seller can be sued for breach of contract in a civil action.

2 The Supply of Goods (Implied Terms) Act, 1973, which amended the Sale of Goods Act, 1893. Some traders had been able to deprive customers of their rights, under the Sale of Goods Act, by writing exclusion clauses into contracts – for example, clauses excluding liability for loss or damage to articles when they were being repaired. Under the 1973 Act such clauses have to be 'fair and reasonable', otherwise the customer can sue for negligence or breach of contract.

3 The Trade Descriptions Act, 1968, which makes it a criminal offence to give a false or misleading description. Descriptions include references to such features as the size, composition and strength of articles. It is, therefore, an offence to describe a coat as 'real leather' if it is made of synthetic materials. Less clear-cut cases have turned on the definition of terms such as 'waterproof'.

The Act also applies to comparisons between prices. It is an offence to advertise a price as a reduction unless the initial price has been charged for 28 consecutive days during the previous six months.

4 The Fair Trading Act, 1973, which set up the Office of Fair Trading, which acts as a 'watchdog' on traders who consistently break the law. Any agreements between organisations to restrict competition must be registered with the Office. The Office's Director General has wide-ranging powers to bring civil actions, in the *Restrictive Practices Court*, against those who do not obey the legal rules. He can, as a last resort, recommend to the Secretary of State for Prices that certain practices should be prohibited.

5 The Consumer Credit Act, 1974, which requires those business engaged in lending money to obtain a licence from the Office of Fair Trading. It also requires those organisations dealing in credit to disclose to their customers the true costs of borrowing the money, and the sources of information on credit worthiness of individuals which the organisation used.

The law on property

People are an organisation's most important resource, but businesses also require other basic resources. For example, all businesses need land and buildings. Most organisations do not own the land on which they operate: they lease the property for a specified period (*leasehold*). During the period of the lease the organisation will have use of the property, and will pay the landlord rent in consideration for its use. An organisation can become the owner (landlord) of property by purchasing the *freehold*. For small businesses especially this can be an expensive acquisition, and many have to borrow the money by *mortgaging* the property. This means that the property is offered as security on the loan, and if the debt is not paid off, the bank, building society or whoever loaned the finance has a claim on the property.

Restrictive covenants

There may be agreements or covenants restricting the use of land, such that the organisation may not build on the land, or all buildings should be of a certain height, or an existing building should not be used as a shop, and so on. In the case of freehold property, restrictive covenants are enforceable in the original contract, and the restrictions are assigned to subsequent owners of the freehold. In leasehold contracts, the landowner may make agreements with the lessee, but the terms create obligations which affect only the parties to that contract. Not all restrictions will be enforced. When making a decision on restrictive covenants the courts will ensure that the covenant is negative – i.e. that it does restrict use, and that the restriction is, in some way, beneficial in protecting the land.

Duties of the occupier of premises

Under the Occupiers' Liability Act, 1957, the occupier of property owes a 'common duty of care' to all visitors, to ensure that visitors will be reasonably safe when using the premises for a permitted purpose. Warnings can free the owner from liability – for example, a notice saying: 'Beware! Overhead Cranes at Work'. However, the warning has to be adequate for visitors to take precautions. Visitors themselves have a duty to take care.

A *trespasser*, however, has to take property as he finds it: the law does not expect the occupier to safeguard a trespasser's interests. Trespass is direct interference with another's possession of land (which includes houses, shops, gardens and paths), and occurs when a person (*a*) enters land without permission, (*b*) remains on the land after the permission has expired, or (*c*) places any objects on land without permission. The remedies which the occupier has against trespass are (*a*) an action for damages, (*b*) an application for injunction to restrain the trespasser, and/or (*c*) throwing the trespasser out, without using excessive force.

Non-physical property

Goodwill. The reputation of a business, and its trade connections, are *intangible assets*, which are commonly referred to as 'goodwill'. When a business is sold, and 'goodwill' is included in the price, the purchaser has a right to the established trade connections. The value of 'goodwill' is determined by the comparative success of the business.

Trademarks. A trademark is a sign used in connection with goods and services, which helps customers and clients to identify a particular producer. Trademarks are registered for a set period, during which they can be sold, especially when the business is put up for sale.

Patents relate to inventions. Inventors apply for a patent to the Patents Office where experts examine the invention to ascertain its validity. When the validity is resolved the Crown grants the inventor monopoly rights (a patent) for a set period. The purpose in granting monopoly rights is to encourage the full disclosure of new products and processes, with protection against 'pirating', while at the same time allowing the inventor a period in which to earn financial reward for his creativity. Patent rights can be sold, or another party can be granted a licence which allows it to use the invention.

Copyright is similar to a patent, except that it does not have to be applied for. A composer or writer has a monopoly right for fifty years in music, and for life plus fifty years in literature. As with patents, copyright can be sold or assigned.

Questions on Part Five
1 Assess the role of the Civil Service in the formulation of government policies.
2 Outline the main functions of the Bank of England.
3 'As far as the United Kingdom is concerned, the disadvantages of the EEC outweigh the advantages.' Discuss.
4 Using Fig. 16.4, describe the main components of, and analyse the trends in, public expenditure between 1961 and 1981.
5 Outline the main components of the National Income, and explain the practical importance of this concept.

6   Explain how the government's policy towards public ownership integrates with the broad aims of government economic policy.
7   Describe the main trading relationships of the United Kingdom and assess their relative importance.
8   Briefly outline the essentials of a valid contract, and explain what is meant by 'unequal bargaining situations'.
9   Distinguish between administrative supervision and judicial control of the actions of public bodies.
10 Identify the principal rights and duties which arise out of the contract of employment.

PART SIX
The Impact of Technological Change

18

Technological Change

The need for change

Organisations are always changing: they are constantly re-defining their goals and policies, developing new products and services, acquiring new resources, appointing new people, and introducing new systems and techniques of management. In order to survive organisations have to be dynamic.

The stimulus for change comes from various sources:

1 The changing needs of customers and clients

The demand for a product or service rarely remains constant. For example, there is an ever-increasing demand for energy. Even though most sources of energy are extractive, and therefore not permanent, people expect to be able to heat homes, offices and factories in winter, to own and run private cars, and to have the power to drive electrical appliances and machinery. The increasing demand for power causes changes throughout business. For example, domestic and commercial energy users are encouraged to devise methods of saving fuel; energy producers look for improved or alternative methods of production; the government makes a controversial decision to invest in atomic power, and at the same time stimulates research into alternative sources of energy such as solar, wind and wave power.

The changing nature of demand is best illustrated by the notion of a product's life-cycle (see Chapter 4). The life of different products varies considerably. For example, most pop records have a very short life which is measured in weeks rather than years. On the other hand, some products (such as Pears' Soap) have been on the market since Victorian times. Different brands within products have different life-cycles – different models of cars, for instance, have lives which vary for five years to twenty years. The important point to remember is that very few successful products remain successful indefinitely. The changing nature of demand is a permanent feature of business activity.

2   The need to solve problems

There are political, economic and social problems which require the application of technology, and which have stimulated extensive change throughout certain sections of business. One of the best examples, where political aspiration caused extensive technological change, is President Kennedy's decision to land a man on the moon 'within a decade'. The solution to the problem required immense inventive genius, and led to developments in such areas as microelectronics and communication satellites which have brought change throughout the world.

3   The need for efficiency

The search for efficiency stimulates change. The development of Jumbo jets and High Speed trains are examples of innovations which improve the competitiveness of the producer and, at the same time, improve the transport service.

The most significant development in recent years has been the improvements in microelectronics. These improvements have such widespread implications for business that they provide the best example of the impact of technological change on organisations. Consequently the remainder of this chapter examines the effects of the changes in microelectronics on business and society.

Many believe that the development of microelectronics will cause an industrial and social revolution which will be as far-reaching as the changes brought about in the eighteenth and nineteenth centuries by the invention of mechanical power. Although no one can be sure of the long-term effects, microelectronic technology will cause significant economic and social changes during the next decade.

Microelectronic equipment consists of large numbers of highly complex electronic control circuits, which are packed into a very small space. The circuits use very little power, they are very reliable, and they can be manufactured in large quantities at low cost. The significant growth has been in the power of a single silicon chip: the number of component parts of an electronic circuit which could be placed on a chip of silicon only one quarter of an inch square has grown astronomically since 1960, as Table 18.1 shows.

Table 18.1 Miniaturisation in the microelectronics industry, 1960–1985 number of parts per square quarter inch of silicon chip

Year	No. of parts
1960	10
1970	700
1976	10 000
1977	30 000
1981	100 000
1985	250 000

The table also illustrates how rapid modern technological change can be.

The growth in the power of the silicon chip has had a very significant impact on computers, however, this is only a small part of the impact which microelectronics has had on all types of organisations, and on all kinds of market. One of the most important developments in microelectronics has been the development of the *microprocessor*, a microcircuit which can be programmed to carry out many different functions. Any product or process which involves elements of measurement is being affected by either the microprocessor or microelectronic instruments. The Advisory Council on Applied Research and Development identified the following industries which are being significantly affected by microelectronic developments: energy, food processing, agriculture, transport, telecommunications, car production and domestic equipment. The Department of Trade and Industry goes even further, and says that it is difficult to point to any sector of business which will *not* be affected.

Examples of the effects of developments in microelectronics can be found in products, production methods and information systems.

Products

1 Domestic appliances. Many domestic appliances use electronic controls (for example, there are timing devices in washing machines, dishwashers, cookers and toasters). The microchip not only increases their reliability, but also makes them easier to control and use.

2 Motor cars. Developments in microelectronics means that the electric system in cars is more reliable, and that electronic devices such as 'trip computers' are becoming standard features in modern cars. In addition, garage mechanics are able to carry out electronic diagnostic maintenance, which is quicker and easier than previous methods of diagnosis.

3 Lighting and ventilation systems. The heating and lighting of homes and places of work is made safer and cheaper by microelectronic control systems, because the fire warning devices and thermostats are more sensitive and more reliable than previous systems.

4 Automatic vending machines. The silicon chip has improved the reliability of vending machines; consequently retailing and other commercial service facilities are being affected by the changes in technology. Food, cash and many different kinds of products are becoming readily available, on a 24-hour basis, from automatic machines.

5 Replacement of existing products. Some products have changed dramatically in style, and in character, as a result of the application of microelectronics. For example, electronic calculators, digital watches and electronic tills have replaced mechanical products, because they can perform more functions, are more reliable, and often cost less.

6 New products. Microelectronics has led to the invention of new products. This is particularly true of 'leisure' markets, where electronic toys, electric pianos and TV video games are replacing the more traditional leisure games and toys.

7 Personal computers, and Prestel. The management of domestic affairs is gradually changing. Personal home computers, and the

British Telecom's Prestel service, enables people to acquire and make use of a wealth of information. For example, they can determine which investment or savings scheme to join, keep accurate financial records, and obtain up-to-date market prices. The purchase of goods by electronic mail order is now possible; and learning packages have been compiled in all kinds of subjects, so that studying at home is becoming easier and more effective.

Production methods and processes

1   Assembly-line operations.   The production of those products which are manufactured by mass production techniques, such as cars, television sets and durable household goods, is affected by the changes in microelectronic technology. For instance, many functions which have involved manual/mechanical operations – counting, sorting, inspecting, testing, weighing – have become electronically controlled. In addition, electronic 'robots' are replacing many jobs previously undertaken by semi-skilled workers.

2   Clerical operations.   Another range of semi-skilled occupations affected by the advances in electronics are clerical operations. For example, cash dispensers are replacing counter occupations in commercial banks, and word processors are replacing some secretarial functions.

3   The handling of materials.   Automatic warehousing and electronic materials-handling is increasing, and the storage and retrieval of stores and equipment is being made fully automatic in many firms. Electronic stock control reduces the opportunities for pilfering; and gives immediate information on the stock level of each item, and when re-orders are due.

4   Automatic transport.   Automatic pilot systems have been devised which rely far less on human control than the traditional mechanical systems. Electronic traffic control in air, road and rail transport means that transport systems are more efficient and much safer.

Information systems

In Chapter 10 it was noted that money is the lifeblood of organisations: if organisations do not receive a flow of cash they go out of business. Information plays a similar role. The flow of facts, figures and words through an organisation's administration is its nervous system.

The nature and flow of information determines how 'sensitive' an organisation is to customers, employees, changes in the market, levels of sales, and so on. The functions of *information processing* are receiving, sorting, analysing, filing, retrieving and communicating. The purpose in performing these functions is to *plan*, *record* and *control* the activities of the organisation (Table 18.2).

For many organisations the greatest impact of technological change has been in the processing of its information. During the last thirty years there has been a constant increase in the cost of administration. In 1950 for example, office costs formed 20% of

Table 18.2   Examples of information processing in the organisation

Purpose	Type of Information
Planning	
Financial Planning	Departmental expenditure
	Budget standards
	Income received
Production Planning	Market Research statistics
	Product Mix data
	Orders received
	Orders despatched
	Work-in-progress
Recording	
Payroll	Wages and salaries
Invoicing	Order despatched
	Accounts not paid
Turnover	Sales statistics
Purchases	Orders placed
Control	
Stock Control	Purchases received
	Stocks used
Quality Control	Production levels
	Reject levels
Budgetary Control	Budget standards
	Expenditure patterns

total costs in most businesses. They now account for 50% of total costs. Consequently, information processing is an area where the application of electronics is having a substantial economic effect on all types of business organisation. Table 18.3 compares the traditional methods of processing information with electronic methods.

The advantages of electronic information-processing are:

1 Speed. Information on almost any aspect of an organisation's system can be sorted, analysed and retrieved almost instantly.

2 Accuracy. Employees' mistakes are the main cause of errors in information. There is far less human involvement in electronic information processing, consequently errors are reduced. For example, in word processing, standard letters are typed only once and then stored for future use.

3 Reliability. Micro-electronic equipment is more reliable than humans and mechanical equipment. People at work become tired and distracted and often make mistakes, while mechanical equipment has many moving parts, any one of which can fail causing the machine to break down.

4 Flexibility. Electronic information-processing means that the analysis of information is both accurate and sophisticated. Microprocessors can be programmed to perform many operations which previously would have been too complicated or taken too long.

5 Improved quality. The finished copy of written communication is greatly improved by word processing. In addition the content can be improved. For example, financial and other statistical information is easily up-dated in reports. Information becomes less historical, and therefore is more useful.

The 'information revolution' is not confined to the internal systems of organisations. Developments such as the Post Office's Prestel service mean that customers and clients have access to up-to-date information on prices, transport timetables, entertainment guides and all kinds of other market information. The growth in external information makes consumers and organisations more knowledgeable about market conditions, and therefore markets tend to become more perfect and competition increases.

Table 18.3   Electronic versus traditional methods of information processing

Function	Traditional	Electronic
Receiving	Internal and external post	Computer terminals in departmental and branch locations transmit internal information to central computer. Examples: banks, building societies, retail outlets, hotels and restaurants.
Sorting	Clerical operation	Coded information can be sorted at considerable speed, with accuracy.
Analysing	Analysis is often made by managers and technical experts, and can be laborious and time-consuming.	Computers can perform standard statistical analyses at high speed, and with great accuracy. Examples: financial ratios, budget variances, orders received.
Filing	Filing by hand into filing cabinets, and card index trays	The memory in a micro-processor can store large amounts of information on small 'floppy discs' or cassettes.
Retrieving	Clerical operation subject to human error	Information is readily available in video or printed form, although print only used when necessary. Examples: stock position, daily sales, cross-referencing, accounts overdue.
Communicating	Labour-intensive operation with secretaries and typists	Electronic mail and word processing means that communication with 'first rate copy' is available. Examples: invoices, letters to customers and clients, internal memos.

The organisation's response

The microelectronic revolution has wide-ranging implications for all kinds of products, production methods and information systems, and it has made technological change even more dynamic than ever. In order to survive during a period of rapid change, businesses have had to become more aware of how technological changes affect their organisation systems, as well as the effect on products and services. In many organisations the Research and Development function is expanding. R&D not only concentrates on designing and developing products within existing conventional processes, but also includes an analysis of the radical changes which are taking place in other products and production systems with a view to incorporating these innovations into the organisation's existing strategy.

Technological change affects all types of business. Even small organisations which cannot afford R&D teams have had to improve their awareness and understanding of the implications of change.

Table 18.4 summarises the internal and external sources of knowledge which can be used to meet the problems of technological change.

The Government's role

Britain's capability as an exporting nation, and the creation of wealth, is dependent on the ability of business organisations to adapt to technological change. Consequently the government plays an important role in technological development. For example, most basic (pure) research is undertaken in the public sector by institutions in Higher Education, and by government-funded research bodies. Developments in electronic technology are seen as crucial to the expansion of the economy. In connection with microelectronics, in the late 1970s, the Labour Government provided financial support to encourage the development of the British microelectronics industry. Since 1979 this policy has been maintained by the Conservative Government. The most significant support for electronic technology was made in 1983 in the Alvey programme, which has been described as Britain's $350 million answer to Japan's advance in information technology.

The extent of the government's contribution to the programme depends on the progress of the research and development, and a financial commitment from industry and commerce. The government offered to spend $200 million provided British business spent $150 million. The funds have been managed by three Government departments – the Department of Trade and Industry (DTI), the Ministry of Defence and the Department of Education.

Table 18.4 Responding to technological change: internal and external sources of knowledge

Source of knowledge	Products	Production methods	Information systems
External: Consultants Higher Education Professional bodies Research associations Government bodies Competitors	(*i*) Product ideas from successful competitors. (*ii*) Cooperate with outside agency in the research of new products. (*iii*) Purchase a patent.	(Problem for capital intensive organisations) (*i*) Consult technical experts. (*ii*) Lease equipment.	(*i*) Employ consultants, e.g. computer bureaux. (*ii*) Purchase 'software' packages.
Internal: Internal R&D Value analysis teams Exhibitions Trade fairs Market research	(*i*) Traditional methods in large organi- sations. (*ii*) But no guaranteed return on expenditure. (*iii*) 80% of new product developments fail.	(*i*) Internal change requires flexibility and imagination. 'Brain storming' techniques used.	(*i*) Expensive and complicated to design own system.

19

Conflict and Change

Microelectronics have created a new basic industry which is revolutionising business. Their development is increasing the movement of labour from manufacturing to the service sector; and some experts predict that eventually only 10% of the working population will be engaged in the wealth-producing industries (see Chapters 3 and 16). The social and economic implications of this shift are considerable. This chapter assesses these implications, and examines the nature of the conflict which change, inevitably, creates.

Economic implications of change

1 Increased productivity
Developments in technology generally lead to increased efficiency and growth. It is estimated that the invention of electronic memory devices has increased productivity in offices by 50%. Not only has the quantity of information increased, but the quality has also improved. Business information is now more accurate and more up-to-date than ever before.

Improved information from external sources such as Prestel creates greater market efficiency. As customers and clients become better informed about prices and market opportunities then competition increases, and this stimulates business efficiency.

2 De-skilling of occupations
The increase in information means that employees have to improve their skills in sifting, absorbing and using large quantities of data.

However, for many occupations, the electronic revolution has reduced the skills which are needed, not increased them. For example, secretarial and clerical functions are being replaced by word processors; Post Office employees are by-passed by the electronic transmission of documents; and the skills of print workers are now carried out by electronic typesetting.

3   Unemployment

Some predict that unemployment will continue to increase as a result of technological change. For example, the Cambridge Economic Policy Group predict that by 1990 4.6 million people will be out of work in Britain. Siemens, a German multi-national corporation, forecast that 40% fewer office workers will be required by 1990. There are instances which support these predictions. For example, the introduction by British Telecom of System X (fully electronic telephone exchange equipment) means that less than 4% of the 1980 telephone exchange workforce will be required by 1990. Similarly NCR, a company which produces cash registers and weighing machines, believe that their total workforce will be reduced by 50% because electronic equipment requires fewer people in its construction.

4   Creation of new jobs

The electronic revolution has created new jobs in the electronics industry, and in those industries which have been able to adapt to the new technology. However, the major change is in the service industries. As wealth has increased, the leisure and social service industries – travel, sport, welfare, hotel and catering – have been employing an increasing proportion of the working population.

Not all people believe that unemployment will continue to increase, and the evidence to date is conflicting. Rapid advances in technology tend to alter the *nature* of employment rather than reduce it. The main implication of technological change is that it changes the nature of many occupations, and requires people and organisations to be both adaptable and flexible.

Social implications of change

1 Education and training
Technological change, particularly the information revolution, has implications for education.

(*a*) *Computer-assisted learning.* Programs are being devised to cover many different types of subject. These learning programs, unlike normal television, require participation by the student and make learning without a teacher much easier and more effective.
(*b*) *Social skills.* The skills needed in many occupations are changing. Greater emphasis is now placed on developing skills which electronic devices cannot replace such as social skills, and on inter-personal relationships (see Chapter 11).
(*c*) *Continuing education.* The need for adaptability and flexibility in people means that many more will continue or return to education and training after leaving school and college.

2 Leisure
As material wants are satisfied by increased wealth, people are demanding non-material services: there is increased emphasis on physical and mental welfare, and on entertainment such as sport and travel. The growth in travel agents, leisure centres and keep-fit clubs illustrates this change of emphasis in life styles.

3 Attitudes to work
Technological change causes a shift in the nature of occupations and also tends to make organisations more remote from employees. It often creates a series of sub-routine tasks which neither stimulate the employee nor sustain his/her interest. These factors, as well as the satiation of many people's material needs, have caused changes in employees' attitudes to work.

The changes in attitudes which are outlined below are not uniform throughout society, and do not apply to everyone. They are examples of change in different sectors of society, and in some instances conflict with one another. This is not surprising. It would be unrealistic to believe that attitudes change throughout society in a consistent pattern.

(*a*)　*Decline in craft skills careers.*　Many traditional craft skills, in engineering and printing for example, are becoming redundant. As a result many young people do not want to spend many years on low pay as apprentices to master craftsmen. Similarly a decreasing proportion of young people apply to become full-time students in Higher Education. Career opportunities are not as clear as they used to be, and consequently many feel that it is pointless to spend time becoming a specialist in a discipline which might be overtaken by technology.

(*b*)　*Unemployment.*　An increasing number of people, unable to find employment, are becoming unemployed for long periods. The bottom layer of Fig. 19.1 shows how the number of long-term unemployed (those unemployed for over one year) increased four-fold from 1972 to 1981. Some use this as evidence to support the opinion that unemployment is becoming more socially acceptable. The inability to find work does not appear to carry the social stigma that it did during the inter-war years.

(*c*)　*Shorter working week.*　Increased early retirement, and the demand for a shorter working week, illustrate how more and more people regard life outside the working environment as more important than being at work. Although many employees take advantage of shorter working hours to work more overtime, there is a shift away from the work 'ethic' to more leisure activities. Work is becoming less important in people's lives.

(*d*)　*Flexibility in work.*　Many employees do not want to be restricted by rigid timekeeping and other working rules. Consequently some organisations have introduced flexible working hours which gives the employees some responsibility for the decision on when they attend work.

4　Attitudes to authority

People now demand more involvement in company affairs. The demand for flexible working hours is an example of the changing attitudes that employees have towards authority. The traditional authoritarian style of management is no longer acceptable to employees in many organisations (see Chapter 15).

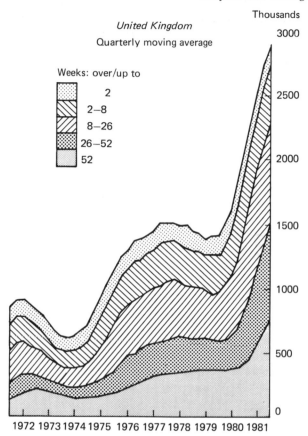

Fig. 19.1 Unemployment: by duration

Source: *Social Trends*, 1983

(*a*) *Consultation.* The demand for devolution in national and local government illustrates how people want more involvement in the decisions which will affect them. Similarly in organisations many employees feel that they should be consulted about important decisions; and as a result many organisations are extending their consultative arrangements. The changing attitude towards consultation is supported by the European Commission. In its proposals for company law harmonisation, the Commission maintains that employees have a right to information about, and consultation in, decisions which will affect them. In line with this proposal, the employment Act, 1982, requires company reports to contain a statement on the steps the directors have taken to develop employee involvement.

(*b*)   *Participation.*   The rapid growth in Higher Education during the 1960s has meant that many more employees are highly educated, and are less deferential and more critical of those in authority. There is a general change in attitude towards those in authority: many feel that decisions in business should be made more democratically. In some countries of the EEC – for example Germany – decision-making groups in organisations must, by law, include members who are appointed by, or subject to the approval of, all employees. However, organisations in the United Kingdom are not statutorily obliged to have 'worker directors' on Company boards (although the European Commission recommends that they should be). Following the Bullock Report on industrial democracy in 1977 the Labour Government of the day encouraged organisations to adopt a voluntary policy of employee representation on decision-making bodies.

(*c*)   *Direct action.*   Some groups have gone beyond conventional democratic involvement, and resorted to direct action against authority. Strike action in particular is now used by people in a wider range of occupations than ever before. During the 1970s a new method of direct action developed: 'worker control' of organisations. As technological and economic change caused the liquidation of firms, and the redundancy of employees, some groups of workers – for example at Meriden Motorcycles and the Upper Clyde Shipbuilders – took control of the organisation in an attempt to manage it by themselves.

Conflict resolution

The social and economic effects of change, such as unemployment and direct action, create tension and stress. In a democratic society change makes conflict inevitable: the interests of individuals and of organisations will not always coincide. For example, the interests of organisations can conflict with the following groups:

1 Customers and clients

Most producers want high profits which, in effect, means that they would like to charge high prices. Customers and clients on the other hand want low prices. Equally producers want to produce at low cost, which often means poor quality products or services. But customers and clients want high quality goods and services. In a free economy, market forces generally resolve this problem: firms have to adapt to the changing needs of consumers. Sometimes, though, in the 'conflict' between consumer and producer, the producer uses unfair methods; in this instance legislation exists to protect the consumer (see Chapter 17).

2 Competitors

Market competition is recognised as a desirable form of conflict. The main problem for an organisation occurs when a competitor introduces a new product, or becomes more efficient because of the introduction of new production methods or systems. The law does not generally resolve the conflict between organisations. It is assumed, in a free economy, that those businesses which are unable to respond to change, and become inefficient, should go out of business. Consequently there are, on average, over 12 000 liquidations and bankruptcies every year: these are cases where organisations have lost in the 'conflict of competition'.

3 Society

The policies of organisations, and of governments, sometimes conflict with the interests of sections of the community. The existence of *pressure groups* illustrates how conflicting interests are managed in a democratic society. When individuals or groups feel that their interests are threatened, they attempt to persuade decision makers to take account of their sectional views (see Chapter 7). For example, cuts in education expenditure in 1979 caused the Teachers' Union to campaign against the Government; the decision of the NCB to open a new mine in Leicestershire generated a campaign against the decision by local residents.

Technological change often spoils the environment with noise, fumes and visual pollution, and this frequently causes conflict between organisations and pressure groups. An *injunction,* which is an order requiring some person to refrain from breaking the law, is sometimes used to prevent organisations from carrying out actions which might be detrimental to sectional interests. In 1953 in Derby, for example, this remedy was used to deal with the pollution of the rivers Trent and Derwent caused by public and private effluence (Pride of Derby and Derbyshire Angling Association Ltd *v* British Celanese Ltd).

Another legal form of conflict resolution is a *Public Inquiry*, which is a technique used by Parliament for giving objectors to a scheme a fair hearing before a decision is made. For example, an Inquiry was held into the siting of the third London airport.

4   Employees
The most frequent form of conflict which occurs in business is the conflict between employers and employees. Technological change has both economic and social effects which make conflict an inevitable feature of organisations. Some of the main features of employer/employee conflict are:

(*a*)   *It affects all levels.*   Traditionally automation has mainly replaced unskilled and semi-skilled workers. But the developments in microelectronics are creating devices and systems which replace jobs in management and in highly skilled occupations such as those in inspection and control.

(*b*)   *Resentment.*   The relative importance of jobs changes as technology develops. Skilled craftsmen, such as watchmakers, find that years of training and experience count for very little. The electronic revolution has de-skilled many occupations – print workers, secretaries, postal workers. Such de-skilling can reduce an employee's sense of personal value, and cause dissatisfaction and resentment.

(*c*)   *Trade union reaction.*   Some trade unions react against change, especially if they find that their membership is declining as their members' occupations are automated. The threat of unemployment, and the lack of security, can create great conflict between employers and employees. There are many instances where trade unions, in resistance to change, have refused initially to cooperate with the employers – for example, print workers in the Times Newspapers dispute in 1978–9; the dock workers' refusal to cooperate with containerisation; and the Post Office workers' rejection of electronic sorting equipment.

Employers can attempt to resolve the inevitable conflict which change brings by:

1 Communication. Ignorance breeds rumour and fear. By constantly informing employees of decisions which will affect them, organisations can reduce the fear and hostility which insecurity and ignorance create.

2 Retraining. Organisations can examine the different needs of employees and provide facilities which enable people to learn new skills and new techniques. Skills in team work and cooperation, as well as improved understanding of the nature of an organisation's operations, are necessary in a changing environment.

3 Participation. It is generally agreed that participation improves employee cooperation (see Chapter 11).

There are three types of employee participation. Firstly, there is share participation (part-ownership of the company). The European Commission recommends that private organisations should encourage employees to become part-owners of the enterprise for which they work, so that they can readily identify with the firm's successes. Secondly, there is the type of participation which was recommended by the Bullock Report in 1977: employees take an active part in policy decisions. Lastly, there is participation in the working environment. Structured work groups are formed, and the groups' responsibilities are increased. Emphasis is placed on common tasks and on job rotation. This form of participation makes the individual's role more flexible, and the employee becomes more adaptable, and more responsive to change.

4 Negotiation. The conflict between employers and employees is often resolved through collective agreements. However, in Britain, unlike other countries in the EEC, negotiation and collective bargaining are mainly concerned with salaries and conditions of employment. The European Commission recommends that collective agreements ought to be much wider, and cover such aspects of change as investment plans, location, takeovers and mergers, as well as plant closures.

Communication, participation and negotiation do not resolve all the problems which change creates. When conflict is not resolved by these measures the parties seek independent *arbitration*, and employees can resort to an *Industrial Tribunal* (see Chapter 17).

Questions on Part Six

1   Give four examples of how conflict can arise in business, and explain how each one might be resolved.

2   'Technological development now creates far more problems than it solves.' Do you agree with this statement? Explain your answer.

3   Give examples of how attitudes to work and authority have changed since the Second World War, and assess the impact of these changes on communication between employers and employees.

4   Define 'conflict resolution' and assess the importance of legal rules in the management of human resources.

5   Define 'dependent population' and 'working population'; and outline the social implications of a growth in the dependent population.

6   Examine Fig 3.1 and assess the social and economic implications of the information in the figure.

7   Explain what is meant by 'information processing', and assess the social and economic implications of developments in information technology.

8   Outline and explain the circumstances when State intervention into private business can be justified.

9   To what extent do you think that the activities of trade unions can be controlled by legal rules?

10   When the Government formulates policies, do you think that the needs of business can be separated from the needs of Society? Explain your answer.

Appendix One

Population Statistics

Table A1.1 Population changes and projections 1901 to 2001

United Kingdom   *Millions and thousands*

	Population at start of period (millions)	Average annual change (thousands)				
		Live births	Deaths	Net natural change	Net civilian migration and other adjustments	Overall annual change
Census enumerated						
1901–11	38.2	1.091	624	467	−82	385
1911–21	42.1	975	689	286	−92	194
1921–31	44.0	824	555	268	−67	201
1931–51	46.0	785	598	188	+25	213
Mid-year estimates						
1951–61	50.3	839	593	246	+6	252
1961–66	52.8	988	633	355	−15	339
1966–71	54.5	937	644	293	−71	222
1971–72	55.6	862	661	202	−30	171
1972–73	55.8	808	672	136	−4	132
1973–74	55.9	752	664	88	−78	10
1974–75	55.9	721	671	50	−71	−22
1975–76	55.9	689	681	7	−22	−15
1976–77	55.9	655	660	−5	−28	−33
1977–78	55.9	664	665	–	−17	−17
1978–79	55.8	720	672	48	−2	46
1979–80	55.9	743	658	86	−22	64
1980–81	55.9	738[3]	659[3]	79[3]		

Table A1.1 – *continued*

United Kingdom   *Millions and thousands*

Average annual change (thousands)

	Population at start of period (millions)	*Live births*	*Deaths*	*Net natural change*	*Net civilian migration and other adjustments*	*Overall annual change*
Projections						
1981–86	56.0	813	705	108	−29	79
1986–91	56.4	901	716	185	−30	155
1991–96	57.2	896	717	179	−30	149
1996–2001	57.9	827	710	117	−30	87

Source: *Social Trends*, 1983

Table A1.2   Sex and age structure of the population

United Kingdom   *Millions*

	0–4	5–15	16–29	30–44	45–59	60–64	65–74	75–84	85+	*All ages*
Males										
Census enumerated										
1901	2.2	4.4	4.8	3.6	2.2	0.5	0.6	0.2		18.5
1911	2.3	4.6	5.0	4.3	2.7	0.6	0.7	0.2		20.4
1921	2.0	4.6	4.9	4.3	3.4	0.7	0.9	0.3		21.0
1931	1.8	4.2	5.4	4.5	3.8	0.9	1.1	0.4		22.1
Mid-year estimates										
1941	1.7	3.8	5.4	5.5	3.9	1.1	1.4	0.5		23.3
1951	2.2	3.9	4.9	5.5	4.5	1.1	1.6	0.7		24.4
1961	2.2	4.5	4.9	5.3	5.1	1.2	1.6	0.7	0.1	25.7
1971	2.3	5.0	5.6	4.9	5.0	1.5	2.0	0.7	0.1	27.1
1976	1.9	5.1	5.8	5.0	4.8	1.5	2.2	0.8	0.1	27.3
1980	1.8	4.8	6.0	5.4	4.8	1.3	2.2	0.9	0.1	27.3
1981[2]	1.8	4.7	6.0	5.5	4.8	1.4	2.3	0.9	0.1	27.4
Projections										
1986	2.1	4.1	6.4	5.7	4.5	1.4	2.1	1.0	0.2	27.5
1991	2.3	4.1	6.2	6.0	4.6	1.3	2.2	1.0	0.2	28.0
1996	2.3	4.7	5.6	6.2	5.0	1.3	2.1	1.0	0.2	28.4
2001	2.1	4.9	5.3	6.5	5.2	1.3	2.0	1.0	0.2	28.6

Table A1.2 – *continued*

	United Kingdom								Millions
0–4	5–15	16–29	30–44	45–49	60–64	65–74	75–84	85+	*All ages*

Females

Census enumerated

2.2	4.4	5.2	3.9	2.4	0.6	0.7	0.3		19.7
2.2	4.6	5.4	4.6	2.9	0.6	0.9	0.4		21.7
1.9	4.6	5.5	5.0	3.6	0.8	1.1	0.5		23.0
1.7	4.2	5.7	5.2	4.2	1.0	1.4	0.6		24.0

1901 · 1911 · 1921 · 1931

Mid-year estimates

1941: 1.7 3.7 5.4 5.8 4.6 1.3 1.7 0.8 25.0
1951: 2.1 3.8 4.9 5.7 5.1 1.4 2.1 1.1 26.1

1961: 2.1 4.3 4.8 5.3 5.5 1.5 2.4 1.2 0.2 27.3
1971: 2.2 4.7 5.4 4.8 5.2 1.7 2.7 1.4 0.4 28.6
1976: 1.8 4.9 5.6 4.9 5.0 1.7 2.9 1.6 0.4 28.7
1980: 1.7 4.6 5.7 5.3 4.9 1.5 2.9 1.7 0.4 28.7
1981[2]: 1.7 4.4 5.8 5.4 4.9 1.6 2.9 1.7 0.5 28.9

Projections

1986: 1.9 3.9 6.1 5.6 4.6 1.6 2.8 1.8 0.5 28.9
1991: 2.2 3.9 5.9 5.9 4.7 1.5 2.7 1.8 0.6 29.2
1996: 2.1 4.4 5.3 6.1 5.1 1.4 2.7 1.8 0.6 29.6
2001: 2.0 4.7 5.0 6.4 5.4 1.4 2.5 1.8 0.6 29.7

Source: *Social Trends*, 1983

Appendix Two

Supply and Demand Analysis

Demand

(i)   Changes in demand caused by changes in price

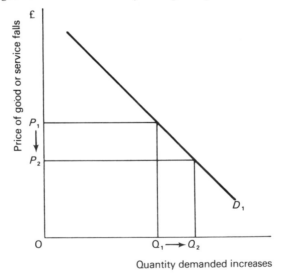

Fig. A2.1   Extension along an existing demand line

In Fig. A2.1, when the price falls from P_1 to P_2 more people by the product, and Q_1 increases to Q_2. However, as shown in Fig. A2.2, when the price of a product increases, then fewer people buy the product and the market contracts.

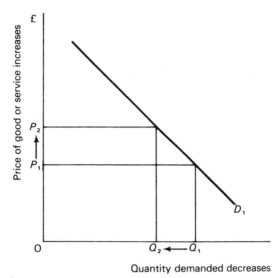

Fig. A2.2 Contraction along an existing demand line

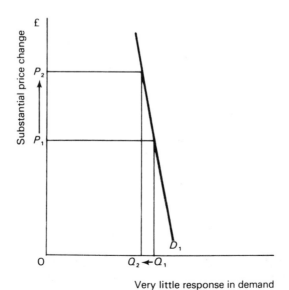

Fig. A2.3 Inelastic demand line

Something
necessary.
Bread.

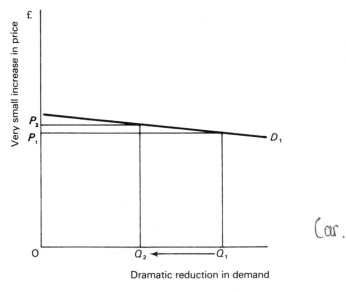

Fig. A2.4   Elastic demand line

(*ii*)   *Elasticity of demand*
Elasticity of demand measures the response of demand to changes in price. Demand is *inelastic* when a change in price causes only a small response in demand (Fig. A2.3). When the proportionate change in demand is greater than the price change, then demand is *elastic* (Fig. A2.4).

(*iii*)   *Shifts in demand:*   Changes in demand caused by changes in the market.
Changes in demand which occur even when the price remains constant are called *shifts* in demand. Shifts occur primarily because of changes in fashion, income, the price of other goods, advertising and the introduction of new products. When a shift occurs (as in Figs A2.5 and A2.6) the whole relationship between price and demand changes, and a new demand line is formed.

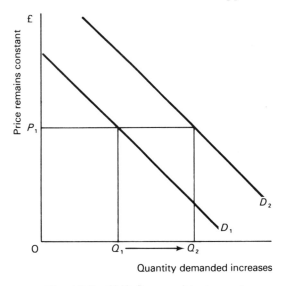

Fig. A2.5 Shift (increase) in demand

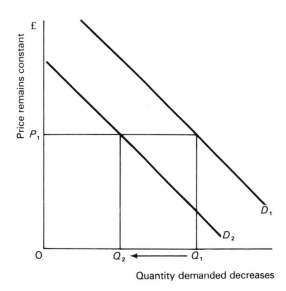

Fig. A2.6 Shift (decrease) in demand

Supply

(*i*)   *Changes in supply caused by changes in price.*

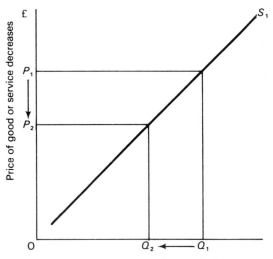

CONTRACTION

Fig. A2.7   Extension along an existing supply line

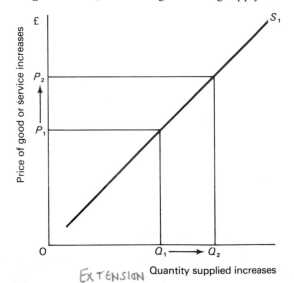

EXTENSION

Fig. A2.8   Contraction along an existing supply line

price don't change — trends fashion Season.

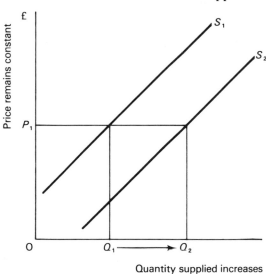

Fig. A2.9   Shift (increase) in supply

If we assume that costs remain constant then, since profits equal price less costs, a price increase leads to an increase in profits; in the longer term, profits attract more firms into an industry and supply increases (Fig. A2.7). Conversely, a fall in price squeezes profits, firms have to leave the industry and supply decreases (Fig. A2.8).

(ii)   Shifts in supply
Even when the price remains constant, producers can change the amount they produce. The factors which cause a shift in supply are primarily related to efficiency. For example, improvements in production brought about by capital investment can cause an increase (shift) in supply (Fig. A2.9). Conversely, inefficient management and industrial disputes can lead to a reduction (shift) in supply (Fig. A2.10).

Interaction of supply and demand

Figs A2.11–15 provide examples of the market acting as a mechanism. Fig. A2.11 shows how price – in a competitive market – will stabilise at the point where supply equals demand (point of equilibrium). Disturbance of the equilibrium is brought about either by shifts in supply (e.g. new technology, strikes) or by shifts in demand (e.g. changes in income, fashion).

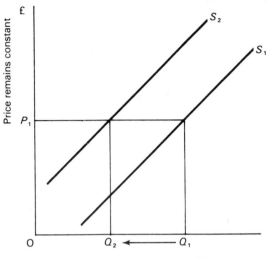

Fig. A2.10 Shift (decrease) in supply

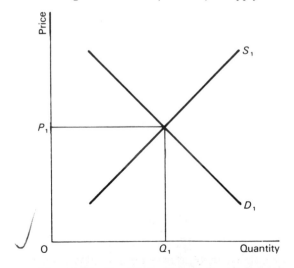

Fig. A2.11 Equilibrium of supply and demand

Example 1: Reduction in supply

Figs A2.12 and A2.13 illustrate how a reduction (shift) in supply causes the price to rise, and as a result demand contracts until a new equilibrium point is reached at $P_3 Q_2$.

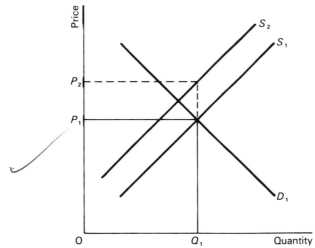

Fig. A2.12   Reduction in supply: in the short run, customers continue to buy the product and the price is forced up to P_2

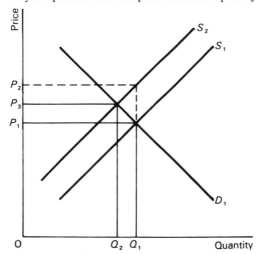

Fig. A2.13   Reduction in supply: in the long run, P is considered too high by many buyers and demand contracts to a new equilibrium at $P_3 Q_2$

Example 2: Reduction in demand

Similarly Figs A2.14 and A2.15 show a reduction (shift) in demand causing the price to fall, and as a result supply contracts until a new equilibrium point is reached at $P_3 Q_2$.

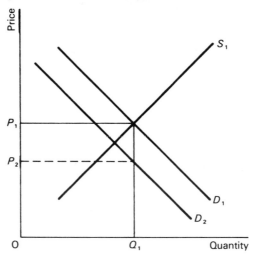

Fig. A2.14   Reduction in demand: in the short run, suppliers are unable to adjust to the shift in demand and the price falls to P_2

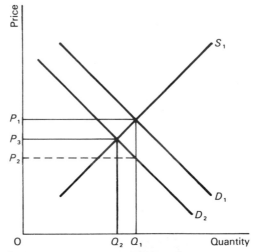

Fig. A2.15   Reduction in demand: in the long run, P_2 forces many suppliers out of business and supply contracts to a new equilibrium at $P_3 Q_2$

Appendix Three

Break-Even Analysis

Consider two companies which manufacture identical products which are sold for £3.00 each. The fixed costs, of both firms, are £100 000; and the variable cost per unit for Company A is £0.50, and for Company B is £1.00. The production capacity of both firms is 60 000 units.

From this information the following tables and diagrams can be constructed:

Company A

Output	Fixed costs (£)	Variable costs (£)	Total costs (£)	Average costs (£)	Average revenue (£)	Total revenue (£)	Profit/ Loss (£)
1 000	100 000	500	100 500	100.50	3.00	3 000	−97 500
10 000	100 000	5 000	105 000	10.50	3.00	30 000	−75 000
20 000	100 000	10 000	110 000	5.50	3.00	60 000	−50 000
30 000	100 000	15 000	115 000	3.83	3.00	90 000	−25 000
40 000	100 000	20 000	120 000	3.00	3.00	120 000	0
50 000	100 000	25 000	125 000	2.50	3.00	150 000	+25 000
60 000	100 000	30 000	130 000	2.16	3.00	180 000	+50 000

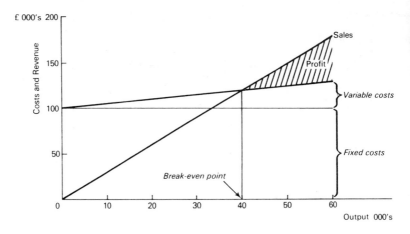

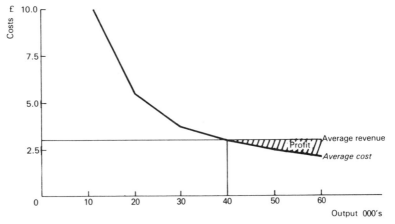

Company B

Output	Fixed costs (£)	Variable costs (£)	Total costs (£)	Average costs (£)	Average revenue (£)	Total revenue (£)	Profit/ Loss (£)
1 000	100 000	1 000	101 000	101.00	3.00	3 000	−98 000
10 000	100 000	10 000	110 000	11.00	3.00	30 000	−80 000
20 000	100 000	20 000	120 000	6.00	3.00	60 000	−60 000
30 000	100 000	30 000	130 000	4.33	3.00	90 000	−40 000
40 000	100 000	40 000	140 000	3.50	3.00	120 000	−20 000
50 000	100 000	50 000	150 000	3.00	3.00	150 000	0
60 000	100 000	60 000	160 000	2.67	3.00	180 000	+20 000

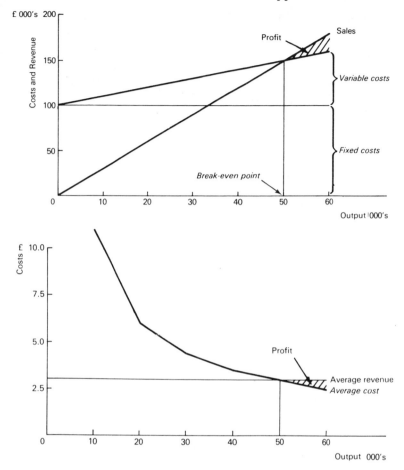

The diagrams illustrate three fairly obvious but important features of break-even analysis:

(*a*) A constant price is the average revenue.
(*b*) Average costs fall as the fixed costs become a smaller proportion of total costs.
(*c*) The break-even point always occurs when average costs equal average revenue.

These examples, although useful in showing the basic relationship between costs and profit, are simplified illustrations of real business activity. In practice the price of a product or service is rarely constant; and, although it is reasonable to assume that average costs will fall initially – because fixed costs become a smaller proportion of total costs – in the long run variable unit costs will increase as the diseconomies of scale set in.

Appendix Four

Financial Records and Analysis

Profit and Loss Account, and Balance Sheet

**Profit and Loss Account for XYZ Ltd
for the year ending (date)**

Trading Account

	£	£
Income from sales		232 000
Costs: Raw materials	122 000	
Wages (direct)	68 000	
Fuel and Power	6 000	196 000
Gross Profit on Trading		£36 000
Gross Profit (b/d)	36 000	
Income from other sources	5 000	41 000
Expenses not incurred in manufacturing:		
Debenture interest	800	
Directors' fees	8 000	
Depreciation:		
Plant and Machinery	5 600	
Motor Vehicle	600	
Wages and Salaries	12 000	
Rent and Rates	1 500	
Hire of equipment	1 500	

Light and Heat	1 000	
Advertising	1 200	
Post and Telephone	750	
Other expenses	2 050	35 000
Net Profit before taxation		£6 000

Appropriation Account

Net Profit (b/d)	6 000
Taxation (40%)	2 400
Net Profit after tax	£3 600

Net Profit after tax	3 600	
Balance from previous year	13 500	17 100
Deduct appropriations:		
Dividends proposed (gross)	3 000	
Transfers to reserve	1 100	4 100
Balance on the Profit and Loss Account		£13 000

Balance Sheet of XYZ Ltd as at (date)

Fixed Assets:	£	£
Premises at cost		10 000
Plant and Machinery at cost	34 200	
less depreciation	16 800	17 400
Motor Vehicle at cost	5 000	
less depreciation	2 400	2 600
Long-term Capital		30 000
Current assets:		
Stock in trade	46 200	
Trade debtors	32 100	
Balance at Bank	1 000	
	79 300	

deduct Current Liabilities:

Trade Creditors	<u>52 300</u>	
Working Capital	27 000	
deduct Reserve for future taxation	<u>2 000</u>	25 000
Net Worth of the Company		<u>£55 000</u>

Financed by:

Issued Share Capital:	
Ordinary Shares (20 000 at £1 each)	20 000
Preference Shares 5% (10 000 at £1 each)	10 000
Profit and Loss Account	13 000
General Reserve	4 000
Loan:	
10% Debentures	<u>8 000</u>
	<u>£55 000</u>

Ratio Analysis of XYZ Ltd

Test of Liquidity

(i) Current ratio
Current Assets : Current Liabilities
79 300 : 52 300
1.5 : 1.0

(ii) Acid Test ratio
Current Assets *less* Stock : Current Liabilities
79 300 − 46 200 : 52 300
0.7 : 1.0

(iii) Average period of collection of trade debts
Debtors : Annual Sales
32 100 : 232 000
Period = 1:7 (almost 8 weeks)

Tests of Profitability

(i) Rate of return on capital
Net Profit : Capital employed
6 000 : 30 000 + 27 000
6 000 : 57 000
0.105 : 1.0 (or 10.5%)

(ii) Profit to Sales
Net Profit : Sales
6 000 : 232 000
0.025 : 1.0 (or 2.5%)

Gross Profit : Sales
36 000 : 232 000
0.155 : 1.0 (or 15.5%)

Capital Gearing (ignoring reserves)
Ordinary shares : Preference shares ·· Debentures
20 000 : 10 000 + 8 000
20 000 : 18 000
1.1 : 1.0

Depreciation

The purpose of depreciation is to reduce the cost of fixed assets to a scrap or realisable value. If we examine the final accounts of XYZ Ltd it can be seen that the amount of money used to reduce the cost of the motor vehicle, in addition to being deducted from the initial capital outlay in the Balance Sheet (£5000 – £2400), is treated as a legitimate expense in the Profit and Loss Account (£600). The method used by XYZ Ltd is the *Reducing Balance Method.*

This method recognises that the value of an asset is higher during the first few years of ownership. The depreciation charge is a fixed percentage which is charged on an annual basis; consequently each year the actual cost of depreciation falls. For example:

Motor Vehicle cost	£5 000

Annual depreciation charge is
fixed at 20%.

Year 1 (20% of 5 000) charge	1 000
Balance	4 000

Year 2 (20% of 4 000) charge	800
Balance	3 200

Year 3 (20% of 3 200) charge	600
Balance	2 600

and so on . . .

In the XYZ Ltd Profit and Loss Account the depreciation charge is £600 and the Balance Sheet shows the vehicle to be worth £2 600, so it is three years old.

An alternative method which XYZ Ltd could have used is the *Straight Line Method* of depreciation. The scrap value of the vehicle is estimated and deducted from its initial cost. The remainder is written off over the expected life of the asset on a constant (fixed instalment) basis. For example

Motor Vehicle cost £5 000.
Estimated life is 5 years
Estimated scrap value in five years time is £750

The annual depreciation charge will be:

$$\frac{5\,000 - 750}{5} = \frac{4\,250}{5} = £850$$

£850 will be charged to the Profit and Loss Account each year, and will be deducted from the cost of the motor vehicle each year until after five years it is completely 'written off'.

Appendix Five

Investment Appraisal Techniques

Pay-back method

The pay-back period is the length of time it takes for the earnings on an investment to cover the cost of the investment. The investment project with the shortest pay-back period is considered to be the most attractive. The technique has the advantage that it is fairly easy to understand, and it enables firms to assess future cash flows because it takes account of the cash received. It is particularly useful in periods of rapid technological change when capital equipment can quickly become obsolete, and therefore the project which brings the quickest return is the most attractive.

The technique's main disadvantage is that, because it does not pay attention to any cash flows which occur after the pay-back period, it does not measure the long-term profitability of an investment project.

Example

A firm has to make a decision between two investment programmes each costing £3 000. It is estimated that programme A will yield a constant, but relatively low return of £750 per annum for five years. Programme B will provide a relatively high initial return which will diminish as follows:

	Programme B	*Programme A*
Year 1	£1 450	£ 750
2	950	750
3	600	750
4	300	750
5	100	750
Total return	£3 400	£3 750

As the graph shows, the pay-back period for A is four years and for B three years. The decision is to invest in B even though after 4½ years A provides a better return.

Average rate of return method

The average rate of return is the ratio of net profit to capital cost. There are alternative methods of calculating the profit and the capital costs. For example, the capital could simply be the initial sum invested or it could include capital outlays over a period of time. Similarly, the returns could be an estimate of only the first year's profits, or they could be an average estimated yield over the assumed life of the project.

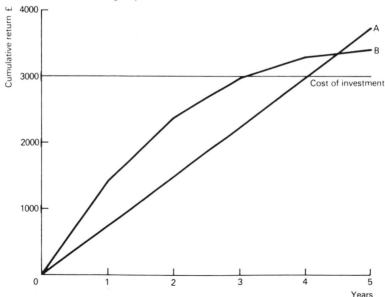

Example

A firm has to make a decision between two investment programmes. The initial cost of both programmes if £2 000, and
their estimated life is five years. It is predicted that the repairs
and maintenance costs will be a constant £200 per annum. The
average annual costs and the estimated returns on each programme
are:

Year	1	2	3	4	5	Total
Average capital cost	£400	400	400	400	400	£2 000
Repairs and maintenance	£200	200	200	200	200	£1 000
Estimated annual cost	£600	600	600	600	600	£3 000
Estimated yield, programme A	£600	600	700	1 000	1 000	£3 900
Estimated yield, programme B	£900	800	700	600	600	£3 600

Average rate of return

	Year 1	Year 5
Programme A	100% (600 : 600)	130% (3 900 : 3 000)
Programme B	150% (900 : 600)	120% (3 600 : 3 000)

Programme B is likely to be preferred to programme A even
though in the long run A provides a better average rate of return.
This is because it is more probable that predictions of events in the
near future (short term) are more reliable than long-term estimates;
and programme B looks a safer prospect in the short term.

The average rate of return method is considered to be more
satisfactory than the pay-back method because it pays attention to
cash flows. However, it does not take account of the incidence of the
cash flows: the method becomes more effective when the timing of
the cash flows is taken into account, and when care has been taken in
the selection of which years to assess.

Net present value

The pay-back method and the average rate of return method do not
recognise that cash in hand is worth more than cash received in
future periods. Discounted cash flow techniques (DCF) do recognise this fact, and by using discount tables cash flows can be
discounted at a rate which reflects the cost of capital.

Example

An investment project costs £3 000, and it is estimated that it will yield an annual rate of return for five years.

Year	Net cash flow (£)	Discount factor (10%) from tables	Present value of cash flow
0	−3 000	1.0000	−3 000
1	+ 800	0.9091	+ 727.3
2	+ 800	0.8264	+ 661.1
3	+ 800	0.7513	+ 601.0
4	+ 800	0.6830	+ 546.4
5	+ 800	0.6209	+ 496.7
		Net present value of yield (net) £	+ 32.5

Internal rate of return method (IRR)

IRR is the rate of interest which, when used to discount the cash flows of a proposed investment, reduces the net present value (npv) to 0. The discount rate is found by trial and error. Using the example above, we know that a discount rate of 10% gives a npv of +32.5. The IRR must be somewhere near to 10%. In the following example a rate of 12% gives a npv of −116.2. We can assume that the rate which give a npv of zero is nearer to 10% than to 12%, and, as the example shows, a discount factor of 10.4% gives a npv of 0.

Year	Net cash flow (£)	Discount factor (12%)	Present value of cash flows (12%)	Discount factor (10.4%)	Present value of cash flow (10.4%)
0	−3 000	1.0000	−3 000	1.0000	−3 000
1	+ 800	0.8929	+ 714.3	0.9058	+ 724.6
2	+ 800	0.7972	+ 637.8	0.8205	+ 656.4
3	+ 800	0.7118	+ 569.4	0.7432	+ 594.6
4	+ 800	0.6355	+ 508.4	0.6732	+ 538.6
5	+ 800	0.5674	+ 453.9	0.6098	+ 487.8
		npv	=−116.2	npv =	0*

* figures do not add up exactly to zero because of rounding.

If the cost of the capital (plus a premium for risk since the cash flows are estimates) is higher than the IRR – in this example 10.4% – then the proposed investment should be rejected.

Index